MW00333216

Becoming an Ancestor

Plate 1. Pineda women ready for the seven-year Mass for the Dead for Jesús Ramírez Escudero, "Ta Chu." 2004. Photograph by Anya Peterson Royce.

Becoming an Ancestor
The Isthmus Zapotec Way of Death

Anya Peterson Royce

Published by State University of New York Press, Albany

© 2011 State University of New York

All rights reserved

Printed in the United States of America

No part of this book may be used or reproduced in any manner whatsoever without written permission. No part of this book may be stored in a retrieval system or transmitted in any form or by any means including electronic, electrostatic, magnetic tape, mechanical, photocopying, recording, or otherwise without the prior permission in writing of the publisher.

For information, contact State University of New York Press, Albany, NY.
www.sunypress.edu

Production by Eileen Meehan
Marketing by Anne M. Valentine

Library of Congress Cataloging-in-Publication Data

Royce, Anya Peterson.
   Becoming an ancestor : the Isthmus Zapotec way of death / Anya Peterson Royce.
       p. cm.
   Includes bibliographical references and index.
   ISBN 978-1-4384-3678-4 (paperback : alk. paper)
   ISBN 978-1-4384-3677-7 (hardcover : alk. paper)   1. Zapotec Indians—Funeral customs and rites—Mexico—Mexico—Juchitán de Zaragoza.   2. Zapotec Indians—Mexico—Juchitán de Zaragoza—Religion.   3. Zapotec Indians—Mexico—Juchitán de Zaragoza—Social life and customs.   4. Funeral rites and ceremonies—Mexico—Juchitán de Zaragoza.   5. Juchitán de Zaragoza (Mexico)—Religious life and customs. 6. Juchitán de Zaragoza (Mexico)—Social life and customs.   I. Title.

   F1221.Z3R69 2011
   305.897'6807274—dc22   2011003106

10 9 8 7 6 5 4 3 2 1

For Na Rosinda Fuentes de Ramírez and Delia Ramírez Fuentes
And for all my Juchitán family
who have shared laughter, tears,
stories, and wisdom for more than forty years
who have loved me into seeing and listening
and understanding, and taught me to recognize
the difference between what is essential and what is ephemeral.
And for Ron, touchstone and partner

Contents

Maps

Plates

Acknowledgments

I first encountered the Isthmus Zapotec of Juchitán at a performance of the Guelaguetza in Oaxaca City in July 1967. It was enough to take me and my husband, Ronald R. Royce, to Juchitán the following summer. My acquaintance now spans more than forty years. Twenty-seven when I began, I have spent more than half my life calling Juchitán home and its people family. The epilogue gives the names of all those family and friends who have died since 1967. My debt to them is profound for they were my teachers, and they have accompanied me through the writing of this book. One of them, Na Berta Pineda de Fuentes, welcomed me to her home and was a patient teacher, never losing hope that I might eventually come to understand what mattered. Her daughter, Na Rosinda Fuentes de Ramírez; Rosinda's husband, Ta Jesús Ramírez Escudero; and their daughter, Delia Ramírez Fuentes, became my family, loving me without conditions, providing both a physical home and a home for the heart. Delia is my sister and my best friend. She has read drafts of everything I write about Juchitán, including this book, making insightful comments and correcting errors wherever they appear. She makes sure that I know when events I should know about are happening, facilitates meetings, meets my obligations when someone dies and I am not there, and makes it possible for me to do my "work" when it means one less pair of hands to help. It is impossible to list all the ways in which she makes my work possible and better than it would otherwise be.

My large, extended Pineda family has also been constant in their support. Those not mentioned elsewhere who have sustained me and my work in ways large and small include Antonia Ramírez de Fuentes; Na Irma Fuentes; her husband, Enrique Lemus; their son, César; his wife, America; and daughters, Sugey and Monserat; their other son, Enrique; Gloria Pineda; her children, Karime, Jibrán, and Rosinda; and husband, Vicente Fuentes Ramírez; Mayella's children, Daniella, Eva, and Diego; Rosi Fuentes; and Profesora Bertha Orozco Fuentes. Na Mavis Fuentes and her husband, Ta Berna López, and their children are my family in Mexico City. They have met every flight and seen to it that I get on the evening bus to Juchitán, refreshed and fed.

Many people, including many in Juchitán, have provided me with source material difficult to find. Delia Ramírez Fuentes buys every new book published locally or in Oaxaca, saves invitations illustrated by local artists, and acquires anything that has to do with Zapotec culture. Vicente Fuentes Pineda also provides copies of publications as does his son, José Fuentes Ramírez. José has also given me wonderful paintings and prints by local artists, introducing me to many of the artists. On my trip to Juchitán in May 2008, José was an invaluable colleague, photographing events while I filmed them. Alma Delia "Mayella" Fuentes introduced me to the work of Julio Bustillo and took me to meet the poet Enedino Jiménez. Na Berta Fuentes vda de Orozco gave me a copy of Gilberto Orozco's wonderful book. Father Vichido gave me a copy of his autobiography. Marina Meneses Velasquez generously gave me a copy of the book in which her article appears. Local historian Gonzalo Jiménez López has been very generous in giving me photographs, both contemporary and of times past, that have been invaluable as well as copies of his books, essays, and videos. Doctora Edaena Saynes Vasquez has been a source of valuable observations about the Isthmus Zapotec language, especially as it is used in Juchitán. Gifted poets Irma Pineda Santiago, Victor Terán, Macario Matus, Victor de la Cruz, and Enedino Jiménez inspired and enlightened me with their poetry and their conversation. Ramón Vicente de la Cruz, manager of the internet café El Ratón, gave me a copy of the film *Ramos de fuego*, and his café linked me to the Internet world.

Indiana colleagues have been equally generous. Raymond J. Demallie found a copy of Kamar Al-Shimas's *Mexican Southland*, a real rarity. Paul Gebhard gave me his beautiful screenfold Peabody edition of the Nuttall Codex. These artifacts of Isthmus Zapotec culture past and present remind me of its beauty and variety.

Two Juchiteco friends who are also gifted photographers, José Fuentes Ramírez and Cristina de la Cruz Pineda, have loaned their talent on occasions when one camera was simply not enough or when I was a full-time participant. Some of their photographs appear in this book.

Various libraries and cultural institutions have contributed in important and unique ways: at the University of California at Berkeley, the Bancroft Library and the George and Mary Foster Library of Anthropology hold treasures for anyone working in Mexico; at Indiana University, the Herman B. Wells library with its scattered gems including the Herbarium Library and the Geography and Map Library as well as its own fine Mesoamerican collections acquired with intelligence and zeal by a series of librarians including Emma Simonson and Glenn Read; the Foro Ecológico of Juchitán with its botanical gardens of local flora; Artes Gráficas of Oaxaca City, the library and paper-making venture sponsored by painter Francisco Toledo; Juchitán's new Librería El Buho with its treasures of books on the Isthmus; the Lidxi Guendabianni of Juchitán, provider of conferences, books, art, exhibits, and a series of directors who have been generous with their help and expertise

My research has been supported over many years by various agencies including the American Council of Learned Societies in conjunction with the Social Science Research Council and the National Endowment for the Humanities for their International and Area Studies Fellowship, Indiana University fellowships and grants-in-aid from the College Arts and Humanities Institute, Media Production Services, New Frontiers in the Arts and Humanities, Research and the University Graduate School, and the President's Council on International Programs. Being a Phi Beta Kappa Couper Scholar in 2006–2007 gave me the opportunity to lecture on the topic of Zapotec death to faculty and students at the University of Houston and California State University at Fullerton.

Places where one can simply be quiet and let thoughts flow where they will at their own pace are rare. This project benefited from two such places. The Mount Calvary Monastery and Retreat Center in Santa Barbara, California, lets me find solitude within community supported by the kindness, humor, and generosity of the brothers resident there. Brother Nicholas Radelmiller read the entire manuscript, making excellent observations and comments, especially with regard to liturgical practices. The White Magnolia School of the Plum Blossom Confederation of Tai Chi, under the leadership of Dr. Miriam Marsolais, let me bring mind and body together. It was a class and then a conversation with Miriam that made me think of the river as a metaphor for Zapotec persistence and change.

The gifted women of the Five Women Poets—Joyce Adams, Patricia Coleman, Anne Haines, Debora Horning, Deborah Hutchinson, Antonia Matthews, and Leah Helen May—have been my circle of writing colleagues who have read all the many poems inspired by Juchitán and the Juchitecos.

On annual returns to Berkeley, I had the opportunity of talking about death in Mesoamerica and the ideas taking shape in this book with wonderful scholars and ethnographers Elizabeth Colson, George Foster, and Laura Nader. Elizabeth Colson read the whole manuscript, and her ability to see the important questions as well as the gaps in an argument have immeasurably improved the book. George Foster and I talked about the indigenous origin of the wet-dry opposition that is so crucial to the Isthmus Zapotec view, and he was most gracious in acknowledging that my argument for it was convincing. Laura Nader spoke from the depth of her own experience with the Zapotec, her perceptive questions forcing me to rethink where the ethnography was leading me. Here in Bloomington, my colleague Raymond J. DeMallie, having read more than one draft, led me back to the evidence more than once. Della Collins Cook joined me in the field for a project on birth seasonality. Her perspective as a bioanthropologist and her expertise on mortuary practices in general have enlarged my vision. All these colleagues are and were the best of field ethnographers, appreciating the value of description as the only ground for saying anything of value.

Long-term field research is not as common as one might think. I doubt that many of us who do it understood that we would spend lifetimes living and sharing the lives of those whose stories we would tell. Mentors and colleagues become precious models and valued sounding boards as we encounter the peculiar challenges, ethical and ethnographic, of such long engagement. Working with longtime colleague Robert V. Kemper, editing the collection of essays *Chronicling Cultures: Long-Term Field Research in Anthropology* (2002), provided a unique opportunity to talk about the different shapes these involvements took, to talk about the place of such research within the field as a whole, and to see how individual scholars had crafted their responses to such lifetimes of ethnography.

In 2005 I was invited by Dr. Bren Neale, University of Leeds, to present a paper at an international seminar on longitudinal qualitative research where I discovered international colleagues whose work was leading them to address the same questions. Serving now on the international board of Timescapes, a five-year study funded by the Economic and Social Research Council of Great Britain, has expanded even further the examples of approaches and findings. I am grateful to Bren Neale for being such a generous and visionary colleague.

Friendships with Juchitecos whose work (*dxiiña'*) is essential to the remembrance and celebration of death taught me not just which and how many vocations are involved but how much the quality with which they are performed matters. These include prayer leaders Na Eusebia and her daughters, Na Feliciana and Señorita Margarita; bread maker Na Rosalia Espinosa; Na Victoria de la Cruz Martínez, who crafts the all-important chocolate tablets; and musician-composer-singer Hebert Rasgado, compassionate veteran of many wakes and memorials, who himself was sung along his way in 2008. He and his friend and fellow musician Feliciano Marin spoke and sang as I filmed them. The last song they sang was "La Última Palabra ("Guenda nabani")," one of the staples of wakes. They sang it with two voices and one guitar. The three of us were silent after the last notes had died away, touched by one of those deeply moving moments of clarity.

The Foro Ecológico de Juchitán was the vision of Julio Bustillo who believed that a place where Juchitecos of all ages could learn about their environment and realize the crucial importance of caring for the earth and all its creatures was so essential that he dedicated his life, talent, and energy to making it a reality. He died too young, and now his father Ta Mario Bustillo, mother Na Yolanda, and others carry on the work he began. I have spent many quiet mornings in those gardens along the river.

So many people have helped me in many ways over my years in Juchitán. These include all the socias and socios of the Vela Pineda; Na Lugarda Charis

Altimirano; Roberto Guerra Chiñas; Isabel "Chave" Luis López; Ta Feli-Félix López Jiménez; the directors and staff of the Lidxi Guendabianni; the priests and staff of San Vicente Ferrer (the parish church that shares a wall with my family's house); municipal presidents and the members of their governments; all the writers, painters, and musicians whose works have lifted my heart; and many others who extended friendship and kindness.

Through all the field research, writing, and thinking, one person has been the touchstone, my husband, Ronald R. Royce. Since the first tentative explorations into Isthmus Zapotec history and culture, we have worked together, learning, sorting out, finding the gaps, figuring out the next questions, grieving for departed Zapotec friends and family, celebrating their births and marriages. His profound knowledge of the Isthmus Zapotec language has made it possible for me to work through it to fundamental understandings. His insistence on examining alternate explanations has given this book the depth that comes from listening to many voices. I am grateful for his knowledge, for the balance he brings to this collaborative work, and for his presence in my life.

In the end, ethnographers are given the gift of people's stories. These stories are never told in obvious ways. They are told in the daily acts of sharing, committing, negotiating, and balancing the idiosyncratic personalities of people with the work of the community. They are told in the rituals surrounding important points in people's lives and in communal celebrations. They are told in the process of finding a place and an identity within larger, impersonal, and sometimes hostile contexts. They are told in the community of memory that acts as a guide for present and future actions. They are embodied in the people and embedded in their language. Both ethnographer and people live in the ground of all this yet must find the grace that lets them imagine, and the quietness and courage to listen in the silences and live in the disjunctures. I am grateful to the Isthmus Zapotec of Juchitán for the example of their grace and courage.

Anya Peterson Royce
Bloomington, Indiana
December 2010

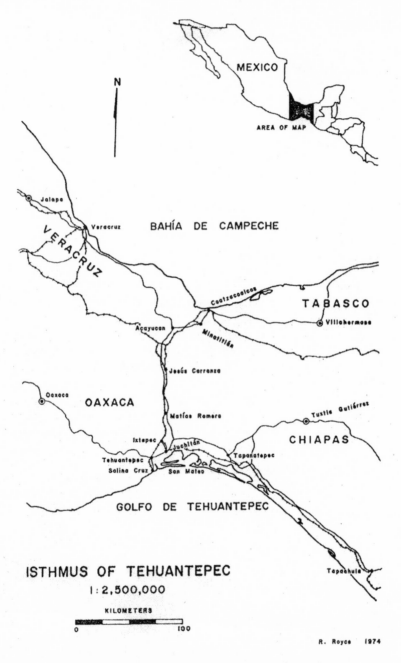

Map 1. The Isthmus of Tehuantepec. Map by Ronald R. Royce.

Note on
Isthmus Zapotec Orthography

Texts of poetry and songs appear in the orthographic systems used by the authors of those texts. Names of persons, celebrations, institutions, or associations are spelled according to local usage. Names of localities are written as found in publications of the government of Mexico. All other Zapotec words follow the spelling given in the *Vocabulario zapoteco del Istmo* (Pickett 1971). This work employs the popular alphabet approved during the Mesa Redonda of 1956, held in Mexico City under the sponsorship of the Consejo de Lenguas Indígenas, the Summer Institute of Linguistics, and the Sociedad Pro Planeación del Istmo.

Preface

The hundreds of generations of Isthmus Zapotec who have been born, lived their lives, and then joined the communities of the dead are linked to each other through an unbroken chain of ancestors and memories of places where community was honored. Never isolated, never local, they experienced periods of stability in which they flourished, periods of upheaval when they were scattered and threatened with extinction, and periods of great opportunity and transformation.

Becoming an Ancestor is about Isthmus Zapotec beliefs about death and how it is commemorated. It is also about grieving. Beliefs, commemorations, and grieving, while marked at particular points, unfold across time. Values of community, transformation, and balance are made tangible in this arena of belief and practice. Those values, in everything surrounding death, are crafted with sure aesthetic sensibility and a profound respect for being present. Focusing on death, we see especially clearly the peculiar continuity within transformation and change that characterizes Juchitán history and culture. The practices and beliefs in the domain of death cut across all other domains; indeed, we might speak of them as part of the deep structure of Isthmus Zapotec community.

The Isthmus Zapotec of Juchitán were part of the fifteenth-century exodus from Zaachila, a major center in the Valley of Oaxaca; a small force of Valley Zapotec swept into the Isthmus driving the inhabitants out onto the lagoons as with the Huave or into the Sierra and beyond in the case of people who were most likely Mixe and Zoque.[1] Once there, they settled into their new environment and exploited its possibilities, yet at the same time did not lose sight of their values, such as community and relationship, which had allowed them to create a strong, powerful, and enviable culture in the Valley of Oaxaca. The floodplain of the Río de los Perros, which divides modern Juchitán lengthwise, and then curves eastward carving off a chunk of the city called Saltillo, provided a rich subsistence and trade base for both early inhabitants and the Zapotec of the fifteenth century.

---

1. For a thorough examination of the ethnohistorical and archaeological evidence for this migration, see Judith Zeitlin's excellent book, *Cultural Politics in Colonial Tehuantepec* (2005). As the title implies, she applies the same careful approach to the entire Colonial Period, 1500 to 1756.

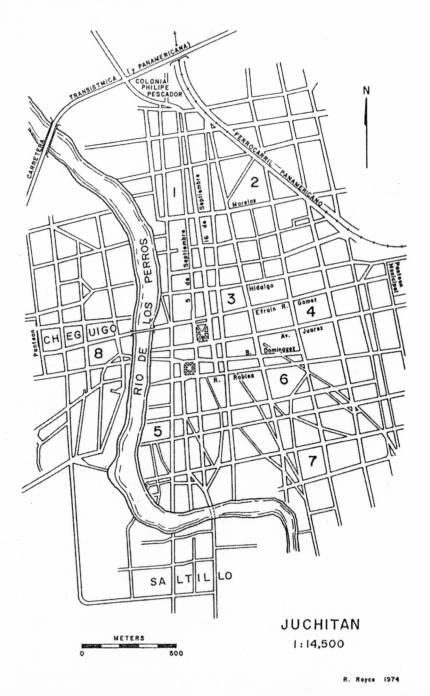

Map 2. The city of Juchitán showing the two main cemeteries and the eight sections. Map by Ronald R. Royce.

The rich floodplain soil in the rainy season allowed the cultivation of maize and other crops, supplemented by hunting and fishing. What gave those economies an advantage, however, was the possibility of trade because of the valued regional commodities such as salt, dried fish and shrimp, marine shells, feathers, and animal skins of the sort not available in more temperate climates (Zeitlin 2005:27). Looking at the ethnohistorical record, we see the central role of salt well into the twentieth century as an economic force as well as a contentious political bargaining point.

Important for understanding gender roles in contemporary Isthmus Zapotec society, something that seems to baffle outsiders, is the early and continuing range of economic strategies. Households, generally extended, were cooperative units with men growing and harvesting crops or hunting and fishing and women processing and marketing the products. This extended to the more exotic commodities such as salt or salted fish. To take fullest advantage meant complementary and equally valued roles for women and men. Having women involved in long-distance trade meant that they became bilingual and bicultural in ways that women in more traditional roles in other indigenous communities did not. This was undoubtedly a source of empowerment. Marketing and trade are still important economic activities, and the market is still predominantly female, but Juchitán's economy now has white-collar and professional opportunities. The long tradition of women's equal economic participation continues to shape their participation in these newer opportunities (Royce 1975, 1981, 1991). Women are just as likely as men to finish secondary school and preparatory and to seek professional degrees. Being a full economic partner in a household gives women a strong base, and, when necessary, an independent one.[2]

Complementary and equal roles, especially in a land typified by machismo, have made casual observers conclude that Isthmus Zapotec women dominate their men and their society. This has resulted in dozens of inaccurate and hurtful magazine articles and films that have exoticized Istmeñas. If one spends only a few days in a city like Juchitán, one might easily come away with this distorted image. Women are more visible on the street and in the market. Women are more visible at all social gatherings, especially the great cycle of fiestas called velas, where wearing the most formal and elaborate version of traditional dress (traje bordado) is required. Deeper than surface phenomena, however, is the fact that women move and go about their work with an aesthetic style that

---

2. For further reading about gender and the economic roles of women in Oaxaca, see Lynn Stephen, *Zapotec Women: Gender, Class and Ethnicity in Globalized Oaxaca* (Valley Zapotec of Teotitlán del Valle), 2005; Beverly Chiñas, *The Isthmus Zapotecs: Women's Roles in Cultural Context* (Isthmus Zapotec of San Blas Atempa), 1973; Judith M. Brueske, *The Petapa Zapotecs of the Inland Isthmus of Tehuantepec* (Isthmus Zapotec of Santa Maria Petapa), 1976; Marinella Miano Borrusco, *Hombre, mujer y muxe' en el Istmo de Tehuantepec*, 2002; and Veronika Bennholdt-Thomsen, ed., *Juchitán, la cuidad de las mujeres*, 1997. In the latter, see especially the essay by Marina Meneses Velasquez, "El camino de ser mujer en Juchitán."

is striking. All accounts by persons who have crossed paths with the Isthmus Zapotec have noted not only the physical beauty of the women, but also their striking carriage and movement. Miguel Covarrubias (1940), who married a Juchiteca, wrote of them, "They glide majestically with a rhythm and poise that defy description, motionless from the waist up, their ruffled, ample skirts rippling and swaying with their lithe steps" (pp. 150–51). He also notes that the women seem to age more gracefully than in other Indian and mestizo groups, explaining it by the fact that they work hard all their lives as the owners and traders of the markets. It is still the case that women are physically active from very young to well into their senior years, a practice that sustains their fluidity, flexibility, and confident demeanor.

Watching women friends sitting and talking is a visual feast of graceful gestures of hands, arms, and heads. Women going about their business, walking from home to market, to visit friends, or to attend Mass move with an elegance that is hard to forget—posture erect, chins high, legs striding purposefully. This is especially true if they are wearing traje—then their lower legs and feet part the long, gathered skirt allowing a glimpse of the full white petticoat beneath. Women, whatever their work or craft, take care to make it pleasing. Sometimes, as with bread making or embroidering traje or cooking for large fiestas, the beauty comes from mastery of the craft, economy of motion, rhythm. Those women the community identifies as "the best" are virtuosos of their craft, so deeply have they ingrained the elements of the craft that they perform it with a kind of nonchalance all the more attractive because they demonstrate not a trace of self-consciousness. These are examples of the aesthetics of ordinary life. Those aesthetics are heightened, reified, made dense on occasions that call for dance and performance that goes beyond the ordinary and become moments of display (Royce 2008).

This sense of the aesthetic struck me unforgettably the first time I saw the women and men from Juchitán perform at the Guelaguetza in Oaxaca in 1967: "the dancers were splendid, full of grace and authority. In all that they did, from placing the lacquered gourds . . . at the side of the stage, to dancing the understated sones, to acknowledging the admiration of the crowd, they displayed the kind of assurance that comes from knowing who one is. Neither a false snobbery nor an ingratiating demeanor, their carriage and character were formal, grave, yet gracious. . . . [This sense of occasion] acknowledges the gravity and importance of the work, *dxiiña'*, of sustaining community, the work of being Zapotec" (Royce 2002:8).

The embodiment of that assurance draws attention at the same time that it eludes our usual analysis. In March 2006, Delia and I visited Na Rosa just to say hello. The visit turned into a lesson in bread making for me. Rosa was kneading the dough for *yemitas* in a big, wooden server when we arrived. After asking her permission, I began filming her at work. When I put down the camera, she said to me, "You need to learn how to make bread." Pum! She slapped down the lump of dough. "Go wash your hands, yes, and take off your bracelet. Now, here is your dough, knead it." Self-consciously (because Delia had retrieved the camera and was filming my efforts), I tried to imitate what seemed simple when Rosa did it. Just when it began to feel comfortable, Rosa took the ball from me, "Now you have to divide the dough—here," and she sliced the big round lump into three identical pieces with a blue plastic deck-of-card-sized tool—whap! whap! whap! She picked up one piece and rolled it between her hands making a long, cylindrical shape. Twisting off the top two inches, she threw the piece onto the wooden surface that she had oiled with liquid lard. She handed me the remaining length of dough—"Now make the yemitas." I twisted off two-inch pieces and tried to shape them into the sym- metrical miniature loaves that Rosa produced by the hundreds. I managed to fill two rectangular baking sheets with misshapen but delicious yemitas, which I could take home and distribute to the family.

Rosa made her yemitas with the same care and attention that she uses as she prays as a member of the Association of the Sacred Heart or when tend- ing her garden of healing plants and flowers. Juchitecos seek the beautiful and appreciate the craft required to create and sustain it. This is part of what "calls our attention." The power of this sensibility as it is manifested everywhere, in the ordinary and the extraordinary, is heightened by another sustaining characteristic, the quality of being present. Women praying the nine days of prayers for a departed friend or relative are fully in that moment, bringing all their energy to the work of supporting the spirit of the dead and sustaining the community of the living.

Being in balance, being in harmony—beliefs about death exemplify this Isthmus Zapotec sought-after state. It is a pull toward symmetry, economy, and rightness, equally necessary for the dead as well as for the living. The passage from life to death is accomplished in an unhurried and deliberate manner, accompa- nied by the fragrant greenness of flowers, the rising clouds of incense, and the soft cadences of prayers all lifted in unison. Women and men work together, each with a set of tasks, to make the death of their loved ones a good one.

This is an ethnography of death, what the Isthmus Zapotec of Juchitán believe about it, how they commemorate it, and how they grieve. While Juchitecos will articulate "rules for appropriate behavior," they also acknowledge and expect subjective and individual ways of confronting death and loss. This is a pattern seen across other domains such as gender roles, the structure of identity, the economy, and change and persistence. The reader will see these domains enacted and embodied, embedded in the lives of the Juchitecos as they converse with and about dying, death, and the ancestors. As befits its central- ity in every society past and present, there is a very large body of work and theory on death. Although many points of similarity exist between the Isthmus

Zapotec case and other societies, especially with regard to natural symbols such as water and dryness, I agree with Sarah C. Humphreys (1993) when she talks about comparative studies of death: "it is clear that comparison will have to deal not with discrete "symbols" or even symbolic oppositions, but with complex combinations of social experience, practical observation, speculation and metaphor for which the notion of 'natural symbols' may provide a heuristically fruitful starting point, but not a ready-made blueprint" (p. 179). My task here is to understand the shape of dying, death, and grief as Juchitecos see and understand it. My discussion of theories and other ethnographic examples are couched in terms of how they illuminate Zapotec practice and belief. As part of this comparative process, the reader will gain an understanding of some of the most significant synthetic and ethnographic works on death.

Why death? Its importance in the lives of the people of Juchitán, increasingly apparent over the years of my association with them, simply calls for its own book. In this one domain, one begins to understand what matters—community, transformation, a complementarity of roles, beauty, and the work of relationship. I offer it to my family and friends and all the people of Juchitán as part of what they have defined as my work for the community. I offer it as well to others that they might see a different way of responding to the death that claims us all. Some may find satisfaction in seeing their own practices echoed here, and others, following the Isthmus Zapotec model, may be inspired to reach out to others in times of loss and grief. It is a way of being that roots people in the ground of community while applauding their seeking after transformation. It ensures that each generation becomes the ancestors for the next, offering comfort and intercession in return for being held in the memories of those who love them. In the midst of loss, it promises that community will survive and relationship will be restored.

Dxi rati guendaguti lu guendanabani

Nuu dxi, miati' ruxui'lu qué risaca xquendanabani
ne rini'xpiaani' ma' gue'tu' laa, laaca rizaaca huaxa
ra canazá sica ti gue'tu' lu guenda nabani xti
qué ziaadxa' tu gabi laa: saca guenda nabani,
guendaguti riguixhebiá' ni.
Raqué nga, guendaguti rati lu xhigaa guenda nabani
ne miati', sti bieque riasa, rigu'ba' bi, ricaa xneza.

—Maestro Enedino Jiménez

When Death Dies a Natural Life

Sometimes a person believes
that life has no purpose
and imagines death,
but it happens in your state
of death in life,
someone says to you: it is death
that gives value to life.
Then death dies a natural life
and a person takes up life once more.

—Translated by Anya Peterson Royce

1

Introduction

Palm Sunday 1997: the sky is electric blue, cloudless on this early morning. I was in the courtyard of San Vicente Ferrer, the parish church, just having returned from the cemetery where I helped the family arrange the armloads of flowers necessary for this day of remembrance. I waited for the arrival of the Palm Sunday procession, winding its way through the streets after distributing palms to all participants at the small chapel of the cemetery. I could hear them now, voices raised in those joyous songs welcoming Christ the King to Jerusalem. The higher pitched voices of children rise above with cries of "Vivo Cristo Rey." The church behind me is filled with flowers, white gladiolas, dozens of them, jasmine and frangipani scattered at the feet of all the saints. The fragrance swells with the heat of fat beeswax candles. All is ready and the crowd is dancing with anticipation. A scout returns, "They are just turning the corner!"

Then, as if my ears deceive me, I hear the low, elongated notes of funeral sones. Jesús Urbieta, one of a cadre of talented young painters who died in Mexico City two days earlier, is being borne by silent comrades to rest a moment in the Casa de la Cultura where his paintings had often hung. The parish church and the Casa de la Cultura sit next to each other, separated only by a wrought-iron fence. The two processions arrive simultaneously. San Salvador, borne on the shoulders of the men who care for him, heavy garlands of frangipani hang around his neck; jasmine, frangipani blossoms, and petals of roses of Castile rain down on him, making his way sweet. The children in white shirts too big for them wave their palms. Beaming women carry huge vases of white flowers. The Glorias fill the courtyard announcing the happy arrival. Urbieta too is carried on the shoulders of his closest comrades, men who have cared for him. His coffin is heaped high with flowers of the wild (white jasmine, long, ropy palm flowers, tuberose, hibiscus, frangipani) all on a bed of the healing herbs (dill and cordoncillo). Everyone brought jasmine, *guie' xhuuba'* in Zapotec, in honor of the club Urbieta had founded by that name to help young artists. Urbieta has begun his journey to his new home among the dead. Christ, in the midst of celebration, has begun his death.

—Field notes, March 23, 1997

1

The Isthmus Zapotec, concentrated primarily in the southern Oaxaca city of Juchitán, are a rarity within Mexico. They have survived 2,500 years of attempts to exterminate them, bring them into submission, assimilate them, and exoticize them, to reach a place where they can and do name themselves and claim their place. As do all peoples who persist through shifts and changes in the larger political and economic contexts, the Zapotec have maintained certain fundamental values and outward markers of who they are, while exploiting opportunities—technological, economic, political—that give them a competitive edge in national and global arenas. Theirs is a culture marked by fluidity around a solid core. Over the centuries, this combination has allowed them to bend, rather than break.[1]

Fundamental Values

Three values are essential to this strategy of calculated change and persistence: community, transformation, and balance. All of these require action to maintain a healthy state. Zapotec is a language of action; people's behaviors and attitudes assume an active stance toward whatever surrounds them. Community, *guendalisaa*, is created only by people's actions. The Zapotec word literally means "making kinship." As people go through their daily lives, they are keenly aware of obligations to make kinship or honor relationships. This value is difficult for Westerners or anyone raised in societies that privilege the individual to grasp. This sense of obligation in no way prevents them from crafting lives that fulfill their own dreams; indeed, the Zapotec community of Juchitán expects innovation and exploration of new areas from its members and sustains them in those endeavors. Such accomplishment can only benefit the community as a whole. Imagine the positive contributions of generations learning all the new technologies and new ways of thinking about old fields, who, at the same time, continue to feel connected and obligated to their home.

Intimately connected to those notions about community is the value of transformation that carries both the meaning of personal change as well as a

---

1. After forty-two years of field research with the Isthmus Zapotec of Juchitán, my own association has taken on the same responsibilities and obligations to the living and the dead as theirs. My grandmother, Na Berta Pineda, whose forty-day Mass I have described in chapter 2, was a superb mentor, witty, wise, and always ready to sit and talk, or better, to dance. Her daughter, Na Rosinda Fuentes vda de Ramírez, has taken me into the family as her other daughter. Delia, Rosinda and Chu's daughter, is my sister and my best friend. These women have helped me understand what commitment means, accepting me as the young, inexperienced anthropologist I was in 1967, and now continuing to teach me as I try to give others a sense of what it means to be Zapotec in the twenty-first century. They have loved me unconditionally.

change of substance. Zapotec call people who are wise *binni guenda biaani'.*
Literally, we could translate this as people (creating) light, or, if we want to
reference a broader, Pan-American Indian tradition, they are the people through
whom light flows. I know wise people who are bread makers, dancers, poets,
healers, prayer leaders, musicians, and cooks. While their occupations and
degree of formal education vary wildly, they share certain qualities. They have
mastered the craft of what they do—they are artists of making bread or dancing
or healing; they are always open to learning new things, thinking of their lives
as a process—the healer who was my friend loved to learn about other healing
traditions, and as part of his apprenticeship worked with healers in Guatemala;
they are not afraid of change, of transformation; they listen and are willing to
act as guides for others who seek them out. They believe absolutely in their role
as vessels for the light and practice making themselves into the best possible
instruments. Finally, they are humble about themselves, believing that the gifts
they have are only loaned to them—they do not own them nor do they make
any claim to privilege. Not everyone is a binni guenda biaani', but everyone
knows people who are, respects them, and occasionally goes to them for help.
Valuing personal risk-taking and transformation has to have been a strategic
advantage, especially as it is embodied in individuals who were women and
men and *muxe'* (third gender)[2], formally educated or not, wealthy or poor, and
found in all occupations.

Balance is the third and last, and, in some ways, is the value that helps
the other two find positive and steady forms, and remain in equilibrium. Ta
Feli or Ta Feli Chomo (Felix López Jiménez),[3] the healer with whom I worked
most closely, told a wonderful story of the balance of forces on the level of
human survival. He talked about the different powers allocated to water and
to wind, powers that when in moderation are helpful and when out of propor-
tion are dangerous. Water is a young woman, he said, who, when humans are
behaving as they should, sees that they have water necessary for growing crops,
for fishing, for drinking, and so on. But when humans do things that upset

---

2. The *muxe'* have long constituted an important part of Isthmus Zapotec society. When I first
began working in Juchitán in 1968, the men who were defined and who defined themselves as
muxe' practiced particular occupations, most notably that of designing and embroidering the regional festive dress, designing the floats, flowers, and decorations for the large fiestas called *velas*,
making the little clay figurines called *tanguyú*, making special kinds of bread, and cooking for
special occasions. Most did not marry although some did. Of those who did not marry, some were
sexually active in homosexual relationships. Some cross-dressed and many more wore the kind of
gold jewelry worn by women. This model has changed over the years to include more attributes
of Western gay lifestyle.

3. Sadly, Ta Feli died on March 11, 2004. His niece Minerva is keeping the healing alive as well
as his *espiritista* temple.

her, she gets angry and causes great floods. It is Wind's job to calm her and make the waters recede. He does this by blowing across the waters, containing them. In the seasonal climate of the region, we see all the possible variations of wind and water, from the disruptive and destructive *bi yooxho* or powerful north wind to the gentle *bi nisa* south or water wind, from rain that supports the crops to rain that periodically floods the city.

This is precisely what happens in the domain of health and illness. Good health is the result of the balance of elements: hot and cold, wet and dry, or emotions such as anger, fear, melancholy. The contrast here between anger and hatred reinforces the importance of balancing strong emotions. Hatred, be *nanna la'dxi'*, literally "it hurts inside," is something that, even though one might direct it toward someone else, it still hurts one. It requires an ongoing and powerful emotion, which is not healthy. Anger is quick to flare and, in the healing process, quick to recede.[4] When one of these is too strong, the person is open to illness, and healing is a matter of restoring the balance. Healers have a whole stock of treatments based on these oppositions. Most Zapotec can also diagnose and recommend treatment that will bring a person back into balance.

Balance, like community and transformation, operates across all domains. So, for example, while Juchitán is famous for its strong, often radical, political positions, the desires and actions of the few who push for political change are tempered by the views of community members who are respected for their knowledge and whose commitment cannot be questioned. How this kind of consultation happens is a good demonstration of the importance of relationships and family. Seeking the opinions of others or the right of family and relatives to offer opinions is not limited to politics. It is the first thing that happens when someone is sick or when someone is contemplating a major personal change. The balance between younger generations who acquire new kinds of expertise and older generations who have a different kind of knowledge is maintained by the implicit acknowledgment of the importance of the community—the city at the largest level, family at the closest to the individual level—and one's obligation to it, at the same time that transformation is also acknowledged and valued. Consensus is not always achieved but inclusive discussion is always expected.

Isthmus Zapotec society lives in this tension between accommodating, indeed, initiating change and sustaining the values and tangible symbols of an ancient tradition even as they change them. The secret of their success is that it has never been an either-or proposition, change or stay the same. Disagree-

---

4. In this context, hatred is an emotion that defies the system. *Nanaa la'dxi'* or *duele dentro*, "it hurts inside" is something one does that hurts oneself; hating someone, who usually does not know about it, causes one pain. People do not accept it as a healthy emotion because it requires an ongoing and powerful emotion, which cannot be healthy for anyone. Anger is another order of things. It is quick and one comes back into balance afterward.

ments arise frequently because of deeply felt positions, but they are mediated by the complicated network of relationships.

Death and dying—Zapotec beliefs about them and the ways in which they acknowledge, grieve, act upon, and remember the individuals and the process— can only be understood within the context of community, transformation, and balance. Death is ever-present in the lives of the Zapotec, in ways in which members of many Western societies, ignorant of the trinity of Zapotec values, cannot even begin to imagine. The beliefs and practices represent an amalgam of Zapotec, Western, Roman Catholic, and global influences. One cannot use-fully separate one from another because they are not layered in consistent or predictable ways. Who and what the Zapotec are today is the result of centuries of a flexible attitude toward themselves and their global partners, sprung out of the active living of community, of transformation, and of seeking balance. They have not acted precipitously out of the passions or challenges of the moment nor have they been satisfied to remain in the comfort of a way of life that got them by. Their history is not a series of lurches, false starts, reactions, or short-term successes. It is, rather, like a great river that swirls and eddies at the edges as it encounters obstacles and opportunities, but which has a deep and smooth current at its heart. If we do not understand that, then we will understand nothing about what matters, about what it means to be Zapotec. Theirs is not a patchwork culture; neither is it a patched-together culture. Like all persistent peoples, the Zapotec enjoy a way of living that has its own integrity; it has the capacity to surprise itself, at the same time that memory and community provide continuity.

Domain of Death

Death provides a window onto the working of Zapotec culture and social insti-tutions. What happens in the domain of death is repeated across all domains, lending support to my argument for integrity and consistency. Death also touches people at the most basic level. As René Le Corre observed about Breton death observances, "Religion for the dead is the religion which has survived best today, and it is that which preceded the Catholic faith" (cited in Badone 1989:159). More than birth, marriage, illness, coming of age, indeed, any of the rites of passage, death seems to have some persistent and powerful place in society's imagination. As Rodney Needham (1973) noted, death is unique among rites of passage because we never can know the final state.

C. Nadia Seremetakis (1992) gives us a thoughtful reflection on two of bodies of theory about death. She examines those who have treated death as one component of an overarching social organization (Durkheim 1947; Bloch and Parry 1982; Huntington and Metcalf 1979) or those, their critics, such as

Rosaldo (1984) and Danforth (1982), who view death as a window onto the affective, emotional domain of individuals. In the first case, death is perceived as an appendage of other social institutions, and in the second is seen as personal and independent of the communal. She suggests that a historical view such as that of Ariès (1981) places death center stage as one of the deep structures of premodern social life. The institution of death, she argues, functions as a space of local resistance to centralizing institutions such as the church and the state (p. 14). Seeing death as part of the deep structure of Zapotec culture allows us to understand that peculiar continuity within transformation that characterizes the history of Juchitán and its people. For our purposes, it provides a point of entry into how and why Zapotec culture has created and sustained itself, while other cultures distant and close have not managed to achieve the same integration and continuity.

Death in Mexico

Much has been written about death in Mexico, the majority of it concentrated on the Day of the Dead, which has become a mainstay of the tourism industry. Mexican writers such as Octavio Paz have speculated about Mexican attitudes toward death—mocking, challenging, not fearful—and the reasons why it should be so. Popular artists such as José Guadalupe Posada (1852–1913) took death in new directions with startlingly macabre drawings of skulls and skeletons, known as *Calaveras*. His most famous, reproduced everywhere was the *calavera catrina*, a fashionable lady skeleton in a big picture hat. The images were accompanied by verses that fell into the category of political satire. Painters such as Diego Rivera and Frida Kahlo incorporated death in their work in both blatant and subtle ways, allowing the observer to uncover multiple meanings. Sergei Eisenstein dedicated the epilogue of his most ambitious and unfinished film, *¡Qué viva México!*, to Posada. Eisenstein himself, like a long list of foreign writers, filmmakers, artists, and social commentators, was responsible for solidifying the idea of Mexicans mocking and celebrating death.

Today much of Mexico becomes a giant commemoration of death on November 1 and 2. All the images beloved by the artists and writers are for sale in markets, large and small, where ordinary wares have been set aside to make way for the accouterments of death—sugar skulls, *pan de muerto* (bread of the dead), decorated candles, cutout tissue paper in Posada-inspired designs, fruit, marigolds, calla lilies, little skulls and images molded from honey and amaranth, carved caskets, altars, whole families of skeletons, cockscomb, incense, coconuts. In the Oaxaca market, I once found skeleton dolls sporting all the regional dresses of Oaxaca's indigenous groups. There is no question that the Day of the Dead is a major holiday throughout Mexico. Chloë Sayer, in her edited volume (1990) provides colorful evidence of its popularity. It is also true that it was observed for quite some time before it emerged in its present form. Mexican anthropologist Claudio Lomnitz (2005) presents an intriguing ethnohistorical analysis proposing what he calls the "nationalization of death" on the part of the Mexican government as a way of consolidating its power. He also gives us rich material on the domestication of death through family ritual and popular culture. Stanley Brandes (1997, 2003, 2006) traces the history of this major holiday, its influences, and the paradoxes it presents within Mexico and in the United States, where it has become a statement of ethnicity. He also takes up the perplexing issue of the relationship of Day of the Dead to what death means in the Mexican context. More specific to Oaxaca is Kristin Norget's 2006 book about the Day of the Dead and other death rituals in a neighborhood of Oaxaca City. She also provides an excellent review of the different theoretical approaches to death.

This book will come back to regional and national celebrations of the Day of the Dead and Mexican attitudes about death only infrequently.[5] Its purpose is, rather, to explore Isthmus Zapotec beliefs about death and their ways of acknowledging and remembering it. Drawing on forty-two years of field research in the Isthmus Zapotec city of Juchitán, I juxtapose fine-grained ethnographic descriptions with more general observations of patterns and symbols. I trace the same structures and symbols that surround death across other domains of Zapotec life. Finally, I am concerned to show, through the examination of death and what people say and do about it, the basic integrity of Zapotec culture, how it came to be, and how it persists, reinventing itself as the larger environment changes.

Historical and Contemporary Practices

All of the sources we can examine to understand pre-Columbian observances of death by the ancestors of contemporary Zapotec—archaeological, ethnohistorical, and historical—indicate that death has always loomed large in the Zapotec worldview, engendering a wide range of practices and beliefs. We know that observances included particular rites for burying the dead as well as communal rites of remembrance. It is worth quoting a passage from Burgoa, virtually in its entirety, because it is such a careful description of one of these communal observances:

---

5. For an examination of Day of the Dead and other death rituals in one of the neighborhoods of Oaxaca City, see Kristin Norget's 2006 book *Days of Death, Days of Life: Ritual in the Popular Culture of Oaxaca*. Norget also provides an excellent review of the different theoretical approaches to death.

On the eve of this lugubrious celebration, they killed a great number of birds, especially turkeys, and dressed them with dry ground
pepper, squash seeds, and spearmint leaves or avocado which they
cooked for the *totomole*; the turkeys with the ground chile were
covered with corn dough, covered with avocado leaves, and put to
cook in jars or clay ovens. These were called *petlatamales*, and each
family put the ones they had prepared in gourd containers. When
night fell, they put them on a table made of cane as an offering
for their dead. They prayed to the dead for forgiveness and asked
them to return and enjoy the food. They asked them to intercede
with the gods whom they served in the other world to bring good
crops and good fortune to the living. They knelt in front of the
offering, eyes cast down, praying, all night long. They never lifted
their heads because if they saw the dead who came, they would
be angry and ask the gods to punish them. The next morning,
they had a big fiesta and talked about how successful the night's
celebration was. They took the food and gave it to strangers or the
poor, or not finding anyone, threw it into hidden places. The food
was blessed and, having given it to the dead, it would be a great
sin to take it back. (Burgoa 1934:391–92)

What Burgoa does not tell us is the location of the night vigil. Setting that
aside for the moment, the remainder of his description fits quite closely with
contemporary Isthmus Zapotec practice on the Day of the Dead and the days
preceding it. Families prepare tamales—of chicken or beef (both of which were
Spanish introductions)—some of which go on the altar as food for the dead along
with fruit and bread. Prayers are offered in front of the altar for nine days up to
and including the Day of the Dead. The prayers include petitions to the Virgin
Mary and to Christ on behalf of the departed. On that last day, visitors come
and are given tamales and bread. The family offering the altar and the prayers
does not eat any of the food. When the altar is taken down, all the food on it
is sorted into separate portions, which are sent to those women who had come
to pray (see chapter 6 for the extended discussion of these Day of the Dead
practices). What makes the Isthmus Zapotec unique is their observance of Day
of the Dead in their homes, rather than in the cemeteries as is the case in the
rest of Mexico. Juchitecos visit the dead in the cemeteries during Holy Week,
an example of reciprocal feasting, one of the fundamental aspects of community.

We have scattered historical accounts of rituals for individuals, and, of
course, we have the archaeological sites themselves and their contents, from
which we can begin to draw a picture of early practices. Distinctions were made
according to the social status or role of the individual. The bodies of kings and
princes were carried to Mitla on the shoulders of men, with an honor guard

of the most distinguished nobility. The procession was accompanied by somber music and the laments of the grieving people. A companion would recite the accomplishments of the deceased so that everyone along the route would be reminded. The tombs themselves were subterranean, cruciform structures with niches carved out of the walls of the main room and the cross-spaces. The walls were richly decorated with murals commemorating Zapotec royal ancestors (Marcus 1978:187). The niches were filled with funerary urns—fired clay vessels that represented various personages and that had vaselike containers on the back. Funerary urns and incense burners were placed on the floor of the tomb as well. Grave goods included fine jewels and fabrics and offerings of copal.

Most people were buried with less pomp and material goods, but their tombs were also subterranean and the walls were plastered over with a kind of stucco. Stone steps led down into the tomb so that relatives could come and make their offerings of food and drink, copal, flowers, and maize.

Ancestor worship was one of the important features of pre-Columbian Zapotec society. The dead were buried under patios close to the living. The departed were visited regularly by their relatives and brought gifts of food, fine goods, flowers, and drink. Their images appeared in murals in the tombs and perhaps also in the anthropomorphic funerary urns. Altars, called *pecogo* in pre-Columbian Valley Zapotec, were close by the tombs and were the locus of family observances.

All of these elements are present in contemporary belief and practice. The procession of the body of Jesús Urbieta, which began this chapter, would not have been out of place in pre-Columbian Mitla. Departed relatives, images kept close to the family on the home altar, are consulted often for advice as well as for intercession with God and the saints. The further distant from death they are, the more their lives and words take on aspects of binni guenda biaani' whose wisdom serves as a prescription for action. Poet Enedino Jiménez (2004) captures this strong attachment when in his poem "Siado' guie'" ("The Flower of Dawn") he writes about the voice of the ancestors—*xtiidxá ca rigola za*—awakening understanding. Every Thursday and Sunday the cemeteries are filled with people bringing flowers and company to their departed relatives. Photographs in tombs and altars are a constant reminder of family members absent through death. And the altar itself in its full communal presentation during the Day of the Dead is called *biguié'* (spirit-flower), a continuation of the old pecogo.

Values and Zapotec Death

Dying is a gradual process of becoming dry, wetness being an essential property of the living. The departed then is transformed from some being that is *nayaa* (wet, green, fresh) to a being which is *nabidxi* (dry). All the flowers, water, willow branches, banana leaves, and green cocos that figure in the funerary rites throughout the first two years are nayaa and function to make the deceased's journey a smooth and gradual one rather than an abrupt transformation. In addition to the body's physical transformation from wet to dry, the deceased also is moved from the space of the living to the appropriate living space of the dead—the cemetery. Again, this is accomplished over considerable time broken into periods each with its own set of rituals—the nine days of prayer, the forty days of mourning followed by a Mass, the Mass on the first anniversary, then again on the seventh, the two years of Day of the Dead altars, and the Holy Week visits to the cemeteries.

Wetness and dryness, life and death are not limited to the Isthmus Zapotec. In the Greek village where Seremetakis (1990) conducted her examination of death, the dead person is referred to as *xerós*, which means dried out or stale in standard Greek. *Xerénome* means I am drying out, I am dying, that is to say, I am drying out due to aging, extreme cold or heat, hard work, crying (p. 179). These people practice a double burial, that is, defleshed bones are exhumed and "reburied" in an ossuary. Such is not the contemporary Zapotec practice though there is some evidence that it was common for high-status individuals in pre-Columbian times. S. C. Humphreys (1993:178), in her notes on the several studies that comprised an earlier edition, observes that an association of water with life and dryness with death occurred frequently across a disparate range of societies. She also notes the complexity of these associations and their distinctiveness. Juchitán adds yet another way of looking at water and dryness and its relationship to death and life.

In Juchitán, the dead person remains part of the community. All of the observances listed previously and the weekly cemetery visits to replenish flowers and water, the tending to the home altar with its photograph of the dead—all these indicate that the dead are very much connected to family and the larger community. Perhaps the clearest demonstration is the reciprocity involved in the dead being invited to the homes of the living on Day of the Dead and the living being invited to the homes of the dead during Holy Week. There is no difference between this and the reciprocal feasting that takes place continually among the living. How much the dead are treated as members of the community can be seen in the ways in which children or young, unmarried adults are acknowledged in death. In both these cases, fireworks accompany the body and livelier sones are played to take the place of the wedding that they will not have. The community is honoring the responsibilities it would have had toward them had they lived.

Balance characterizes the process of mourning as well as the attitude toward the feelings of the departed. In the first hours after death when the body is laid out in front of the home altar, relatives and friends come to pay their respects. Weeping and lamenting the death are expected and appropriate. Sometimes mourners may be so overcome that they throw themselves on the coffin or cry uncontrollably. There is a point past which such behavior is regarded as too much and people will step in, trying to calm the person, gradually leading him away to a quiet place. Grieving may be bound at some level by codes of behavior, but it is and should be a very personal response. The work of musicians and prayer leaders in these contexts weaves a fabric of notes and words that holds people in a safe space. Musicians understand their work at wakes and memorials to be directed toward both the living and the dead, singing the dead along their way and holding them in the grief of the living. Prayer leaders define their work as much more than reciting prayers; they hold the people together in their grief, making a proper space in which they can mourn without disrupting the important work of transformation and passage (see chapter 3).

Just as there is this sensitivity toward the living who have suffered a loss, there is the same sensitivity toward the dead who, after all, are now in a liminal place, neither living nor dead. People understand the sadness, indeed, the literal sense of dislocation, felt by the departed and balance the spirit's need for companionship and familiar surroundings with the need to begin the process of separation. There is a real concern that the dead, in their cemetery homes, be happy, and conversations will often include reference to how appreciative the deceased was for the flowers and the visit. *Espiritistas* have the ability to call up the spirits of the dead and, in fact, do so regularly around the Day of the Dead. People go on the chance that their family member might be one of the passing spirits bringing a request that they will need to honor. Several adepts of the espiritista temple go into a trance state (*se duerman*), working one at a time. Another member of the temple is there to interpret and provide guidance for the people who have come. Three older men stand to one side, acting as spirit-bouncers. When there is an unhappy, bad, or mischief-making spirit, they may distract it, make it leave. The initial response, however, is always to try to discern what has caused the spirit to feel so helpless, aggrieved, or angry. The arriving spirits speak through the adept, and after an exchange of greetings and establishing who the spirit is, the spirit is asked what he wants. The first answer, in almost every case, is a drink of water. It is assumed that he is thirsty because he has been walking, but it may also be that his family has not been keeping fresh glasses of water on the home altar. Other quite specific requests may be made.

In a sense, the novena and the entire forty days of prayers become a grace period, with the spirit still there, close to the home altar, embodied in the flower body laid out on the floor, listening to the prayers, smelling the flowers, and drinking their moisture. The last lifting up of the flower body and the Mass on the fortieth day tell the spirit that it now has to go to its new home. Little crosses made from palm leaves are placed in the windows to discourage the spirit from returning but, at the same time, a votive candle burns day and night in front of the altar, a light for the dead.

Structural Oppositions

Certain fundamental oppositions run throughout Zapotec culture and become foregrounded in beliefs about death and the rituals that embody belief. These are wet (*nayaa*) and dry (*nabidxi*) on the one hand, and wild (*gui'xhi'*) and town (*guidxi*), on the other.[6] In moments such as death or a serious illness, these oppositions are either out of balance or are in transition from one state to another. Whatever the state, these moments must be treated carefully because the consequences of doing nothing or doing a ritual improperly are grave. The fact that these oppositions, or rather, the symbols that stand for them, are at the heart of much Zapotec song, poetry, and painting highlights their importance and provides further evidence of their centrality to Zapotec culture.

Wet

The living, young girls, flowers (especially those of the wild) the sea, the south wind, and *bi nisa* (water wind)—all these are quintessentially wet and are imbued with positive qualities. We have already seen instances of this quality being invoked in practices having to do with death, and we will examine them and others in greater detail in subsequent chapters. One is wettest at birth and life is a process of gradually drying out; death hastens that process somewhat, explaining the need for "wet" objects and ritual because the dead are in greater need of it. Young girls have all the good qualities of freshness—they are described in conversations, literature, and song as *nayaa* (fresh), *nanaxhi* (sweet-smelling), and *nagá'* (*frondoso*—lush or leafy). The *traje bordado* (embroidered skirt and huipil) especially but not exclusively appropriate for unmarried girls is embroidered with flowers of all colors, shapes, and sizes. The girls are flowers. Married women can retain the quality of nagá' or lushness. Dieting or losing weight through illness robs one of that quality. I made one trip to Juchitán after a successful diet and was told that when I came before I was nagá' and beautiful. Now I was *naguundu'* (wilted or dried up), and so I needed to eat more. Thinness is associated with being dry once one is an adult woman. Young boys are not described in these terms nor do they figure in the songs or painting.

Most flowers and many fruits have the quality of being nayaa. Those that have it in greater abundance are those that are found in the wild or gui'xhi'. Rosinda told me about gathering fruit and flowers from the wild when she

---

6. In addition to these, hot (*nandá'*) and cold (*nananda*) provide an opposition that characterizes certain beliefs and practices, particularly in the area of illness and healing. Because they are not as well-integrated and are limited to only a few domains, I regard them as later notions that have been incorporated in those areas where they supplement the other oppositions or certain important values. An underlying explanation might be that the seasonal variations that are recognized in the Isthmus have to do with wet and dry rather than with hot and cold.

was a child—wild cherries, icaco or *pépé* (fruit of a local tree), guayaba, wild figs, nanche, sugar cane, several kinds of jasmine, cordoncillo, frangipani, palm flower, *guie' bi'chi'* (dragon's blood), and basil. Willow branches are also important for certain death observances. There is also a wonderful flower of legend—*mudubina*, a kind of water lily. Women make necklaces of them by taking one long-stemmed blossom and folding and peeling the stem so that it makes two strands with the flower at its center. They fasten the ends and wear it around their necks with the blossom in front. It feels remarkably cool and wet, especially welcome in the hot climate that characterizes most of the year. The other flower that is worn around the neck is the frangipani or *guie' chaachi*. Individual blooms are strung and the strings are tied to make a necklace—these are adornments of both saints and humans. Their freshness and sweet smell are said to have great healing properties.

Water (*nisa*), of course, is nayaa, but the sea (*nisadó*), and the rain (*nisa guie*), are especially so. This is to be expected because both are climatological forces of significance for the continued well-being of Juchitán. The other major climatological element with this wet property is the south wind (bi nisa), literally "water wind." This is the gentle (and female) wind that comes off the Pacific bringing much-needed rain, and not the inundations that are more likely to come from the north particularly during the summer hurricane season. This wind and the rains it brings characterize the season the Isthmus Zapotec call *gusiguié* ("rainy season," literally, "season of flowers"). All these manifestations of water appear again and again in literature and painting. We can also trace them back to the earliest symbols that appear at the ancient site of Monte Albán I (500 BCE–100 BCE), in particular, glyph C, so named by Mexican archaeologist Alfonso Caso in 1928, and associated with water in its different manifestations.[7] For example, in its simplest form, it has wavy or zigzag lines that represent water. It is also associated with the day-sign Water (Leigh 1974).

---

7. Alfonso Caso was the Mexican archaeologist who excavated the pre-Hispanic city of Monte Albán. In his 1928 study of Zapotec hieroglyphs, he named one that appears most frequently and consistently through all the stages of Monte Albán, glyph C. Following earlier writers, Caso believed the glyph to represent a stylized jaguar, and his interpretation held sway for many later writers. Howard Leigh (1974), in his careful reconstruction of the evolution of glyph C, finds no evidence of anything other than water and water-aspects associated with this glyph. Leigh describes the simplest form of the glyph as having undulations or zigzags that represent water; it is also sometimes associated with the day-sign Water (*Nisa*, in Zapotec). In Monte Albán IIIa (200–500 CE), the day-sign for Alligator (*Chila*, in Zapotec) appears in conjunction with glyph C, leaves, and flowing double streams. Alligator is the first day of the Mesoamerican calendar and is also referred to as Sky Monster. Marcus and Flannery (1996) describe *Cociyo* or Lightning as the most powerful and sacred of the forces in the early Zapotec universe. Lightning's companions include Clouds (*Zaa*), Rain (*Niça Quiye*), Wind (*Pèe*), and Hail (*Quiezabi*). The other major set of forces was associated with Earth (p. 19). A cosmos with supernatural forces such as these is what one would expect of an agricultural society, especially one living in the physical environment of the Valley of Oaxaca.

Dry

Old people, the dead, the ancestors, tuberculosis, toads, and the north wind—these are all examples of dryness. In some cases, this is part of a natural process and not regarded as bad, as in old people whose other qualities such as wisdom and transformation compensate the dry state of their bodies, and the ancestors who continue to intercede and provide models of proper behavior for the living. Ancestors are so dry as to be beyond any negative sense attached to dryness. Diseases such as tuberculosis are obviously bad because they accelerate the process of becoming dry in an unnatural manner. Toads (*bidxi*) embody an unpleasant dryness, whereas frogs (*bidxi ñee gaa*) are wet. Toads loom large in the literature and painting, including the Classic Period murals at the site of Cacaxtla. They appear frequently in the paintings of Francisco Toledo who calls Juchitán his home. The north wind has a season named for it, the season of the *nisadó', nortes*. This is a fierce, drying wind that howls across the Isthmus from north to south for five or six months of the year. With its dry, sometimes gale-force winds, it brings the onset of colds, bronchitis, eye diseases, and chronic coughs. In Zapotec, it is the *bi yooxho* or the "old wind," and is thought of as male. The season characterized by nortes is called *gusibá* ("season of the tomb"). Together, the year is divided between the rainy season or *gusiguié* and the dry season or *gusibá*. Two major communal celebrations mark the beginnings of the two seasons: Holy Week or *Nabaana Ro* ("time of great mourning") initiates the gusiguié, whereas the Day of the Dead signals the beginning of the gusibá.

Wild

The wild—the uncultivated, unworked land, mountains, caves, rivers, and the sea—is where one goes for knowledge. The rabbit stories, once a mainstay of tales told to children, epitomize this belief. Rabbit is set a task and he goes to the wild—a cave or the monte—to find the solution. When healers "travel" in their minds to find the causes of someone's illness or to augment their knowledge of illness, health, and healing, they go to the wild. Ta Feli, the healer I knew best, would describe rivers with their rushing waters and banks of lush foliage or sometimes the inside of a huge mountain as places he was drawn to by his *cumplimiento*, or vocation as a healer, and as someone whose dedication kept the world from tipping to the side of evil. The wild is inhabited by certain flowers (those listed here as the wettest), nondomesticated animals—jaguar, iguana, armadillo, snakes, turtles, deer, wildcats, monkeys, rabbits, and some birds—eagles, hawks, ravens, owls, and the water ouzel or *bere lele*. The wild is both a place of danger and a place of wisdom. Children are admonished not to wander near riverbanks or caves or the *monte* because that is where the *duendes* (mischievous spirits who appear as small people) gather. Unhappy or lost spirits of the dead may be there too, or *bidxaa* (a kind of witch who turns into an animal and causes harm to people) who frequent the wild, but especially crossroads on the edges of inhabited places.

There used to be more of the wild but as Juchitán expands, adding more and more suburbs, and other cities grow, the wild has become more circumscribed. The category remains an important one, however, remaining very much alive in people's imaginations. One bird, the bere lele, illustrates the deep import of the wild-tame opposition. The bird is basically wild but will allow itself to be "tamed" by one person. They are scarce so, while many people would like to have one, few in fact do. And the bird, when it bonds, does so with only one person. They have a song, more, a cry, which consists of notes cascading downward. The blind Juchiteco flute player, Cenobio López, composed a piece called "Bere lele," which imitates this cry. When the owner dies, the bird begins this cry, refuses to eat or drink, and almost always dies, despite the heroic efforts of relatives. The first time I encountered this was at the death of Don Silahyn, an old man who had been one of Ta Chu's goldsmiths. At the moment of his death, his bird crawled under his bed and began its lament. It tried to follow the funeral procession but was kept back. His daughter-in-law took it with her to Coatzacoalcos where it died three weeks later. The second encounter was on Good Friday at the Capilla de la Misericordia to which Christ's body is taken after his descent from the cross. I was sitting in the chapel with Delia when I heard those same notes. It was a bere lele in the patio of the adjoining house. The bird figures in painting, literature, and music. Indeed, Zapotec think of themselves as being like the bere lele, essentially wild, but willing to live in community, on their terms.

Before the Spanish arrived, there were only three domesticated animals—the turkey, the honeybee, and a dog that the Aztec bred for food. Most animals, then, fell into the wild category. Many of them were hunted for food—iguana, armadillo, rabbit, deer, and turtle both for its flesh and its eggs. Although the supply is decreasing, all of these are still an important part of the Zapotec diet, supplementing beef, pork, chicken, and all manner of fish. The Foro Ecológico (Ecological Forum) has begun a program of breeding and raising iguanas to bring their numbers back to the abundance of an earlier time. Foro personnel also instruct Juchitecos on how to raise their own iguanas.

Tame or Town

Cultivated land, the town, domestic animals (cows, pigs, cats, dogs, domesticated birds such as chickens and turkeys), Western medicine, cultivated flowers usually trucked in from Puebla of Mexico City—these, in addition to innovations such as movies, videos, computers and Internet cafes—are all town things. What is interesting about this category is that everything in it is essential for the contemporary Zapotec way of life as part of a Mexican and global economy. Cultivated land and domesticated animals allow a degree of stability and predictability that is simply not possible under the conditions that characterize the wild. It is what makes community possible, and without community Juchitecos would never have been able to maintain and develop their sense of a unique identity. Revered local writer Andres Henestrosa retells a legend of how the Zapotec avoided capture and enslavement by one of the pre-Conquest Empires. They all gathered in a huge circle, and, accompanied by flute and drum, danced, individuals and small groups leaving the circle until finally no one was left. Only by dispersing could they avoid capture, but they honored the community that bound them by coming together in one last dance.

As with everything else about Zapotec culture, both the wild and the town are necessary for people's sense of well-being. It is, in fact, those things of the wild that make daily life more interesting, especially the fruits, flowers, and animals. Those same things make it possible to heal, to commemorate the dead, and even to make *velas*[8] truly Zapotec. It may be too that one might find the home of the ancestors, the *binni gulas'a'* (the Cloud People), there in the wild.

The dead must negotiate the transition between these two realms, finally coming to rest in their home in the gui'xhi', in time to become ancestors. The multilayered, complex set of rituals surrounding dying, death, and the dead make the transition possible. When they are observed properly, the transition is slow and smooth, allowing the souls to remain part of the living community while they are slowly joining the community of the dead.

Rituals

Observances and practices having to do with death fall into two kinds—communitywide and those of individual families. Both kinds involve reciprocity, transformation, display, and balance. For both, any single death begins a cycle of observances that lasts at least seven years and possibly more, depending on the sentiments of family members.

---

8. *Velas* are one of the most important symbols of being an Isthmus Zapotec. They are annual fiestas that include a vespers service and a Mass, a parade, an all-night dance, and a daytime dance. Each family belongs to a *vela* society and, in the year preceding the four days of festivities, engages in preparations ranging from decision-making meetings to sending out the invitational bread to collecting the required donations. The all-night dance requires the most formal of the regional *traje* for women and black slacks and a white shirt for men.

Community Rituals

Two large communitywide and reciprocal commemorations of death occur every year. One occurs during the Day of the Dead and All Saints and the other during Holy Week. In the first, the dead are invited back to the homes of their living families. In the second, the living are invited to visit the dead in their cemetery homes. The reciprocity here is exactly the same as that one finds in the round of fiestas, velas, weddings, baptisms, and so forth. An invitation obligates one to attend and to reciprocate. The Holy Week rituals and visiting parallel Christ's entrance into Jerusalem described at the beginning of this chapter and his death on the cross. He is mourned in the same way as a beloved Zapotec ancestor. The existence of the two celebrations, the details of the practices, the extension into other realms of Zapotec society argue for a very old, pre-Hispanic origin. The Holy Week rituals are unique to the Isthmus Zapotec as are certain elements of the Day of the Dead observances.

These two celebrations require not only the participation of the living mourners and the dead, but also hundreds of others who bake the special bread;[9] acquire and sell the flowers; cut and cart banana stalks, banana leaves, and coconuts to market; clean the tombs and build the altars; walk the Via Crucis (Stations of the Cross); lead the prayers; dress and care for the saints; make thousands of tamales; and cook up batch after batch of *dxiña*', the syrupy fruit confections especially appropriate for Holy Week. Lately, it also includes outsiders who set up trampolines and other amusements for the children. These are ordinary people, Juchitecos and outsiders, priests and lay priests, who shift into high gear to make these celebrations possible and beautiful.

Family-based Observances

Families participate in the communitywide observances, but they are also involved in cycles of commemorations within their own family and extended

---

9. Bread, in Juchitán, comes in many forms. Some of those carry no special significance—*bolillos* (hard rolls) or *pan Bimbo* (white bread) both of which may be used for sandwiches, or *pan dulce* (sweet bread) that, together with sweetened coffee, usually comprises the light evening meal. Bread, the making of it, the giving and receiving of it, takes on great significance in observances having to do with death. Six kinds of special bread are associated with death ritual that will figure in the chapters that follow. This is a brief introduction to them: *pan de muerto* (bread of the dead)—a thick round or oval loaf decorated with a cross, tear-drops or bones made of dough; *roscas*—a ring-shaped roll or pastry, sweet, for use on the altar; *marquesote*—sweet bread in a rectangular shape, decorated with egg white writing the name of the deceased, also part of the altar; *yemita*—a small, round bread with lots of egg yolks, sweetened, given to guests; *pan bollo*—a roll, a slightly rounded square shape, given in twos to guests; *torta*—a large rectangular bread characterized by more fat and sugar than any other of the special breads, given as part of Masses for the dead to the guests.

family. These begin with the death of a family member and the laying out of her body in front of the home altar. Ideally, this happens in two stages; in the first, the departed loved one is dressed and laid briefly on the floor then on a cot; in the second, she is transferred to a coffin also in front of the altar. The funeral follows and initiates nine days of prayers in the altar room with a *ba' yaa* (moist, green, fresh body) laid where the coffin had been. The chief mourner stays in that room for forty days, people coming and going, expressing their condolences, bringing flowers and candles. The end of the forty days is marked by a Mass, followed by a gathering at the home, and a last round of prayers. Another Mass marks the year anniversary, and the last marks seven years. Some people have fifteen- or twenty-year Masses; some like to mark every year up to and including the seventh. In addition to these practices, families visit the cemetery with fresh flowers and glasses of water every day for the first forty days and then every Thursday and Sunday thereafter. Someone in the household must tend to the altar at home, changing the flowers, the votive candles, and making sure a glass of water is available for the spirits.

A network of relationships involves individuals in these practices of relatives and friends so that some death-related observance will require a person's attention at least once a week, usually more often. There is no appropriate age at which involvement begins; young children attend wakes and funerals, carry flowers and pictures in processions, and girls may be drafted to tend the altars. Even though the practices are complex and marked off, the fact of death is natural, and its domain all-encompassing.

Death in Literature and Painting

Given the pervasive nature of death in Zapotec society, it would be strange not to find it occupying a central place in art. The images are quite different from the Posada calaveras or the rhymes that accompanied them. They spring from the complicated web of beliefs, actions, and symbols that surround death. Death figures prominently in the work of internationally known artist, Francisco Toledo. He painted processions of elephants led by skeletons. Sometimes, he drew skeletons draped with a toad. Images of the wild, juxtaposition of dryness and wetness, abound in his work.

Although like Francisco Toledo and Rufino Tamayo, many of the younger Juchiteco artists have been trained in conservatories in Mexico and abroad, the themes most of them choose to depict have deep connections with themes that define Zapotec culture and much of that is iconography connected to death. Here not only is death itself depicted, but also those symbols associated with it—flowers and water paramount among them, but also symbols of the more general dichotomy between things of the wild and things of the city.

Wild and tame is a particularly important distinction. It symbolizes how Zapotec feel about their own character and underlies many of the practices associated with death. The parallel they draw between the bere lele, a kind of water bird, a bittern, and themselves is perhaps culturally the most fundamental statement of this tension between being of the wild with all its freedom and danger, and being of the community with its restrictions and safety.

Zapotec paintings turn on the balance between wild and tame, of the wild and of the town, individual, and community. In the specific symbols, they also embody the tension between wet and dry. Birds, fish, iguanas, and toads both surround human figures and are part of them. Women have bird heads, become fish, and metamorphose into iguanas. Men in black hats are dogged by ominous black birds. Painters transgress the boundaries between wild and tame all the time. There are very few "homely" paintings, no communal dance scenes as in Brueghel, no representation of everyday activities. Zapotec paintings are bursting with animal and human life. The animals that fill Zapotec art tend to be animals of the wild, and mostly but not exclusively animals that are the favorites of autochthonous peoples—snakes, fish, toads, bats, the trickster, and sexual icon rabbit or hare, iguanas, birds, especially the bere lele, but also the ubiquitous zanate. Insects and shellfish were the favorites of Toledo—wasps, scorpions, grasshoppers, crickets, crabs, and shrimp. When "domestic" animals are depicted, they are often those associated with bidxaa, of the sort that can turn themselves into animals—pigs, large black dogs, horses. Even here, one does not know where the boundaries are—is this simply a pig or is it a bidxaa?

Human depictions include both women and men, but rarely children. In virtually all the paintings, with the exception of some done for commercial spaces such as bus terminals, people have some oddity about them. They transgress the boundaries between the real and the bizarre. Francisco López Monterrosa often paints large-busted, big-nosed women in profile. Their hair is a stream of fish, and they might move through water surrounded by fish, crabs, and shrimp. Their feet are hooves. Toledo's *Mujer iguana* (*Iguana Woman*) is exactly that—a nude woman wearing high-heeled shoes whose head is that of an iguana and whose back has a scaly ridge. In Jesús López Martínez's *El conjuro de Sapandú* (*The Incantation of Sapandú*), a woman sits at the edge of the sea; fish swim up to her and become birds flying off from her head. Oscar Martinez's paintings are filled with men wearing fedoras, people whose torsos are flowers, men whose limbs are often reassembled in odd ways. Victor Cha'ca' gives little wings to humanlike figures who appear as angels or flying insects.[10]

---

10. *Cha'ca'* is the Zapotec word for woodpecker; because Victor Cha'ca' began his career as a woodcarver, he was given this nickname. He signs his work both as Cha'ca' and as Chaca.

Flora is surprisingly limited in the work of Juchiteco painters. Landscapes are nonexistent as are still lifes that feature flowers or fruit. The exceptions are significant—corn, frangipani, and a stylized heart-shaped fruit sometimes shown in cross-section, and often with a spray of water or foliage erupting from the top. The corn plants are young, some at the tasseled stage, and they frequently incorporate a human face. In another of Jesús López Martinez's Sapandú drawings, a young woman is curled inside the seed of a corn plant. These are fairly close renderings of the ancient Zapotec tradition of the Young Corn God who is slain and then reborn. A slightly different variation is Jesús Urbieta's powerful *El lobo y la milpa* (*The Wolf and the Cornfield*). The wolf is fierce, clearly a creature of the wild, but with human eyes and nose. The corn plants are tasseled and one springs from a heart-shaped seed. When frangipani appear, they are usually single blossoms, just as they are frequently used in ceremonial observances.

Two examples incorporate all three symbolic categories. One is a vignette by Soid Pastrana called *El guerrero* (*The Warrior*). This shows a man's torso in profile. His heart is a bere lele, and on the crown of his head sits another bird. He is surrounded by four sprouting seeds, at least one of which is a corn plant. The other Pastrana created as the invitation to the 2001 Vela Pineda. At the top center of the drawing is the face of a Juchiteca wearing the white starched lace headdress in the manner one uses for church. She is flanked by two iguanas. Beneath her is a turtle facing upward. The turtle is flanked by four frangipani blossoms each attached to their leaf. It is a remarkable incorporation of all the significant Zapotec imagery. These images are not pan-Mexican; they are specifically Zapotec, images of an autochthonous people—turtles, toads, snakes, iguanas. These are images that signify emergence from the earth and a return to it. The Young Corn God who is sacrificed and returns to life appears in many forms, in paintings, and on house murals.

In the same way, death appears in poetry and literature, couched in terms of wild and tame, of liminal figures, of wetness, fragrance, and flowers. Juchitán has long been a cradle for the arts, not only painting and music, but also the literary arts. Carlos Montemayor (2005), in his pathbreaking work together with Donald Frischmann on Mesoamerican indigenous languages, wrote, "the Zapotecs of the Isthmus have created what is arguably the most important modern literary tradition of all the indigenous languages of Mexico" (p. 2). Gabriel López Chiñas (1911–1983), Andrés Henestrosa (1906–2008), Nazario Chacón Pineda (1916–1994), and Pancho Nacar (Francisco Javier Sánchez Valdivieso; 1909–1963) established an impressive literary movement writing in their native language in the first half of the twentieth century. Continuing that tradition but now linked to the populist political movements, most notably the Coalición Obrera, Campesina y Estudiantil del Istmo, already hinted at in 1971, but which burst on the scene in 1974, were local writers such as

Macario Matus and Victor de la Cruz.[11] A new generation has emerged: Irma Pineda Santiago, Natalia Toledo, Victor Terán, and Enedino Jiménez, among others, who continue to give voice to the political and cultural consciousness of the Isthmus Zapotec. Poets commemorate the deaths of friends, such as poet Enedino Jiménez writing of the death of Francisco Toledo's mother, using all the symbols of wetness and flowers that one finds in the death rituals themselves. Jiménez's more abstract poem about the blurred or nonexistent boundaries between death and life is the appropriate frontispiece to this work.[12] Irma Pineda, in a magnificent work of translation, made available to Spanish-speakers much of the important poetry of Pancho Nácar (Pineda Santiago 2007). The subjects he chose to write about ranged widely but were grounded in the imagery of flowers, fragrance, water, the wild, and the mysticism of transformation. More directly connected to death is his "Xandu' yaa" ("First Offering"). In her own rich poetry, Irma Pineda (2005) employs the same imagery speaking to matters of living and dying. In "Bedandá guendaguti lii" ("Death Surprised You"), she writes eloquently of what it means for a Zapotec to die far away from her homeland (p. 51). Victor de la Cruz, mentor for many of the contemporary writers, plays with both images and language in poetry that conveys meaning at many levels. His "Chupa si diidxá" ("Just Two Words"), in two short stanzas, encapsulates the turning of the seasons at the end of October, the rituals of

---

11. An excellent account of the Coalición Obrera, Campesina y Estudiantil del Istmo (COCEI), based on written sources but more importantly on extended interviews of the major figures in the movement, is *Autonomía de los zapotecos del istmo* by Gabriela Kraemer Bayer and published in 2008 by the Universidad Autónoma Chapingo. She sets the rise of this political movement not only within the context of other 1960s protest movements in Mexico, but also more globally. It was not the first populist political movement originating in Juchitán and most probably will not be the last but it did bring together political figures, artists, and writers in a heady mix that led not only to the COCEI but also to the creation of the *Lidxi Guendabianni* (Casa de la Cultura) in 1971.

12. Maestro Jiménez died August 27, 2004, while a volume containing this and other poems was being produced. Sadly, then, the volume *Ti guchachi cuxooñé guidxilayú: Una iguana recorre el mundo* became a posthumous publication. It is bilingual in both Zapotec and Spanish. I first met Maestro Jiménez in 2002. One of my friends in Juchitán told me that if I were interested in poetry, I had to meet Enedino. She was quite right. We went to his house one evening and talked about poetry. He clearly loved writing and was gracious in talking about it. He read perhaps ten of his poems to us, holding us mesmerized by the beauty of the sound and the power of the content. It is a rare poet who can craft both sound and content equally well. I told him that I would like very much to translate his poetry into English, working perhaps toward a trilingual publication. He was intrigued by the idea and gave me copies of a dozen poems to render into English. The poems in this book are among those I heard him read that memorable evening. His widow, Na Enilda Vasquez, has also given me her permission to translate and publish these poems of her late husband, believing in the beauty and importance of his poetry. He was a rare poet and a generous soul. I hope that these translations give the reader some sense of his craft and that they may seek out the posthumous volume.

the Day of the Dead, and the tenderness of a lost love (in Montemayor and Frischmann 2005:44).

Isthmus Zapotec writers, poets, and painters create out of their profound knowledge of Zapotec culture, imagery, and language opening a window of understanding for us. Nowhere is this more clear than when they speak about dying and living.

Conclusion

Death pervades all domains of Zapotec culture. It touches the lives of everyone living in the community and those distant from it. It binds the living together in belief and commemoration. It redefines the relationship between the living and the dead. It connects the living to all the ancestors, the binni gula'sa' (Cloud People), before them. Children learn the meaning of death and its symbols through both family and community rituals and in poetry, song, and paintings. Through death, the Zapotec are reminded of the values that have bound and sustained them for 2,500 years—community, transformation, and balance. They are made mindful of those oppositions that frame their sensibilities of who they are. In the daily practice and the large communal celebrations of the dead, the Zapotec understand who and why they are. Without these promptings, people can become so lost in the everyday getting by that they forget the larger purpose that gives them integrity as a people.

A Note on Method

Between 1967 and 2008, I have made twenty-nine field research trips to Juchitán, ranging from one year in 1971–1972 to months to several weeks. I have been there seven times during Semana Santa, four times during the Via Crucis, and five times during the Dia de los Muertos. On virtually every visit, I have attended one or more commemorations of individual deaths. I maintain a lively relationship with my closest family through weekly and monthly telephone calls. And through e-mail and shared photo files, I keep in touch with the younger generation.

I have photographed the city, its events, and Juchitecos since 1974, chronicling changes both in people and places. My husband, Ronald R. Royce, documented the city through photographs, diagrams, and maps during our 1971–1972 visit. I have also videorecorded velas, parades, binni guenda biaani' talking about their craft, and the city since 1991, accumulating some forty hours of video. So, in terms of visual documentation of Juchitán and Juchitecos, I have a continuous record over forty-two years. I have no photographs or film for some events having to do with death, namely, funerals and events occurring during the first forty days. I have respected the sensitivities of my friends and family in this regard. I have recorded each of these observances I have attended, however, with drawings and diagrams in my field notebooks.

Other forms of documentation include field notes; transcripts of interviews; linguistic material beginning with a grammatical frame, and then covering vocabulary across several domains; acquisition of local newspapers, journal issues, and books by local authors in Zapotec and Spanish as well as locally available articles and books about the city and the region; surveys of changes in the physical appearance of the city, including new businesses; acquisition of art produced by local painters, printmakers, and sculptors, both large gallery works as well as invitations, announcements, and posters for events; and similarly, collecting recordings by Isthmus Zapotec musicians and composers, from LPs to DVDs. I have also collected examples of the crafts in which the Juchitecos excel from woven palm to hammocks to pottery. I researched, documented, and collected women's traje (Zapotec forms of dress), acquiring one example of each kind and style of dress from the most formal to the least, with the Zapotec term for each.

Beginning with the field trip in 1974, I have lived with the Ramírez Fuentes family. The senior woman and an important mentor was Na Berta Pineda vda de Fuentes, until her death in May 1982. I stayed with her daughter, Na Rosinda Fuentes de Ramírez, and Rosinda's spouse, Ta Chu—Jesús Ramírez Escudero, and their daughter, Delia Ramírez Fuentes, exactly my age. The compound has changed shape physically over the years as have its human occupants: the senior generation, Berta and her siblings and their spouses, have become ancestors, Ta Chu has joined them, and two new generations have appeared. I have grown up alongside Delia, absorbing what it means to be an Isthmus Zapotec woman by participating in activities, mundane as well as celebratory, embodying both the craft and the aesthetic behind it. I have grown up as an ethnographer there as well—learning to shift between the embodied and the intellectual, the participatory and the reflective.

I share my life and my work with Juchitecos of all classes and vocations, giving talks at the Casa de la Cultura, writing prologues to books by local authors, publishing in Spanish in Mexico, providing copies of photographs and films, translating local poets from Isthmus Zapotec or Spanish into English, making photo CDs of the work of local artists for them to send to galleries, talking with young Juchiteco ethnographers and linguists and sharing materials. What I write, the story I interpret, comes from all this living and collaborating.

2

The First Forty Days

Zapotec is a language best suited to describing action, and the philosophy that it embodies is one of continual creation and transformation. Some of these cycles are long, for example, as in speaking of the world and the Zapotec place within it;[1] some are daily, as in the passing of the sun across the sky or the song of birds as they prepare in the early dawn to fly off to the outlying fields and at dusk when they settle in the city trees for the night. Some are measured by the span of human lives and the passage of the seasons.[2] Endpoints and beginnings are not firmly fixed. Life and death, *guenda nabani* and *guenda guti*, literally, "living" and "dying," are gerunds rather than nouns. Each carries the seeds of the other within itself, and neither is a full stop. Living and dying are the seamless work of the community.

Both the living and the dying have work or *dxiiña'* to do to make the dying good. Good implies harmony, hospitality, a balance between the needs of the

---

1. This is the sense of time that Fernand Braudel and the Annales School speak of as *la longue durée,* meaning events that take place over centuries. The Isthmus Zapotec hold their history in their memory all the way back to the origin myths.

2. There is some support for the melding of the seasons into one another in a continual round in the murals of the Classic Period Zapotec tombs at Monte Albán. Tomb 104, which, according to Caso (1938), depicts Lord 1 M's journey throughout the underworld to the home of his ancestors, does so in terms of wet, dry, and liminal seasons. The journey itself is a cycle because he originally descended from that mountaintop home to join the living and now he returns to it. As noted in chapter 1, contemporary Isthmus Zapotec describe at least two seasons in terms of wet and dry: *gusiguié* (wet, or "time of flowers") and *gusibá* (dry, or "time of the tombs"). Marcus and Flannery (1977) reconstruct sixteenth-century categories of time and find the same categories of wet and dry. The same terms appear then as now, with the slight transpositions from Córdoba's sixteenth-century Valley Zapotec to the Zapotec spoken today in Juchitán—*cocijguije* to *gusiguié* and *cocijobàa* to *gusibá.* They find the same continuity for flower and animal terms. That continuity does not seem to characterize contemporary Mitla Zapotec. The length of time of the journey that the dead make explains the restriction on Day of the Dead observations. If a person dies within forty days of the Day of the Dead, he or she will not be called back until the following year; that is, the *xandu' yaa* is postponed. This is to give them time to complete that underworld trip.

community and of the individual, and meeting one's obligations to relationships. For families who have had a death, all normal activity ceases for the first forty days while the household is caught up in its obligations of hospitality, its responsibilities to the departed, and its own grief. It is in the rituals and commemorations of those first forty days that the well-being of the deceased is ensured. What the living do then begins the transformation and translocation of the dead from the community of the living to the community of the dead. The transformation is from a person composed of *guidi ladi* (skin) and *la'dxi'* (insides), to a *ba'* (body), to a *binni gula'sa'* (ancestor). And in terms of qualities, a being that is *nadxé'* (wet) becomes one that is *nabidxi* (dry). The rituals include preparing the body for viewing, viewing, burying the physical body, preparing the "fresh body" to lie in front of the home altar, overseeing the nine days of prayers, taking the "fresh body" to the cemetery, placing the *lu bidó'* (face of the altar or image of the deceased) on the home altar, setting out a line of flowers of the wild, organizing prayers each Friday, hosting the Forty-Day Mass for the Dead in the church and receiving guests at home, and making daily visits to the cemetery. The crucial elements over these days—earth, sand, flowers of the wild, and water—have the transformative properties of the wild; they are wet, fragrant, and natural. Secondarily, the fragrance of incense, the illumination of votive candles, and the offering of prayers help mediate between the realm of this earth and that toward which the spirit now makes its way.

A successful outcome of the forty-day ritual period finds both the body and the spirit of the deceased united and more or less content in a tomb (*yoo ba'*) in a cemetery. But the spirit is loosed from the body by death. Subsequently, it must "go on a journey," and eventually it must find its way to its tomb. Current Isthmus Zapotec beliefs about this journey are complicated and inconsistent. The details seem simply not to be important. What is important is that after death the spirit of the deceased is in danger of going astray or being lost and needs all the help that family and ritual specialists can provide. The spirit may be confused, distressed, resentful, injured, or otherwise debilitated for what must follow. For the Isthmus Zapotec, a stray or misplaced spirit not only threatens illness or misfortune to individuals, it also represents the loss to the community of a valuable ancestor—a binni gula'sa'. Resident in a yoo ba', yes, but still a member of the family and of the lineage, as well as an additional soul strengthening the community with wisdom and knowledge and presence. The center for the rituals that accomplish this transformation—from resident among the living to resident among the dead—is the household altar of the deceased. How important a site the altar is, especially as a place where the spirits of the ancestors reside, can be seen in the actions of the *xuaana'* (ritual specialist) when he visits the home of the bride, either to formally request her hand in marriage on behalf of the groom or to bless a newly completed marriage. The first action he takes when he enters the room where the household altar stands is to light incense and cense the altar to welcome the spirits of the ancestors to be witnesses to what follows. Rituals surrounding death are based on this same kind of participation and acknowledgement. In these first days, the spirit must be strong and it must not stray. The rituals are intended to provide sustenance, healing, and guidance, and they do so by employing a series of "houses" or refuges for the spirit. As the natural home of the spirit is a body, these "homes" appear as "bodies" or body stand-ins:

1. The body of the deceased, placed on the floor in front of the altar as soon as possible after death[3]

2. The body of the deceased, bathed, dressed, and prepared for burial, in its coffin, placed on a coffin stand in front of the altar[4]

3. The *ba' yaa*, literally, the "moist, green, or fresh *ba'*," a carpet of flowers laid out in the shape of a body on the ground in front of the altar after (2) has been removed for burial

4. The *lu bidó'* (face for the altar), a photograph or portrait of the deceased placed on the altar, and a single row of flowers placed on the floor perpendicular to the altar. These replace (3) after the nine days beginning with the death of the deceased.

As soon as possible after death, the deceased is laid on the floor in front of the home altar. What is crucial here is the contact with the earth, preferably the same earth from which the person came and where the umbilical cord is buried. It is a reconnection not only with home and family, but also with the earth which is thought of as moist and fertile. This is the first instance of surrounding the deceased with moistness. While life is a gradual shift from being overly wet to being overly dry, in life one can restore a balance by observing proper healing practices. Death begins the inevitable process toward ultimate dryness—*binni gulásá* is the Zapotec term for ancestors. It is also the term applied to the small pre-Columbian clay figurines and fragments found in the ground all throughout the region. To make the transition an appropriately measured

---

3. Though occasionally referred to as a *cuerpu* (from Sp. *cuerpo* "body" or "corpse"), the body of the newly deceased is usually denoted by the name of the deceased or a personal pronoun. The Isthmus Zapotec word *guidi ladi,* "the exterior surface or skin of the body," sometimes translated into Spanish as *el cuerpo,* is never used to denote the body of the deceased.

4. The body prepared for burial in its coffin is also sometimes referred to as *cuerpu* (see note 3) and is likewise usually denoted by the name of the deceased or by a personal pronoun. My understanding of Isthmus Zapotec beliefs regarding death suggests that (2) is the underlying meaning of *ba'* in such forms as *ba' yaa* "moist, green, fresh," *ba'* and *yoo ba',* "tomb," but literally "house for *ba'.*" Currently, however, *ba'* is only attested to mean *ba' yaa* and *yoo ba'.*

one, all of the forces of the wild and wetness are marshaled. Recently deceased is the *guidi ladi* and *la'dxi'* (which is also used for the pulp of fruit)—the soft skin and moist insides—that will be transformed into a dry container holding even drier bones together.

After its brief contact with the floor, the body is prepared for burial and placed in a coffin. Few Isthmus Zapotec embalm their dead. They have a real aversion to disturbing the ladxi, and especially the *ladxidó'*. This is the center of the inside body, the place of the heart/spirit/soul. Cutting into it, in any context, would release the spirit in an untimely manner and in an unfamiliar place, causing it to lose its way. The person is dressed in formal clothes with every effort made to choose something of which he or she was especially fond. The coffin is placed perpendicular to the altar, the person's feet toward the altar if he or she were married or away if unmarried. It remains open as all the relatives and friends come to take their leave and greet the family. Women visitors bring white flowers, a candle, and a donation of money. The flowers are normally gladiolas, which seem to have replaced tuberose, but they may be mums or calla lilies if gladiolas are unavailable. From four to eight large vases filled with these flowers flank the coffin together with four altar candles in tin holders; another arrangement of flowers is placed at the end of the coffin away from the altar and a votive candle burns in front of the flowers. In return, women mourners are given bread and coffee or horchata, and men, mescal or brandy and a cigarette. Those who stay for the whole wake must also be fed. When people take their leave of the deceased, they will sometimes scatter single blossoms of *guie' xhuuba'* (Isthmus jasmine) in the coffin as well as some coins to pay the way of the journey and small things that the deceased liked or may need.

A household embarking on these observances has a chief mourner, usually the eldest female, always blood kin—daughter, mother, sister, who is quiet, immobile, at the center of circles of activity that radiate outward from her. Her work is to be still, to receive, to pray, and to grieve. Her closest female relatives tend to her, fanning her, smoothing her hair, bringing her coffee, bread, and comida (a meal), if she will eat it. These forty days are a delicate time. For the sake of the deceased, certain rituals must be observed and observed in the proper order. On the other hand, it is the time when grief is the freshest. The rules of social personhood are set aside in acknowledgement of each person's grief and the idiosyncratic ways in which it manifests itself. It is a time of tension and fragility, this time when the deceased's departure has torn the fabric of family and community, and it demands great generosity and accommodation. It is a time when those closest to the deceased are in the community but not of it. Humphreys and King (1981), in their examination of death and time, speak of the period immediately preceding and following a death as one that presents the bereaved with the most conflicting demands (pp. 266–267). In the case of Juchitán, this period is extended across the first forty days.

Before the Funeral

March 21, 1999: Na Tiquia died in Mexico City. Eutiquia "Tiquia" Castillejos was the wife of Audifaz Deheza, "Dxu Timbre," both of Espinal. Dxu Timbre, who preceded Na Tiquia in death, had been a tax collector in Juchitán and that gave him in nickname: *dxu*—foreigner, male, and *timbre*—stamp. Na Tiquia, despite her Espinal origins, was embedded in the social relationships that constitute membership in the community. She never failed to appear at fiestas, Masses, funerals, and the dozens of other occasions that call for community. Her wit was legendary—funny but never mean-spirited, and her eyes full of smiles. She came home to Juchitán in the afternoon, and the following morning, Na Rosinda, Delia, and I went to pay our respects. We carried' our newspaper-wrapped bunches of white gladiolas and our candles to the house on the avenue 16 de septiembre where Na Tiquia had lived all her married life. Men with black armbands lined both sides of the corridor leading into the altar room. They held the complementary cigarettes and occasionally sipped from the copas of mescal, a quiet presence that gave support to Na Tiquia's oldest son who sat among them. We continued to the large interior skylighted room where Yolanda, Na Tiquia's daughter, sat as chief mourner, surrounded by family and friends. She cried as we each expressed our condolences, receiving the *limosna* (a gift of money) wrapped in a paper tissue, and gesturing for a woman to take the flowers and candles. Na Tiquia lay, feet to the saint, in front of the home altar. The top half of the coffin was open so that mourners could touch her for a last time. She was dressed in a black huipil embroidered with tiny white flowers and her hair was in long braids, just as a proper matron would wear for festive and solemn occasions. "I will miss her," I thought, as I made the sign of the cross. After greeting other friends, we moved to find chairs not in the direct sunlight. Members of the household served us brimming glasses of cold horchata, and we settled in, a community of loss, finding comfort in each other's presence.

April 7, 2003: Delia and I went to sit awhile with Na Concha, who was mourning her husband, Don Rafael Saavedra (Tío Chito), who had died the preceding day. We brought candles, limosna, and white flowers—a combination of alstroemeria and Easter lilies—there were no white gladiolas to be had so white of any kind was the most suitable substitute. Na Concha was sitting, flanked by her older sister and an aunt, and when we greeted her, she commented about me, "first she was the daughter of Na Berta, now she is the daughter of Na Rosinda." Na Concha was acknowledging the fact that I was fulfilling my obligations as a member of the family. We took our seats in a row of chairs facing the coffin that was laid out in front of the home altar, like Na Tiquia, head away from the altar, acknowledging his status as a married man. The coffin, a metal one, was open as is required by Zapotec custom, and flanked by four large candles, one at each corner. Tío Chito was dressed in a dark blue suit with a white shirt and a burgundy tie. He had wasted away in his last illness but still presented a handsome appearance. His coffin was surrounded by two rows of twelve large vases with white flowers. In front of it there was an arrangement of flowers with two vases of roses, one on either side, and in front of the arrangement was the lighted votive candle. When Delia and I went to take our leave of Don Rafael, one daughter laid a rosary in his hand and another scattered guie' xhuuba' blossoms in the coffin. Before he was taken to be buried, someone would place a coin in his hand.

Na Tiquia and Tío Chito, although different genders, were treated in the same way. The mourners also played the same roles: women bringing flowers, candles, and limosna, greeting the chief mourner, and sitting in the altar room; men greeting whatever senior male was the closest to the deceased, sitting outside in the patio or along the external corridor, being given cigarettes and mescal. People come and go as their lives permit; the household is there at every moment to greet them. People sleep in shifts because the body of the departed and the now separated spirit are never to be left alone.

Others in the household arrange for everything that has to be done in the aftermath of a death. Candles, flowers, incense, bread, soft drinks, mescal, cigarettes have to be purchased. Tamales have to be ordered or cooks hired to make them. The band has to be hired. Word about the death has to be gotten out—to immediate family whether living in Juchitán or elsewhere, to more distant relatives, to friends. Word of mouth works very quickly; telephone calls are made; the local radio station carries the announcement, a car with a loudspeaker makes its way through the streets. Someone has to contact the funeral home. Women of the family wash and dress the body for the initial viewing unless the person died in an accident or away from home. The funeral home prepares the body for its presentation in the coffin.

The decisions are made consensually within the family as is usual but everyone will defer to the chief mourner. Na Rosinda decided the Chu would be buried in a wooden rather than a metal coffin. Coffins of wood are custom-made and more expensive. When there was some question about what would go in the coffin with him, she prevailed in the matter of the cane that I had given him. It went in because I had given it to him and he would need it. "It was a gift from his daughter," she said, "and he will need it." There was some initial question because it had a lot of good use left in it, but no one argued with Rosinda's decision. Her own needs stemming from her bereavement took precedence.

The Nine Days

A whole host of other preparations must be made immediately following the departure of the coffin from the house. The departed is carried in procession from the house to the cemetery. The coffin used to be carried by men of the family, then in ox carts, now often it is in one of the hearses of the three local funeral homes. That, however, is up to the chief mourner who frequently prefers that the procession walk and that the coffin be carried. The band leads the procession, walking in two lines on either side of the street. The coffin follows. A prayer leader (*rezadora*) walks in front of the women. Other women carry white flowers. The men normally walk at the sides of the street. Public display of this journey of the departed to the cemetery is extremely important. It is part of maintaining community. People will come out of the houses and businesses to watch the procession pass by. Any major rite of passage—weddings, Quinceaños (fifteenth-birthday celebrations), or major fiestas such as the velas, has this public processional aspect.

Some members of the household must remain behind; these are usually helpers or may be friends of the family. Immediately following the departure of the coffin and the guests, they lay out the ba' yaa in the place vacated by the coffin. Another "body" must stand in for the departed and without delay. This body is built up in layers—first a layer of fine sand, and then one of *guie' daana'* (cordoncillo) or another green healing plant. It has become common in the last five years to use evergreen branches (cedro, most commonly). On top of that base women arrange flowers of the wild—*guie' gui'xhi'*, or more accurately, *guie' ndase*—flowers of the wild in single blossoms or petals suitable for scattering.[5] These flowers are all local and include several kinds of jasmine, frangipani, hibiscus, and petals of *flor de china*. They will sometimes use gardenias and roses of Castile. People will often contrast the white of jasmine with red hibiscus or roses. Sometimes the contrast is between cream-colored and magenta frangipani. All have the qualities of the wild—they are fresh and green—nayaa, and the favored ones are also highly aromatic. Wetness is essential for the spirit of the dead, which still inhabits the home. Each of the layers is sprinkled (*rurubanisa*)[6] with water so the flowers, sand, and healing plants make a moist, aromatic bed that is refreshed each of the nine days of prayers. Flanking the ba' yaa are

---

5. A folk taxonomy for flowers is understood by most Juchitecos. *Guie'* is the general term for flower. It is divided into two categories: *guie' gui'xhi'* or "flower of the wild" and *guie' guidxi* or town or cultivated flower. The category *guie' gui'xhi'* is further divided into *guie' biuxhe* or "simple flowers" and *guie' ndase* or "flowers used for scattering." For a fuller discussion of flowers, especially this taxonomy, see chapter 5.

6. The verb *rurubanisa* can be translated as "sprinkling with water" but in the sense of "falling like dew." This is the verb used for all acts of arranging flowers used in rituals. *Rucheeche,* on the other hand, is the word commonly used for watering as with a hose or watering can or irrigating. The words chosen for particular actions impart a real sense of not only the physical action, but also the connection to the ritual efficacy or a spiritual domain. *Rurubá nisandaayá* is another example: it refers to asperging relics, saints, and also the "substitute bodies" in death rituals with holy water.

giant vases of cultivated flowers or guie' guidxi, usually white. Large beeswax candles in their holders secure the four corners and a votive candle sits on the floor at the end of the ba' yaa.

The prayers are Roman Catholic prayers for the soul of the dead, led by a prayer leader, and prayed in Spanish. Usually a small group of women, family members and close friends, convene every afternoon. They may bring a donation of sugar for the bread and atole, but it is not necessary. Midway through the prayers, one of the women will get up and cense the altar and the ba' yaa. The incense lifts the prayers to the Creator and also serves to greet the ancestors whose presence resides in the home altar. The newly dead spirit hovering close to the ba' yaa is also greeted in this way and comforted by the sweet smell. When the prayers are over, the women sit and talk while a family member distributes bread and chocolate, or, on alternate days, atole in a little bucket.

March 11, 2000: I went with Delia to the home of Lourdes Ferra to mark the end of the nine-day mourning period for Lourdes's mother. We took white gladiolas, votive candles, and limosna, and we were welcomed into the living room that featured one of the largest nine-day offerings I have seen in Juchitán. Against the wall opposite the entrance stood three almost life-sized images: San Judas Tadeo, a crucified Christ, and the Virgin of Guadalupe, each surrounded by flashing red and green lights. There were four enormous silver candlesticks with thick, beeswax candles, vases of white gladiolas and calla lilies, and arrangements of other, mostly white, flowers that surrounded the ba' yaa of mounded gardenias. We went at 1:00 p.m.; Rosinda went at 5:00 p.m. for the prayers; Delia and Irma went at 7:30 p.m.; Father Hector went at 8:00 p.m. to say a rosary. In this case, the entire family went, some more than once.

Tío Chito's nine days was more traditional. Delia and I went, bringing Na Concha more votive candles and limosna. All the entrances to the house had willow branches stacked next to them or twined into the grillwork. It looked as if the house had sprouted a forest overnight. The ba' yaa showed a great deal of care and artistry. The base for the flowers was cordoncillo (guie' daana'), one of the cleansing plants. White jasmine (guie' xhuuba') and creamy frangipani were laid down the center of the long piece (body) and the cross piece (arms). They were flanked by red hibiscus and red frangipani. As it had been with the coffin, the head of the flower body was away from the altar. At either side of the ba' yaa were large vases of white gladiolas, white mums, Easter lilies, and baby's breath. Candles secured the four corners. At the head of the ba' yaa stood a spray arrangement of purple and white flowers and an incense burner to the side. No incense is burned while the body of the departed is in the house, but it is burned each of the nine days following the burial. At either side of the altar table, bundles of willow branches leaned in the corners. The altar had an image of the Virgin of Guadalupe and a votive candle. The lu bidó' (photograph of the deceased) will not be placed there until after the nine days. Again, there has to be a body or a body substitute at all times, but there may not be more than one at any given time.[7]

The close family and the chief mourner remain with the ba' yaa for the nine days, praying and receiving visitors. Others go to the cemetery daily to refresh the flowers and the glass of water. Still others are making preparations for the ritual ending the nine days and anticipating the preparations needed for the Mass for the forty days, each of which involves particular kinds of foods. The men are more likely to return to their work than are the women so they tend to take on those defined actions that can be done quickly. They might go to tend the flowers at the cemetery, for example, because this requires less than an hour in the early hours of the day. Or they might pick up tamales or bread.

In this domain of death, women and men act in accordance with the complementary and equal gender roles that have characterized Isthmus Zapotec society for as far back as we can push the record. Those roles probably grew out of aboriginal arrangements for the Zapotec after they moved into the Isthmus. Men produced something, a crop or fish or a craft item, and women processed and marketed it. The marketing often involved long-distance trade so women moved freely in and out of their home communities. Income and property belonged to the household that produced it. A much greater variety of occupations and employment characterize contemporary Juchitán, but the cooperative pattern still holds. Women are economically active, sometimes dropping in and out of the economy during childbearing years, but never relinquishing their claim to work. Women and men both are necessary for the smooth functioning of both ordinary and extraordinary activity. Their responsibilities may be divided differently across the different domains, but men are generally responsible for activities that have a defined beginning and end, and that, while crucial, are of shorter duration. Women's responsibilities tend to be longer term and have more fluid boundaries. In the case of death, it is the women who live the mourning, providing the continuity and the guidance that lets everyone come and go appropriately. This is quite apart from the emotional investment that characterizes individual experience whether male or female.

---

7. On January 11, 2004, Delia, Gloria, and I went to the nine-day celebration for Señor Humberto López Lena. The altar with its ba' yaa was typical in every way—though perhaps a bit more extravagant in the quantity of flowers that entirely filled the room. The only feature that was out of place was an urn with the ashes of the deceased that sat on the altar. Señor López Lena had died in Oaxaca City, and rather than bring the body back to Juchitán, the family had had him cremated. However unusual cremation is, it does occur and effects changes in how people observe death. Because he had died in Oaxaca City, there had been no lying of the body in front of the home altar before burial. Events occurring at the beginning and end of the nine-day period were conflated, with the urn and its ashes on the altar representing a body that would have been conveyed to the cemetery at least eight days previously. This meant that there were two bodies or body stand-ins present at the same time. It was an uncomfortable accommodation to an unusual situation.

On the ninth day, a rosary is prayed early in the afternoon, then another at 5:30 p.m. The women who come to pray bring a donation, a votive candle, and flowers. At the end of the second rosary, the men in the family gather up the ba' yaa. In Spanish they would say *se levantan la cruz* (they raise the cross) whereas in Zapotec they would use *riasa ba'* (they raise the body). From this act as it is expressed in Zapotec, the ba' yaa clearly stands in for the body, and its characterization as a cross is clearly a later Roman Catholic influence. The difference in meaning between the Spanish and the Zapotec is crucial to understanding the meaning not only of this particular ritual, but also the continuing presence of the departed. It also speaks to the parallel and deep Zapotec observance that runs alongside the later Christian form. Furthermore, it is not simply that a body and a cross look the same or that raising the cross and raising the fresh flower-body occupy the same functional niche. This ritual speaks profoundly to the difference between belief in the continuing presence of the soul among the living as it gathers sustenance (in the form of prayers, incense, fresh flowers, and water) for the translocation to a home with the other ancestors and a notion of the soul departing for one of the three realms of the Christian afterlife. In all of the various works on Mitla that speak about death—Elsie Clews Parsons in 1936, Charles Leslie in 1960, and Ellen Messer in 1975, this end of the nine days of prayers is called the "raising of the cross" and refers to a lime cross on which the body was laid before burial and that becomes the base for the flowers that are placed on it. Fadwa El Guindi (1986) also provides a long description of a funeral and a novena culminating in the raising of the cross. In this case, in Lachigoló, a valley Zapotec town, a specialist in making flower crosses comes on the ninth day to make a cross from reeds, plantain leaves, flowers, and thorns. In the raising, the lime cross is lifted separately and carried on a plate. The flower cross is carried in procession by a comadre or compadre (pp. 114–120). Kristen Norget (2006), in her book on death and life in urban Oaxaca City, offers a detailed examination of what can be a much more elaborated ritual ending the novenario. The original cross of lime, covered with flowers, becomes the center of a tapete, a kind of sand painting, which is raised, the Levantada, in five sections by friends and relatives who are called godparents. During the Levantada, a special hymn, "In Praise of the Holy Cross," is sung, and after the cross is raised, the "Adoration of the Cross" begins (pp. 127–35). Neither of these is part of the Isthmus Zapotec lifting of the ba' yaa.

The men who have lifted up the ba' yaa and family members accompany the gathered-up sand and flowers to a nearby chapel or cross, and then return to the house where they are given coffee and a tamale.

At the Cemetery

While all these activities take place around the home altar, other family members visit the tomb in the cemetery each day. They refresh a glass of water on each

Plate 2. Corona of hibiscus, jasmine, and *reunión de señoritas* in the Panteón Miércoles Santo. 2007. Photograph by Anya Peterson Royce.

visit and refresh the corona of flowers of the wild, guie' gui'xhi'. The shape of the flowers in front of the altar during these nine days represents a body, but the shape the flowers take in the tomb varies. Often, especially during the early days after a death, the shape is what people call a corona, a circle. Within the parameters of the corona, the variations are many—concentric circles of contrasting colors and kinds of flowers; an outside circle enclosing a cross that divides the circle into four quadrants; a circle with a spray of flowers at the top. I have also seen ba' yaa laid out—simple ones, especially when the flowers are more suited to straight lines than circles, branches of a flowering tree, for example; or quite elaborate ones, framed by a single row of flowers on three sides. Within what people regard as appropriate, there is much room for individual taste and for the likes of the deceased. At this stage of the deceased's journey, water, greenness, sweet scents, and healing herbs continue to be critical. When the flowers are laid out, each layer is sprinkled with water. In tombs, which are new and still constructed of earth and palm, the entire tomb is sprinkled, making it cool and bringing out the fragrance of the flowers and herbs. This fragrance, like the fragrance of the incense in front of the altar and permeating the ba' yaa, surrounds the spirit with beauty so that it feels less lost.

Role of the Roman Catholic Church

The role of the Roman Catholic Church in these observances varies depending on the family's relationship to the church and their desires. The coffin of the

Plate 3. Flowers in the shape of a ba' yaa in a tomb in the Panteón Miércoles Santo. 2007. Photograph by Anya Peterson Royce.

deceased is not present at the Mass, which may be either before or after the funeral. In some cases, there is no Mass at this point. Priests do not normally go to the cemetery for graveside offices; speaking over the grave is usually reserved for one of the senior males in the family, although anyone so moved may speak. Families may celebrate a Mass to mark the end of the nine days, and most celebrate a Mass at the end of the forty-day period. Priests may remember two or even more departed at any given Mass. This is also the case with other occasions such as weddings or Quinceaños or velas. The one rule seems to be that one may not have Masses for these occasions mixed in with Masses for the dead. The medieval church had the least control in prescribing what had to happen when it came to death (Weckmann 1992). This remains true in Mexico—one may not be baptized without the church but one may be buried without it.

Between the Nine Days and the Forty-Day Mass

For the forty days after death, the chief mourner remains in the altar room while visitors come and go. Prayers are said, incense is burned, the cemetery grave is tended to, and the grieving continues in the context of a community that understands this and makes provision for it. The family's responsibility to the community is acknowledged in its public rituals of mourning and its welcoming the community to share in the grief. During the forty days, the soul of the departed is still not fully settled in the community of the dead, and it is a time of the deepest grieving (Orozco 1946:112).

The forty-day Mass for the Dead for Ta Mario Marín on March 8, 2006, was sadder than most. I had arrived that morning and joined the family, all dressed in somber *enagua de luto* (Zapotec mourning dress), at the afternoon Mass. On our minds was the previous September when Ta Mario and Na Margarita had been the mayordomos (sponsors) for the Vela Pineda. Ta Mario had been too ill to complete all his duties, and his youngest son Jorge stood in his place, escorting his mother. But Mario had sat at the mayordomo's table with his wife to receive all the family members and guests who came after the Mass offering company and congratulations. The patio of their house was overflowing with women in all the colors of the rainbow, gold jewelry catching the light, laughing, teasing, visiting, and enjoying the sense of family. The men on the street in front of the house were doing the same; everyone was celebrating being a family. Now the church was filled with black-clad women and men with black armbands. The big candles were wrapped in deep purple ribbons. When the Mass ended and the procession assembled, Na Margarita, her hair tied back and covered with a black kerchief, leaned heavily on the arm of Jorge. We walked silently with no music. The altar room was packed with women waiting to pay their respects and other women speaking quietly to each other, balancing tamales, bread, and a soft drink. Ta Mario's altar was very simple and beautiful—a wooden crucifix and an image of the Virgen de Guadalupe, Ta Mario's photograph and vases of white flowers. On the floor were alternating vases of white calla lilies and purple *montecassino* (wild aster), and the purple-wrapped candles. Between them was a narrow file of blossoms—purple montecassino in the center flanked by the same flowers in white—altar at one end and two lavender votive candles at the other. The memories were powerful and the contrasts hard to bear. The following Sunday, we met Jorge cleaning his father's tomb and filling it with flowers. The rest of the family had gone to Mexico City, and he was alone to care for his father.

Na Berta Pineda, Her Death, and Forty Days

When Na Berta Pineda, Na Rosinda's mother and my adopted grandmother, died in June 1982, I returned to Juchitán for the last week of the forty-day mourning period.

Na Berta had been ill with cancer for a year before her death. She had rejected the idea of chemotherapy because it would have meant prolonged periods of absence from Juchitán. Juchitán was where her family and her friends were, and that was where she was going to spend whatever time remained to her. She was adamant in the face of well-meaning urgings from her children to do whatever it took to prolong her life. Toward the end, she sent for friends and took her leave of them. She took care of the practical matter of distributing land and property. I can only imagine how difficult it was for her to balance her need for a dignified and timely death with the pain it would cause her children, especially her eldest, Na Rosinda. Rosinda scarcely left her side. When she did, late one afternoon, to drink a cup of coffee at the urging of her daughter and siblings, Na Berta died.

The family immediately set up the altar in that same large room, placing a cot in front of it. The cot was covered with a sheet blessed by the parish priest. Berta, dressed in her favorite traje morado (purple huipil and skirt) and white lace headdress (bidaani quichi') was laid on it. They surrounded her with gardenias, jasmine, and tall beeswax candles. As people arrived bringing flowers, the family and their helpers set those out in large vases on the floor around the cot. One of the first mourners to come brought two great bunches of purple agapanthus (*agapando*). It was quite by accident, but they made such a wonderful match with Berta's purple traje that the family sent out each day during the nine, then forty days, for these flowers. Her body lay there through the night, people coming and going, a low hum of prayers and quiet conversation, punctuated by renewed expressions of grief each time a new visitor arrived. Just past noon on the following day, she was transferred to her coffin, which occupied the same position in front of the altar.

Women continued to come in a constant stream, approaching Na Rosinda, embracing her to express their sorrow, and leaving flowers, candles, and limosna. As they went up to the open coffin, and then found seats, Rosinda's helpers stacked the candles in a corner, put flowers in vases, and removing the money, returned the handkerchiefs to their owners (if the woman had folded the money into a cloth handkerchief rather than a paper tissue). Men who had been close to Berta came into the altar room briefly to pay their respects, and then joined the other men in the patio where they were given cigarettes and mescal or brandy by the male family members.

Delia said that there were so many flowers that the family finally sent helpers to distribute the surplus to the various churches and chapels of the city. The dozens of votive candles that were not used during the mourning period were stored in cardboard boxes to be taken as gifts to other people's Masses and funerals or as part of the household's normal round of remembrances. Every household keeps a stock of these candles, giving and receiving them throughout the years. The monetary donations help defray the expense of feeding the mourners, helpers, and prayer leaders all the special food that marks the different stages of grieving. Food, flowers, prayers, Masses, and receptions in the home, all take particular forms during the transition of the departed from the community of the living to the community of the dead. People take exquisite care with the rituals that mark important points in the journey because it matters to the feeling of acceptance on the part of the person they have lost, and it matters to the larger community of which they are a part. In this regard, death is treated with the same respect for proper behavior and demeanor that marks virtually every aspect of Isthmus Zapotec life. In some senses, it is even more crucial here where one is ensuring the continued "health" of the dead soul and the community mourning its transition.

Berta's funeral Mass filled the parish church of San Vicente and mourners even filled the courtyard, spilling out into the street. After the Mass, everyone came next door to Rosinda's compound for tamales, soft drinks, bread, cigarettes, and mescal. They had to come in waves because even the large compound could not accommodate everyone at once. Rosinda greeted everyone who came. When night fell and the last visitor had gone, she lay down on the small cot that her brother Vicente had put there in the altar room for her. She scarcely left the confines of that room for the forty days, dozing in a hammock in the heat of the afternoons and sleeping on the cot at night. She was there, ready for all visitors no matter when they came, and keeping vigil for her mother.

Ba' yaa and Altar

When Berta left the compound for the cemetery, the household members who remained laid down the ba' yaa—jasmine of the Isthmus, red sweetheart roses as single blooms and as petals, gardenias, frangipani, the small-leaved pungent basil found throughout Mexico, and sweet-smelling cordoncillo (*Piper* spp.). The fragrant flower-body was flanked by four tall candles. An incense burner sat ready at the end farthest from the altar. Each evening's prayers were led by a rezadora and attended by a faithful group of women.

On the Sunday of my arrival the week before the forty-day Mass, the altar and the space in front of it dominated the long, rectangular room. The altar itself was two-tiered. A glass case with an image of the crucified Christ stood at the back of the top tier. The image was flanked by large glass vases filled with white chrysanthemums. Outside the vases were lighted votive candles. Stepped down from this level was a wider shelf with a photograph of Na Berta. Her photograph showed her dancing a son at a recent Vela Pineda, resplendent in her purple traje and a striking contrast with the Christ of Life Eternal. The framed photograph was set off by two even larger vases of dark blue-purple agapanthus. A small candle burned in front of the photo and was surrounded by individual frangipani blossoms, pale cream against the white paper covering the shelf and visibly striking against the tall purple agapanthus. Mauve frangipani hung in two large loops from the edge of the shelf. In front of the altar, on the floor, sat a tin censor filled with burning incense. Then followed a six-foot-long single line of blossoms, alternating chrysanthemums and frangipani. Their progress was halted by a votive candle, then a dark brown candle that was lit only at night. The whole arrangement showed a sensitivity to Berta's own aesthetic preferences and the continued importance of flowers of the wild at this stage of the mourning.

I spent the morning in the altar room with Rosinda and Delia, needing to be close to them and to Berta. Then I joined the group of women in the patio. Tía Rosa, now the last sister of that generation, hugged me, stroked my upper arms as Zapotec women are fond of doing, then returned to her reminiscences of the Pineda family, a family with a richly deserved reputation for loving parties. Funny stories about past velas were told again, and a debate heated up about whether to have the upcoming Vela Pineda outside under tents or inside in Oscar Cazorla's dance salon: "The Pinedas always have their vela outside—we are the most traditional of all the families," from the older women. "If we are at Cazorla's we won't have to worry about the rain ruining our trajes," from the younger.

Early on Monday morning, three of Rosinda's sisters, Mavis and Berta, both down from Mexico City, and Irma, went to the cemetery to take fresh flowers to their mother. Vicente drove them, one of those short-term actions that are the task of the male relatives. Rosinda and I swept the altar room and changed the flowers. We had armloads of them from which to choose, the flowers brought by visitors, which had been deposited in the big, concrete laundry basins. They seemed inexhaustible.

TAMALE PREPARATION

At 9:00 a.m. Orfia and Corina swept majestically through the big doorway, ready to cook and supervise the making of tamales for the Mass. They are women in their sixties, Pinedas too, who have the reputation of being among the best cooks in the city. They are always hired for Pineda functions, but in this case, they are donating their time out of love and respect for Berta. They soon had us all at work, peeling garlic, an enormous task given that we were making two tamales each for more than 300 people. Orfia and Corina organized their pots and the raw ingredients, looking skeptically at the cooking arrangement, a butane-powered hearth that Irma's husband had devised in one corner of the patio.

By 10:00 a.m., all the garlic had been peeled, and both it and the chiles had been cooked, sautéed in hot sesame oil smoking in a big, shallow iron pot. Other women had begun to arrive—all relatives who were honoring their

Plate 4. Na Orfia Carrasco Pineda cooking *mole* ingredients for Mass for the Dead. 1972. Photograph by Ronald R. Royce.

obligation to contribute their labor and their presence. The patio took on a festive air even though we were all wearing various degrees of mourning. The women made a striking picture, confident, comfortable in themselves, telling ribald jokes and stories in Zapotec, and laughing uproariously. From time to time, they paused to give directions to one of the men of the household, whose activities included ferrying women back and forth by car, getting ingredients, taking the cooked ingredients to the molino where they are passed through a giant food mill, bringing in the rented chairs, and picking up the commissioned bread. Vicente and his compadre Fernando Vera did most of the driving. Irma's husband, Enrique, was on hand to do odd jobs and improvise sun shades and fires for the cooks. Maestro Leonardo, a local schoolteacher and friend of the family, strung a light outside so that the work could continue after nightfall. Within the broad outlines of what men's behavior is expected to be, there is room for considerable variation based mostly on personality, and less so on other commitments.

The same freedom is accorded to women, even in their more sustained roles. Personal desire and particular aptitudes are the basis for how work is divided. For example, making the tamales for the Mass requires many hands but not all occupied with the same task. With the base for the mole simmering, we moved to the back of the compound, away from the eye-watering smoke of cooking chiles and the full heat of a Juchitán afternoon, and we turned our attention to the tall bundles of banana fronds stacked in the patio. Much processing happens to them before they are suitable wrappings for tamales. Each bundle has to be opened and the fronds spread out to "warm" them. When they are

Plate 5. Na Lidia Esteva cooking the *mole* for the Mass for the Dead. 2004. Photograph by Anya Peterson Royce.

Plate 6. Na Mavis Fuentes de López grinding ingredients for *mole* for Mass for the Dead of Na Berta Pineda's husband, José Fuentes. 1972. Photograph by Ronald R. Royce.

at just the right temperature, the frond is stripped from the spine and torn into rectangular pieces big enough to enclose the tamale filling. It became clear immediately that some women had just the knack for this and others (myself included) did not. So, without discussing it, we sorted ourselves: those who could, tore the leaves; others stacked them into two inch-high bundles; still others tied the bundles with a strip of fiber. The little that remained of the fronds was set aside to be used as a base for steaming the tamales.

Relationship also plays a part in determining what one does. When lunch interrupted the banana frond preparations, I was drafted to help serve because of my status as a kind of adopted daughter. Rosinda, Berta (Rosinda's sister), and I brought steaming bowls of caldo de res (a spicy beef broth) to the workers. We sliced the wonderfully tart Isthmus limes and pungent jalapeño peppers as an accompaniment to the soup. The tortilla vendor appeared just in time, and we served baskets of the small, thick, hard tortillas (*gueta bicuuni bola*) meant for breaking into chunks and dropping into the soup. We ate on the porch, protected from the sun, if not from the heat. When we had eaten all we wanted, we turned again to the banana fronds. Tía Rita had arrived to help, and we soon finished bundling all the little rectangles. Vicente packed the large cooking pots of mole ingredients into the car, and went off to the molino accompanied by two women.

Later in the afternoon, Orfia and Corina, to whom everyone deferred, put the cut-up pork on to boil—three pigs. We saved the brains for Ta Chu and the skin for crackling. To justify our raid on the crackling, piping hot from the boiling fat, we served small plates of it to Chu and Vicente. The traditional offering of sweet bread and hot chocolate was also available, and many of the women accepted it. Our numbers had been augmented by later arrivals, who were bringing more flowers and candles. Some were close family and friends, such as Delia's cousin Gudelia and aunts Urania and Bernarda. They joined Rosinda in the altar room and were served chocolate.

In an acknowledgment of our special aptitude, Irma and I arranged the flowers. There were now seventeen vases on and in front of the altar, and we were almost out of both vases and places to put them. Agapanthus and white mums lined the two shelves while individual double-ruffled hibiscus blooms in a glorious deep pink covered the white paper base. Na Berta had loved hibiscus, growing them quite successfully, so we took pains to have them for the altar. We placed four oversized vases of salmon and white gladiolas in a line parallel to the front of the altar. Eight vases of white pompon mums made a double row on either side of a single line of white and yellow mums that marked the place where first the body, then the ba' yaa, had lain. To mark the end of this line, we put a new votive candle and then a vase of deep pink carnations. After much discussion and rearranging, we were pleased with the harmonious balance of color, shape, and size.

When the pork had cooked and cooled, the cooks and four other women cut it into tamale-sized chunks. Even with all the hands, every task took a long time because of the heroic quantities. Soon it was time for the evening meal, which Rosinda provided to all who had helped—fresh shrimp from the nearby lagoons, baked and salted fish with tomato; the large, crisp tortilla peculiar to the Isthmus called *totopo* in Spanish and *gueta biguii* in Zapotec; fresh, salty cheese; and sweetened coffee. We ate in turns, conceding first turn to Orfia and Corina. The men were fed regardless of whether they had contributed to the day's work, here an artifact of the complementarity of Isthmus Zapotec gender roles and an acknowledgment of their place in the family.

Although we had been working all day, we were not finished yet. Now, with the mole cooked, the meat cut up, the banana wrappings ready, it was time to make the corn dough or masa. At 9:00 p.m., with the benefit of Maestro Leonardo's light, we put the corn on to boil. This time, Orfia insisted on a wood fire rather than the butane one because, she said, the latter does not burn hot or fast enough. Soon the whole compound was filled with acrid wood smoke, making our eyes smart and tear. It did have the virtue of driving away the mosquitoes and biting flies, however.

At 10:30 p.m. I was in my room writing notes. Delia was painting her nails and talking to keep me company. I could hear the soft sounds of Zapotec coming from the patio, interrupted from time to time by bursts of laughter. Rosinda was there with Orfia and Corina and her sisters Irma and Berta. I heard them slide their wooden *butacas* (low chairs) across the stones of the patio, and then heard the noise of cots being brought out. Orfia and Corina were staying the night. It was midnight when one of the tropical storms for which the Isthmus is famous descended. I could hear the women scurry to cover the mole, which had been left out in an uncovered container. A little rain on the soaking corn was not a problem. Orfia and Corina moved their cots back to the shelter of the porch and everyone went back to sleep.

DAY OF THE MASS

It was not quite light when I heard the bustle from the patio indicating that the day's work had begun. Orfia and Corina were washing the now softened corn. I took a quick shower, threw on my clothes, and came downstairs, notebook and pencil in hand. I joined the women—Na Yolanda, Tía Rosa, and Tía Eva—who were helping the cooks wash the many kilos of corn, enough for 600 tamales. When we finished, Vicente and Fernando Vera carried the corn to the car and, with Yolanda and Eva, drove to the mill. While we waited, Rosa busied herself transferring the caldo (broth) from the large pot to smaller and more convenient plastic buckets. Every household has many of these in all colors and sizes because they are given, filled with mole, by hostesses to those who pay their respects, whatever the occasion. We chatted too, in Zapotec, which is the choice when the participants are older women and when the banter is likely to include jokes and puns. Out of politeness, women will speak Spanish if there are guests not from the Isthmus or younger women whose Zapotec may not be fluent.

The return of the corn and the men precipitated one of the many morning snacks. We served coffee and sweet bread to everyone, with Vicente and Nando Vera sitting apart from the women. Given their relationship as family and compadre, they could have sat with us had they chosen, but they followed the more general pattern of separation by gender. Enrique appeared and was put to work shifting the corn dough from its large container into the one in which Eva was kneading it. As she kneaded, she added a jícara of mole and a fistful of sea salt to give it flavor and the right consistency. Orfia seemed content to let Eva do the mixing while she seated herself by the fire to tend the heating mole.

By 7:00 a.m. everything was in full swing. There clearly would be no rest for anyone today. Mavis, her sister-in-law, and her comadre, all from Mexico City, went with Vicente to see to Berta's tomb. In the patio, Eva continued mixing the dough. Two men arrived with more wood for the fire. Nando Vera was lying in the hammock, commenting on the activities, heedless of the risk he ran from the elder Pineda women's sharp tongues. Another of the aunts was in Irma's kitchen frying pork skin and keeping an eye on another big pot of simmering mole. Having discharged his obligations to the cemetery group who had gone to arrange the flowers in Berta's tomb, Vicente now returned with the rented chairs, helped by Flaviano, one of Chu's apprentices.

Five hours after the day's chores started, the serious work began—the assembling of the tamales. Orfia and Yolanda, the two best and most experienced tamale-makers, invited me to join them at their table. I hoped that I would be better at this than at stripping banana fronds. I was, and they were pleased. "Each one has her own talent," people say, "each helps make community in her own way." People go to great lengths and show great patience helping individuals find their way of contributing. I watched this at work in the making of the tamales—every woman who wanted to help was found a task she could do so that the high standards could be maintained. No one was ignored or criticized or patronized. I see this process at work in all aspects of Zapotec life—the deep current of community and the individual ways of maneuvering the shoals and eddies of the banks.

Tamale-making requires good hand-eye coordination and a knowledge of how the ingredients will react, but it also allows for artistic license, the flourish with which some women clean the dust from the banana leaves or the way of patting out the masa. At the same time, conversation itself is an opportunity for demonstrating wit and an ability to play with language. The Zapotec words for many of the ingredients provide irresistible opportunities for ribald puns.

Dxita, for example, means both egg and bone, and the women are quick to come up with riddles and puns. Plantains, *bidua machu* (macho bananas) in Zapotec, provide great opportunities for jokes and innuendo.

One of the difficulties of making tamales in such large quantities is that calculating the right proportions of meat, masa, and banana leaves is impossible. Which will run out first and at what point does one finally stop, acknowledging that there will be a little of something left? This time the meat and the leaves ran out at the same time while we still had a great quantity of mole and masa. We took a break while Eva went to the market for meat, and we sent a helper for another bundle of leaves. Because it is always a good time to eat, we had the second, and more substantial, breakfast (almuerzo, in Spanish, and *ruxhirini*, in Zapotec)—pork cracklings, beans, chile and tomato sauce, cheese, and frito (cow's stomach in a broth). As an accompaniment, we had three kinds of tortillas and totopos, *nisiaaba'* (a thick corn gruel served hot), and coffee.

While all this was going on, Rosinda was receiving a steady stream of visitors bringing flowers and candles. She stayed in the altar room where she greeted them, and, from time to time, I would go back to see if she or Delia needed anything. The visitors who were there midmorning were served *horchata*, the cold, refreshing drink made from rice flour and cinnamon.

While we waited for the meat and the leaves, we decided to steam the first of the tamales. Broken and doubled-over banana stalks went into the bottom of the big, galvanized containers along with about four inches of water. We stacked the tamales on top of this nest of stalks, and then covered them with leaves, and finally a cloth. We put the pot on the wood fire, and when the banana leaves arrived, we placed them on top the steaming pot to warm and soften them. Men came and went, getting the cooler for the beer and soft drinks, and bringing more chairs. None stayed long around the women except Enrique who was trying out his new camera by recording the events.

By noon, the second batch of pork had disappeared but we still had masa and leaves. A helper went to the market, this time for chicken because we had exhausted the supply of pork. It seemed a good time for another break, and we were chatting when Tía Paula arrived. She, along with Rosa, was another of the last senior women in the family.

By two in the afternoon, all the tamales were made and steamed. The line of visitors continued without a pause. Everyone who arrived after 1:00 p.m. was given a piece of bread and a tamale in a small plastic bag. If there is an especially close relationship, the visitor might be given more than one tamale but no one was ever given less, even if, on very rare occasions, the family had to send out to the market for some. It was an advantage to have brought the flowers on a metal tray because then one had a way of carrying home the tamales, which are really quite hot, just out of the steaming pot. For a time, I was pressed into receiving the flowers and making sure that each visitor had tamales and bread. Then I joined the members of the household who were serving comida (main meal of the day) to all the people who had been working. By 3:00 p.m. all had been fed and were resting in the shade of the porch. The beer and soft drinks were stacked in the coolers; the overflow flowers were taken along to the parish church for the Mass—eight vases of white gladiolas behind the altar, two in front, a cross of white flowers on the marble floor in front of the altar, each corner marked by a votive candle.

All of us were dressed for the Mass by 5:00 p.m. and spent the remaining time before leaving helping Rosinda greet the visitors who still flowed into the compound. All but Orfia, Corina, and Ta Chu had left for the church by 6:30 p.m., walking literally next door to the parish church of San Vicente. The nave filled up rapidly and people spilled into the courtyard, and then into the street. Men tend to stay in the back so they were represented disproportionately in the courtyard and street. Father Vichido, from Tehuantepec and an old friend of the family, celebrated Mass. While he spoke about the Blessed Virgin and of the importance of service to others, he was really speaking about Na Berta and her long life of service to her community.

RECEIVING GUESTS AND THE LAST PRAYERS

Because the church is so close to the house, one of the problems is getting back in time to greet people coming from the Mass. Delia, Carmela, Mayella, and I left as soon as the Mass concluded so we could begin filling plates before the first guests arrived. As was expected of her, Rosinda stayed behind in the church to greet people. People were not long in arriving, and we had all we could do to push through the crowd, giving each woman a plate of two tamales and a piece of sweet bread. Seven flats of soft drinks, twenty-four bottles each, vanished within the first half hour. The confusion was heightened by the fact that Rosinda had not yet arrived, and women were milling about not knowing to whom they should give their limosna. When she did return and could make her way through the crowd, she sat in her familiar place in the altar room and received people as they presented their handkerchief-wrapped money and the occasional votive candle. She was, as she had been since her mother's death, a figure of calm in the middle of a whirl of activity. This ability to be still and present in the moment is highly valued and respected.

Where people sat told a great deal about relationships and expectations. By 9:00 p.m., the guests had sorted themselves into four groups: the men were outside on the sidewalk in front of the house; the women guests were ranged along the sides of the long patio; the "aunts" (those women who had worked for the last several days preparing for the Mass) sat around the large, rectangular serving table under the back porch roof; and the group, predominately women, who sat in the altar room praying the last round of prayers.

The men arranged themselves in little groups, pulling their chairs together to form semicircles based on close friendship. Vicente and his younger brother José (Chito) served beer, mescal, and brandy to the men, and passed around a bowl of loose cigarettes. Later, two of the household helpers brought the men plates of already unwrapped tamales with forks so that they could eat them on the spot (women take their food home with them on such occasions). The talk revolved primarily around politics.

The second group, the women lining the patio, included older women who were not family and younger women, related but not yet "aunts." An occasional male sat there accompanying his wife. In almost every one of those instances, they were newlyweds, still exempt from the gender separation. Women sat grouped by friendship and family. There is not very much shifting around or visiting, which is hard to do given the number of people as well as because groups sat together at Mass and arrived together afterward.

The back table included the "aunts" who tended to be the older women of the family, and the conversation, in between seeing that their guests were served, was entirely in Zapotec. It ranged over family matters, the vela (major fiesta of the Pineda family), and questions raised by the younger women. When I went to sit with the second group, along the sides, Na Rosa quite firmly made me sit among the aunts.

The group in the altar room was led by the rezadora, its membership shifting over the hours of the prayers. Rosinda never left the room. For most of the time, she was supported by several of her sisters—Mavis, Berta, and Irma, her daughter Delia, and Tía Rosa, Berta's only remaining sister. When guests were no longer arriving and all had been served, many of us joined the prayers at the beginning of the second set. The sensation is comforting because regardless when one enters, one knows where one is; one knows the responses. The words, the strong, steady voice of the rezadora, and the sense of community hold one up. It provides stability in a world that has an empty space in it left by the death of a loved one. It brings everyone together, both the living and the dead. By 11:00 p.m. we had finished the second and last set of prayers. It was time to lift the "body" of flowers from the floor in front of the altar. The rezadora signaled to the men, called padrinos or godfathers, who gathered up the flowers into a plastic basin that they placed back near the altar. As they raised the flowers, a woman censed the men and the flowers both. The same woman then took one of the larger blossoms and extinguished the six large white candles in their two-foot-high holders. This marked the last opportunity to say goodbye to Berta. Rosinda and Berta did this more vocally than others but many joined them. They cried, asking their mother why she had left them. At this point mourners sometimes become distraught, and they are then led gently out of the room to a quiet place where someone sits with them until they regain their composure. When the last of the candles is extinguished, the display of grief stops. How this happens differs from person to person, depending on personality and one's own sense of propriety. Women and men are respectful of each other's feelings and needs, neither needing nor demanding uniformity. By midnight everyone except the family had gone.

RETURN TO THE EVERYDAY

The next morning, I woke to relative silence; no bustle, no chatter. After Rosinda attended to Chu who wanted food packed for a trip to his rancho, she and I returned to the quiet of the altar room. We put fresh flowers in the vases on the altar. The vases placed on the floor and the flower-body that had accompanied them had gone with the end of the forty days. Berta's spirit had gone too. With the lifting of this second flower-body, which like the first is taken to the cemetery chapel, she was freed to go to her resting place in the cemetery community of other spirits. Until this leave-taking happens, candles are kept lit in the altar room so that she does not lose her way. Now only one lighted candle on the altar and a small cross of palm in the grillwork of one window remain—these to keep her spirit happy in its new home. We folded and stacked the wooden chairs, swept and mopped the floor, and made everything tidy.

Mavis and Berta joined us and we sat down to the task of counting the donations Rosinda had received over the last few days. It takes a long time to count, and we found ourselves laughing each time we picked up a discarded tissue that, to our surprise, still had money in it. As many donations as there were, the money still did not cover the expenses of the Mass, all the meals, the bread, and the tamales. Still, it does help defray the large expenditure. It is part of the system of reciprocity that binds Zapotec to each other and that makes possible a decent standard of living for most people. No one who participates in this web of relationship is allowed to go hungry or homeless or, indeed, to die alone. It also makes it possible to meet these impossible to anticipate, one-time, big expenses, which otherwise would be beyond the means of most families.

Later in the afternoon, I accompanied Delia to Emma's house to see how she was doing. We had visited on the day of her mother's death, taking flowers and candles. The scene at Emma's house was a duplicate of the one a month ago in Rosinda's—flowers everywhere, candles overflowing improvised packing boxes, people coming and going, Emma seated in a big comfortable chair, dressed in black, caring for her mother's spirit and being cared for by her own living family.

Rosinda acknowledged the end of the forty days that evening by going to the market to buy the shrimp, the salty cheese, and the totopos for cena, the last meal of the day. With her mother's illness keeping her close, and the obligations posed by Berta's death, Rosinda had scarcely set foot outside the compound for months.

Saturday began as a quiet day. No one went to the cemetery because Saturday is the day that the Virgin makes her weekly visit to the spirits who live there. Rosinda was still cleaning her part of the compound. As she swept around the laundry basin, she found the small cross of palm that the wind had torn from the window. She brushed it off and put it back.

Cemetery Visiting

Early Sunday morning, Rosinda, Irma, and I went to the cemetery, chauffeured by Vicente. We had our arms loaded with flowers—two bunches of white mums, two of agapanthus, a triple bunch of lavender mums, and some cordoncillo from the patio garden. Cordoncillo is used as the base for the flower bodies laid out in front of altars and in the tombs; it is also a cleansing plant used to clean out flower vases, leaving them not only clean of old plant matter but also sweet-smelling. Vicente brought us buckets of water from the nearest water trough, and we set to work cleaning all the vases as well as the floor of the tomb. We filled the two large permanent urns at the back of the tomb with the purple agapanthus, refreshed the pink carnations in the smaller vases on the shelf, and put one very large vase of lavender mums on the floor. Rosinda stepped back, clearly pleased with the effect—dark blue-purple, pink, and lavender. Moving on to Leonarda's tomb (Rosinda's sister who died young), we swept and washed the little houselike tomb and cleaned the vases. We replaced the dying agapanthus with two vases of lavender mums and filled the remaining space with a vase of pink carnations, two of white mums, and a third, in the center, of white mums. Finally, we made our way down a narrow cemetery street to Ofelia's tomb (one of Berta's sisters) where we repeated the cleaning and replaced the flowers. Because her tomb does not yet have a door, the only vase is an old paint can that no one would be tempted to steal. Irma made a wreath of the remaining cordoncillo and white mums that she placed on the floor beside the paint-can bouquet.

On the way out of the cemetery, Rosinda saw a woman with an armload of guie' bi'chi' (dragon's blood). It is a wonderfully fragrant, small white flower that grows in tight clusters on long branches. Because it grows only in the gui'xhi' (wild) and is hard to find, Rosinda begged two stems from the woman. When we got home, she put both on a flat, lacquered gourd tray with bright purple bougainvillea. She placed the tray on the center of Berta's altar and surrounded it with pale orange, bell-shaped flowers called campanillas. The final touch was a red hibiscus that Rosinda hung over Berta's photograph. Now, more than twenty years later, Rosinda takes the same care with her husband Chu's flowers as she did for her mother.

Transitions and Community

Anyone's death begins a journey for that person from her community among the living to her home in the community of the dead. For that transition to be smooth, ensuring that the person is content, and finds her appropriate place, particular observances have to take place, each defined precisely in terms of content and action, and they have to occur in a particular order. Elsewhere (chapter 9) I have described the case of a young mother who left instructions that she be cremated so that all of what has to happen in the normally pre-scribed rituals would not be a burden on her young daughter and her spouse. In fact, the reason people were so uncomfortable with her solution was that it eliminated the desired slow transition. Neither her spirit nor the community of the living had the opportunity to effect her transformation satisfactorily. There was no body to lay out in front of the altar and from which to take one's farewell; there was no way to give the departed all the homely things that make the spirit's journey less fearful; no physical body to travel from house to cemetery accompanied by family and friends, and to be seen off by all the community; no round of prayers to buoy the soul in unfamiliar territory and to comfort the mourners; no tomb to visit with the flowers and water that the dead crave; no tomb to be a home for the departed who then wanders home-less; none of the exchanging of food, flowers, prayers, and grief that lets the community knit itself together.[8]

These transformations require time above all; time to make the physi-cal transformation of the body from living to dying to dead, and to make the transformation of the community around the loss of one of its members. Dying and death are not private matters to be shared among a small number of intimates. All the processions, the opening of the home and its altar to the community, the coming together of the women to prepare food and flowers, the unfailing hospitality of the mourning hosts to all who come to console and be consoled by the company of others—all these during the first forty days, then in subsequent Masses of one, seven, fifteen, and sometimes twenty years, and the Day of the Dead and Holy Week visits, make everyone's death a matter for the community. Even in the negotiation of space, time, and manner of personal grief, family and friends are silent reminders of community. One's personal style can only be crafted against the norms acknowledged by the larger society.

---

8. Irma Pineda Santiago's poem "*Bedandá guendaguti lii*" ("Death Surprised You," 2005) is a tender and melancholy portrayal of what dying away from one's home, family, and friends means for the deceased—to be thrown into a nameless tomb with no belongings, no prayers, no flowers, no songs to accompany your journey, frozen at the beginning of a road, and for the family—your mother looks for someone recently dead to give your favorite clothes, the flowers that will not make your body fragrant, the tears that your ears will not hear because she knows that you wait.

Each death contains the capacity to heal. In the narrowest interpretation, it heals the rent it has made in the fabric of family and community. It heals by bringing people together in shared grief, repeating, reinforcing, and teaching the lessons of relationship and community. It heals by placing a loved one among those ancestors who have powers beyond those of the living, powers of intercession. As we shall see in a later chapter, sitting in the Capilla de la Misericordia on Good Friday evening in the company of women and men and children who honor the crucified Christ in his coffin with their prayers, tears, and flowers makes one understand the power of a beloved soul to hear and to heal. Christ as ancestor is a later import. The care with which the living and the dying treat each other, each with the power to heal and celebrate community, is an ancient Zapotec legacy.

3

Artists of Bread, Flowers, Prayers, and Music

Bread, flowers, special foods, music, and prayer are essential elements for the living, reminding them of their obligations and relationships. In the case of death, these elements also bind the living to the dead in a similar web of obligation. The individuals who craft and perform them are key to the communal work of obligation. They are cognizant of Juchiteco aesthetic demands and strive to meet them. In their work, the most dedicated of them are acknowledged as artists, binni guenda biaani'.

Bread

Na Rosalia moves between the beehive-shaped oven and the long tables and racks. She feeds the oven great platters and tin trays of unbaked bread, and then takes out the hot brown loaves and figures, putting each kind in its proper place (see footnote 9, chapter 1, for descriptions of bread). A smallish woman in her late fifties, she moves with the efficiency of years of experience, long skirt hiked up and tucked into the waistband, towel around her head, directing her crew of ten women and one young boy. Two women tend each large wooden batea, one mixing the batter, the other kneading the dough. Five women decorate the big rectangular loaves of marquesote, writing names on them for Day of the Dead. The boy was whipping bowl after bowl of egg whites for the frosting decorations, hardly keeping pace with the women. It was eight in the evening, October 30, and Na Rosalia was trying to fill all the orders of people anxious to build altars to honor their departed family members. Young girls arrived and departed, carrying orders to the homes of longtime customers. Others come to buy their bread there at the source and Na Rosalia attends to them just as if she had nothing else to do, smiling as she points out the various animal and human shapes of the special bread or holding up a freshly baked yemita, knowing well that its aroma makes it irresistible. She is an artist of bread, a hardworking widow whose creations will grace many altars this Day of the Dead, a feast for the eyes of the living and the palates of the dead.

Na Rosalia is one of those workers without whose efforts the dead would fare rather more poorly in terms of commemorations. Like all the others in the many crafts and services necessary for observances of death, baking the bread of the dead is only a part of what she does to maintain herself and her family. She came to Juchitán from Guevea de Humboldt, a nearby Zoque town, as the bride of a Juchiteco. She settled into the community, becoming fluent in Zapotec, raising a large family, and developing a reputation as a reliable and excellent baker. When her husband died several years ago, she worked very hard to maintain the baking so that her children would all have good educations. When she is not baking, she devotes many hours in service to the church. She is one of the core members of the Hermandad del Sagrado Corazon (Society of the Sacred Heart), one of the important societies during Holy Week, appearing with the Christ of the Sacred Heart on Holy Thursday. The society also coordinates all the celebrations of the Sacred Heart in June.

Her business is thriving, first because her bread is excellent, and second because she is totally reliable. Reliability is essential because no one can afford to be without the appropriate bread for whatever the occasion may be. She has a large space, which is a combination of home, patio for growing medicinal

Plate 7. Na Rosalia Espinosa, artist of bread and member of the Hermandad del Sagrado Corazon. 2006. Photograph by Anya Peterson Royce.

and other plants, and a very large covered area, open on one side, for all the bread-making activity. In that space is a large, beehive-shaped oven made of plastered mud brick that sits on a base of the same material. There are ten-foot-high racks with multiple shelves for storing the cooling bread. Opposite them are the big, wooden bateas (basins) used for mixing the dough, a table on which bread to be decorated can be placed, and several quite large palm baskets for the finished bread. On a table across from the oven are rectangular tin pans (these for the marquesote) and beside them rafts of eggs. Long wooden paddles, used for removing the bread from the oven, lean against the corner. Lastly, stacks of firewood cover almost all of one wall. Na Rosalia bakes throughout the year; pan bollo, yemitas, and bread shaped into human figures or animals are her staples. She has regular customers whose orders are delivered, customers who drop by her compound, and customers who order bread—marquesote, yemitas, and pan bollo for funerals, nine days, forty days, Masses for the dead, and Day of the Dead altars. She plans ahead for Day of the Dead by hiring extra help but sometimes will be caught shorthanded if too many deaths occur in a short space of time. Her children can be, and often are, drafted into helping. Bakers from all sections of the city congregate in the market of bread in the evenings in front of the arcades of the municipal palace. Here, women come to buy bread for the light, evening meal of coffee and sweetened bread. Bakers will bring their bread or more typically, will send one of their daughters, to offer it for sale in the evening.

When individuals order bread for a special occasion, they know the repertory and skill of many bakers. Still, the quality is all-important so bakers will send samples of the kind of bread the person has ordered. The women family members will taste and offer evaluations. Finally, they will reach a consensus and the helper who has brought the bread will convey it to the baker. Everyone agrees that the bread is excellent but wants to adjust the recipe—a little more or less sugar or a little more or less fat—to make it conform to the particular taste of the family and their friends. This exquisite attention to quality and nuances of taste ensures that Juchiteco bakers need not worry about the existence of the very large commercial bakeries, such as the one in the Aurrera (Mexican Wal-Mart franchise) at the north end of the city.

Bread is one of the essential symbols of both the stability of community and the inevitable transformation with regard to death. It is given and received among the living and the living make gifts of bread to the dead. The decorated loaves of marquesote stand in for the departed, and they are also one of the special foods craved by the dead. The moist essence of the bread is absorbed by the dead and so it becomes dry. Bread also figures in other domains such as invitations in the case of important fiestas such as velas and as part of the gift of food that the bridegroom must send to his bride. Bread is sent by the prospective compadres to the godmother or godfather of Baptisms, First Communions,

Confirmations, or weddings. Baking, then, is a full-time occupation for many Juchitecos, primarily women, but also some muxe' (third gender).

Flowers

Flowers are ubiquitous in Juchitán, from fresh flowers for sale every day in both the inside and the outside market, to the flowers that decorate the tombs, the flowers offered to the images in the churches and in the homes, to the exquisite embroidered blooms on the women's traditional huipil and skirt, to flowers and flower imagery everywhere in poetry, narrative, song, and paintings, to the paper and silk flowers now available that decorate many living rooms. Also common sights are single blossoms tucked into women's hair, fresh necklaces of mudubina or *stagabe'ñe'* (water lily), or, more commonly, whole leis of frangipani for important political or social events. Local artist Jesús David García painted a Juchiteca in traje with a water lily necklace for the new bus terminal. There is, finally, the large industry of making *ramos* (branches) of flowers and ribbons that women wear at the back and side of their hair when they are going to their vela, a wedding, or a birthday celebration.[1]

As symbols and metaphors, flowers are associated with women, particularly young women, largely because they, like young women, have the desirable qualities of freshness and a sweet scent (Everts 1990). The flowers native to the region are among the most heavily scented—jasmine, tuberose, dragon's blood, frangipani, wild rose, and coyol (palm flower). Some—hibiscus, bougainvillea, and reunión de señoritas ("gathering of virgins"), are among the most brightly colored, splashing gardens and hedges with scarlet, purple, crimson, orange, and yellow. Young women wear trajes (traditional dress) that are gardens of colors and different kinds of flowers. Married women and older women may choose more subdued colors and patterns or a traje de cadenilla (one whose pattern comes from machine chain-stitched rows), but for their vela they will be as colorful as the younger women.

As we have already seen, flowers are essential in all stages of death observances, bringing their moistness, and with that, the healing power of life to the transformation of the departed. We will see even more specialized uses of flowers in the communitywide commemorations of death discussed in chapters 8, 9, and 10. Outside of those seasonal acknowledgments, death is not predictable. Vendors sell year-round but have special strategies for buying and stocking flowers for the fixed-date observances. All the local vendors are women. The

---

1. The *ramos* are made by women and by *muxe'*. The latter, in particular, are frequently hired to make the paper flowers that decorate *vela* candles and parade floats. They also make and sell leis of frangipani, and embroider the local costume whose design is based on flowers, either real or imaginary.

majority of the sellers who truck in huge quantities of flowers during the special seasons and weekly throughout the year are men, but there are no local men who make their living selling flowers.

There are so many uses for flowers and so many categories of flowers (see footnote 5, chapter 2) that one market is not big enough to contain them all. Women have permanent stalls in a large section on the main floor of the indoor market. Those women also sell flowers outside the municipal palace building on Sundays from very early until 9:30 or 10:00 a.m. All along the north side of the Parque Benito Juarez, the park in front of the municipal buildings, are two rows of flower sellers. Toward the east end of the rows, the vendors offer primarily loose flowers—wild rose, jasmine, frangipani, coyol, gardenias, and healing herbs such as dill and basil. Although a kind of consensus exists about who sits where, places are not so rigidly observed as they are down the other direction or in the indoor market. At the west end, the women vendors have more or less permanent stalls from which they sell cultivated flowers such as gladiolas, chrysanthemums, carnations, wild aster, Asiatic lilies, baby's breath, wax flowers, agapanthus, roses, tuberose, stock, daisies, and, most recently, gerbera daisies. In recent years, this market has spilled over to occupy the arcade under the municipal buildings on the north side of the square.

While there is a relatively constant demand for flowers, certain days of the week require expanded offerings. After the first nine days of mourning, people visit the cemetery twice weekly, on Thursdays and on Sundays. Vendors

Plate 8. Vendors of healing plants. 2004. Photograph by Anya Peterson Royce

Plate 9. Na Roselia Vasquez Ruiz flower vendor. 2007. Photograph by Anya Peterson Royce.

Plate 10. Flower vendors under the arcades. 2006. Photograph by Anya Peterson Royce.

always have extra stock for those two days. Some women who sell regularly in the center of town may go early to the street in front of the cemetery in Cheguigo on those visiting days to take advantage of visitors' needs. Cheguigo has no regular flower market. With the exception of the loose flowers and herbs, which are local and "of the wild," the rest are trucked into Juchitán from the states of Mexico and Puebla. Staples that are needed for the various stages in the process of death and mourning include white gladiolas, white mums, and white lilies. Beyond those, an astounding variety of flowers can be found in the Juchitán markets.

Women buy wholesale from their particular dealers, and then sell retail locally. Trucks of flowers from the cooler climes such as Puebla come once or twice a week, park on a convenient street, and the dealers sell out of their trucks to the flower vendors. Vendors of loose flowers harvest them from the low hills around the city or from plants and trees in their compounds. All arrive before dawn to take the canvas coverings off their stalls and flowers, unpack fresh flowers, and get settled into the routine of the day. The outdoor market has tarps that stretch along the length of the street, providing shade. In the merciless heat of the afternoon, more canvas covers the basins of flowers themselves. Some vendors have arranged the use of space under the arcades of the municipal buildings so one sees large, newspaper-wrapped bundles of gladiolas and chrysanthemums, big containers of baby's breath and wild aster, and greens of all kinds leaning against the wall in the shade. The advantage of being inside the covered market is that it is always shaded. The market tax is higher there, however, and the space and the rules are more rigidly enforced.

Buyers do not shop around for the best buy. They may shop for particular kinds of flowers if it is a special occasion or if the person whom the flowers honor had particular desires. Every woman has her *marchante de flores* (flower seller) from whom she buys regularly, making do with whatever range of flowers that seller may have in the trade-off between short-term variety and bargains for long-term relationships in which the vendor will do favors for the buyer, getting special flowers or adding some to the purchase, or occasionally lowering the price. The same loose, ongoing relationships characterize buyers and sellers of all basic commodities. Vendors do not generally compete with other vendors in terms of price; rather, they will give regular customers better bargains.

A new option has appeared only in the last five years—flower arrangements that can be purchased premade or made to specifications. The vendor with whom a woman has a special relationship will usually make an arrangement; some vendors will make them on speculation. Juchitán currently has two florist shops, but their business is primarily with non-Zapotec or for Juchitecos who want to know in advance that they will be able to have an arrangement of particular flowers. They have not taken business away from flower sellers in either market. The florist shops are not open year-round.

With few exceptions, Juchitecos do not buy flowers to decorate their homes nor do they give them as gifts except on occasions such as the various rituals connected with death. Mother's Day, when a gift of a floral arrangement is appropriate, is one exception to this tendency. They buy flowers for home altars, tombs, and to take to the wakes of others. They buy flowers too to take to the various churches and chapels whenever they are sponsoring a Mass. Particular saints, such as the Virgin of Guadalupe and the Virgin of Juquila or the Señor (Cristo) de Esquipulas, are likely occasions for special flowers. They buy them in pairs because the most common way of arranging flowers is on either side of an altar, either end of a shelf of a big altar, or in symmetrical arrangements in tombs. There is a constant and high demand for flowers. When the occasion does not dictate the kind of flower, people like to buy ones that will last. This is especially true of flowers that go to the cemeteries where, with the exception of perhaps two months in the year, they will quickly bake in the high temperatures. Chrysanthemums and the small carnations, as well as the varieties known as *la holandesa* and *la argentina*, are the most durable, and the local flower sellers keep good supplies of them.

Local vendors maintain their stands during the two large communal celebrations of death, Day of the Dead and Holy Week, but they share their sales with opportunistic vendors who fill the Parque Benito Juárez, spilling over into the streets and the arcades. These are women who buy marigolds, amaranth, and cockscomb in bulk, find a corner of sidewalk for themselves, and sell until their stock is gone. Trucks come and go each day, dropping off bundles. One often sees women shopping for flowers surround a truck to determine if its flowers look better or can be had for less. Holy Week flowers are different—no marigolds or other specifically Day of the Dead flowers, rather, lots of fragrant carnations, stock, tuberose, as well as mums, lilies, gladiolas, and other highland temperate-climate flowers. These may be sold right off the truck or sellers may find spaces not already belonging to the regular cadre and try to entice buyers. Because many of the Holy Week observances occur at the cemeteries, flower vendors crowd the open spaces in front of each cemetery.

Throughout the year, individuals who have plants such as hibiscus, bougainvillea, basil, and cordoncillo or trees such as frangipani in their garden may supplement their income by selling these or trading them for other things. This commerce goes on in the homes rather than in the market. Sometimes, a woman may have a particularly beautiful color of hibiscus or frangipani, and then she may be petitioned for some of the blooms for a friend's altar or tomb.

Flowers and bread mediate relationships among the living and between the living and the dead. When they function in this way, they lose their ordinary status and become special.

Cooks

Bread, flowers, food—all are essential ingredients of death and dying, as they are, indeed, of virtually all commemorations and celebrations.[2] The requirements of even a modest wake or novena or Mass for the dead mean that the women of a household must hire help. Cooks are among the most important of the help.[3] For Na Berta's funeral and for her forty-day Mass, hundreds of tamales were distributed. Each visitor had to be given at least two, the women who helped with the preparation six, and the cook twelve. All the women of the household, augmented by relatives and friends, participated in the preparation but specialists were on hand to direct, participate, and see that all was done well and in time.

Cooks are overwhelmingly female although there are a few muxe' who have quite lively businesses preparing the sort of food that is used on special occasions. One of these has a stand in the market and is also a very popular healer. Most cooks work out of their homes. Those who want to place an order go to their homes and work out quantities and kinds of food, price, and delivery dates. If a household is going to be involved in the preparations and the cooking, then one might hire a cook to come to the home and supervise or help. If the preparation involves slaughtering a pig, a professional comes to dispatch the animal. In 1972 the family held a seven-year Mass for Na Berta's husband. Family came from all parts of Mexico to help but, in addition, there were two cooks to supervise, a butcher to slaughter the pigs, and the wife of the butcher to help and to make blood sausage.

Just as with any other craft, cooks may specialize in a particular kind of food—tamales, for example—and then may further specialize in the kind of tamale. Some will make the mole (sauce); some will make the "filling"; some will do it all. Skill and talent are recognized, and cooks are ranked accordingly. Choosing a cook involves knowledge of those relative rankings as well as any relationship that may exist between a cook and a family. If it is a busy season, people may not have much latitude in choosing a cook. As with other com-

---

2. Giving and receiving food and drink establishes and honors relationship. A visitor must always be offered something to eat or drink, even if she is unexpected or her visit is brief. On occasion, the family has to send someone out to buy soft drinks or fruit if there are none. Not to offer food would be unthinkable. As it is among the living so it is between the living and the dead. Not only are there special foods for the occasions when one remembers the dead—certain kinds of tamales, bread, and *mole*, but there is also the expectation that one will prepare food and offer drink that the dead particularly liked.

3. For an illustration of the importance of cooks, see the description of Ta Chu's seven-year Mass in chapter 4.

mercial relationships, people tend to find one person whom they like and hire her whenever an occasion may arise. A long-term relationship such as this also makes it more likely that this person's services will be available to you even during very busy times.

It is again the case, as with bread, that matters of quality, preferences, and family tradition influence the choice of cook. Families hosting an altar for the dead at the end of October are judged on the kind and quality of the bread and tamales they give to visitors. *Gueta guu beela za*, beef tamales made with lard, are highly praised and coveted, and have become a tradition for particular families. Masses for the dead require mole and not all moles are alike. These aesthetic choices and traditions create relationships between particular cooks and families, some of which extend across generations.

Some of these women and muxe' also sell from stands in the indoor market but one could not buy all the food necessary for any of the occasions honoring the dead from what is available in the market on a given day. This kind of "prepared food" tradition apparently is a long one in Juchitán, probably beginning with some women specializing in making tortillas and totopos for sale as well as the breakfast dishes of iguana stew and baked armadillo. Most years see an abundance of corn, and processing it into a food that people would want to buy ready-made is easier and more profitable. It is similar to the tradition of women gathering up windfalls of fruit to sell in a corner of the market even though they are not regular vendors. Isthmus Zapotec households have, for centuries, relied on the different economic contributions of women and men. In this situation, taking advantage of prepared food is perfectly appropriate for busy women. The latter is also a solution to the problem faced by widowed men who have no household or female relatives to prepare their meals. Preparing food for others provides excellent economic opportunities for women whether they work from home or have stalls in the market or evening snack food tables on the most populated streets. The best of them enjoy reputations as masters of their craft.

Rezadoras

No passage can be effected without prayer. Today, these are almost always variants of Roman Catholic prayers such as rosaries, prayers for the blessed souls in Purgatory, prayers for the various saints' days, or the Our Father, which is part of almost every prayer cycle. Healers can and do add to these with elaborate prayers that sustain the universe and prayers soliciting the aid of different beings. For example, Ta Feli often addressed his prayers to the beautiful young woman who is the guardian of the water. There are also cycles of prayers in the various churches, for example, those prayed in both Zapotec and Spanish by twelve men who are designated as apostles on Holy Thursday and Good Friday. On Holy Thursday the men of the Society of the Sacred Heart lead the songs of pardon in front of the Christ of the Sacred Heart when He is imprisoned outside the church. Much of the prayer that takes place outside the church is the province of male and female lay readers.

A prayer leader may be called when a person's death is clearly imminent. When she prays alongside the dying person, it is called *rusi guundacabe* in Zapotec, *encaminarlos* in Spanish, and "pray them along the road" in English. The rezadoras with whom I have spoken lament the fact that this is increasingly less frequent. Now, the rezadora comes in time for the laying out of the body in front of the home altar. Her job is to pray throughout the vigil, alternately censing the body and the altar in front of which the body lays. If there is no band, the same rezadora walks in the funeral procession from the house to the cemetery. When the family returns to the house, preparations are made for the nine days of prayers and the services of the prayer leader continue. Rezadoras carry little notebooks in which they have copied all the standard prayers needed for most occasions. These include most of the contemporary Roman Catholic prayers as well as some songs that can be traced back to fifteenth-century Spain. These are little more than prompts because they have memorized the prayers as, indeed, have the women in the household and those who come for the nine evenings of prayers. The prayer leader becomes important because she will keep the pace and the rhythm going when emotion may cause the mourners to falter. It is she who signals the change of prayers as well. The censing is usually done during these days by a member of the household, leaving the rezadora free to concentrate on leading the prayers. She will bring the prayers to an end, normally after an hour, and stay with the mourners for a short time while the bread and chocolate is passed out to each woman, the rezadora served first, and while people talk.

People tend to use the same prayer leaders again and again if they are not otherwise engaged. They might like a particular way of saying the prayers or a quality of voice or the ability to keep a quiet, steady pace. And people have a notion of what constitutes a fine performance and base their assessments on it. Rezadoras must have great endurance for prayers that sometimes go on through the night, for praying while walking slowly in procession, for returning every day for nine days, then again for the forty days, for the novena at the Day of the Dead, and so on. As with the other specialists whose work is necessary for the proper assisting and honoring of the dead, prayer leaders must be available whenever a death occurs while depending on the large communal events for a regular income source. They will also most likely have responsibilities as laypeople who belong to church groups, which sponsor cycles of prayers. The Society of the Sacred Heart of Jesus, for example, sponsors prayers every afternoon in June, whereas the Society for the Virgin Mary prays daily in May, joined by members of the Sacred Heart. Laypeople also pray during the commemoration of particular saints, for example, La Virgen de la Soledad in December. Households that own images of saints are expected to offer prayers on the feast day of that saint. Certain images rotate among the houses of women belonging to a circle of that saint and part of having the saint with one is offering prayers.

Rezadoras and rezadores may have other employment. Some grow and sell flowers "of the wild"; others may be healers. The other employment must be flexible because being a rezadora can be a full-time occupation. Some women prayer leaders never marry because the demands are unpredictable and necessitate that the woman will be away for hours at a time, often through the night. This is an interesting contrast with the men who pray almost without stop for two and a half days at the end of Holy Week in their capacities as the twelve apostles. They go home for short naps but spend most of their time in the parish church and church yard. Their wives or female relatives bring them food and whatever else they may require. It would be unimaginable for a husband to perform similar services for a wife.

Prayers at the Home Altar

Rezadoras can also be hired to lead prayers in honor of a particular saint, occupation, or cross that might be venerated by a family. Many such are congregated around May 3, the day of the Holy Cross. The flower of choice for the cross or saint's image is the frangipani, with wreathes of the fragrant blossoms around and over the image. The women who respond to the invitation bring flowers and votive candles, which they place on the altar. When there is no more room, they put them on the floor in front of the altar (Everts 1990:344). The rezadora begins the prayers after the host has censed the altar. The last prayer is a farewell to the image being honored. Afterward, each woman is given bread, tortillas, and the cold sweetened rice drink known as horchata.

An alternative commemoration can take the form of an afternoon gathering, much like a vela, in which there is music and dancing and food that the women consume on the spot. The focal point is usually a *santa cruz* (holy cross).

In Juchitán, the saints who are most popular, that is, who are displayed on household altars, include Esquipulas, San Judas Tadeo, the Virgin of Juquila, the Virgin of Guadalupe, and most recently, Christ of the Sacred Heart. Anyone with a saint's image will offer prayers on the day of that saint. Delia and I went to a prayer session for Esquipulas, taking a votive candle, which we placed on the altar and lighted before finding our seats. There were perhaps forty women[4]

---

4. Generally, men do not attend these kinds of prayers for saints, the exceptions being *muxe'* or a man of the household with a particular devotion to that saint. The prayer leader may be a man. In this case, gender is not as important as knowledge of the prayers for that particular saint.

in addition to the prayer leader who had come to pray. Afterward, we were given food, soft drinks, and gifts from the various women who had gotten a little doll baked into the cake last year. The cake we received had little dolls baked in it, and getting one obligates us to bring a gift the following year. The atmosphere during the prayers was quite solemn, each woman concentrating hard. Once the prayers ended, however, it became a lively party.

Rezadoras also preside over the annual Christmas tradition of the posada, in which the figure of the Christ child is honored. Processions fill the streets taking the baby Jesus to his new home. The gathering at the receiving house is like a child's birthday party, except that prayers are chanted and sung after the party. My friend and field assistant, Roberto Guerra Chiñas, now has three images of the baby Jesus (el Niño Dios). Every Christmas, he hires a prayer leader and hosts all the neighbor children. He feeds them sweets and horchata as they hear the story of the Christ child. "They should know these things," he says, "and they should have treats as well."

These latter home gatherings for prayer and homage are quite similar to those honoring the dead in the important sense that, just as these ask the saints for their intercessions, so do those for the dead ask the departed to intercede. After all, they are becoming not only ancestors, but also saints.

Who are the women and men who choose this occupation? Broadly speaking, the occupation runs in families, but some prayer leaders also take on apprentices, even to the point of having a "school." Finally, some come to the attention of people because they have a good voice or more piety than most, and they are encouraged to learn.

The latter was the case with Emma, the friend of my family, and the one who is most frequently the prayer leader for family commemorations. Emma told me that the family encouraged her. She had faithfully attended church since she was very young and had learned all the prayers. The family asked her to lead the prayers for Na Berta's death observances. She did not know all the required prayers, so she brought her booklet with the prayers for the souls in Purgatory. She has since added several special prayers to her own handwritten book. The prayers she knows are in Spanish. There is a special set of prayers in Latin when the ba' yaa is lifted at the end of the nine days, and these she does not know.[5] Emma has a strong voice that has the power to sooth. Her equanimity creates a sense of community with the women all believing in the efficacy of their prayers.

Na Feliciana and Señorita Margarita come out of a family of prayer leaders. Their mother, Na Adolfina, who died in 2004 in her late eighties, was a legendary rezadora, who learned the craft from her mother, Na Eusebia. Na Eusebia

---

5. I know of no prayers for any occasion in Zapotec. Most are in Spanish and a few in Latin.

gave classes to whomever wished to learn, charging one peso a week. Margarita never married and lived with her mother until Na Eusebia's death, taking care of her. She is a respected rezadora and has as much work as she can handle. Na Feliciana married and lives in Cheguigo. She too is sought after for her knowledge of a variety of prayers for different occasions and has had apprentices learning from her. Her daughters are not interested in this kind of work, she said, and her last apprentice quit because people did not pay her. Feliciana's handwritten prayer book has been passed down from her grandmother, and it includes all the prayers needed for the rituals associated with death. Sitting with her, I listened to her talk about what she does, I heard her pray some of the prayers, and I began to feel what others must feel as she prays for their loved ones—the presence of someone who knows loss and who can guide others through it. She is someone who mends the tear and helps people to establish a different kind of relationship with the dead. "Rezadoras do more than pray," she said, "they hold the people together, and they accompany the departed on the beginning of their journey. You have to be strong in the face of great grief or you will cry too, and then you cannot do what needs to be done."

Na Feliciana is so busy from October 22 to November 2, the period of honoring the dead by inviting them back to their homes, that afterward she can barely speak. Those days for her mean prayers from 8:00 a.m. until 9:00 p.m. every day, moving from one xandu' to the next, returning home each night exhausted. Holy Week is not so demanding. Prayer leaders are involved only in the Good Friday procession when they walk with the Virgen de Dolores. These are the communitywide observations in which Na Feliciana plays a role. She also is sought after whenever someone dies and she knows the prayers for children as well as for adults. If she goes to the laying out of the body, then she will follow that soul through all the rituals during the next forty days. She is hired too for saints' days—the Virgen de Guadalupe, San Vicente Ferrer Valenciano, the Santa Cruz, Esquipulas.

She and her sister Margarita work very hard at their craft. They are constantly learning new prayers and teaching young girls who want to learn. Like their mother and their grandmother, being a rezadora is a full-time job that requires discipline and dedication, knowledge, and heart.

Rezadoras are essential mediators between the world of the saints and the ancestors and the world of the living. Their presence allows the grieving and the devout to approach those worlds beyond, finding comfort and healing in the cadence of the prayers and the company of friends.

Musicians

Musicians hired to sing and play for the departed and for their living relatives and friends are exclusively men. They come in different arrangements—small bands with trumpets, saxophones, clarinets, and drums that play both regional sones and popular Latin American pieces, guitar trios, self-accompanied solo singers, and, more rarely, mariachi ensembles. All have other employment, either as musicians or in another occupation. Playing for funerals, Masses for the dead, wakes, and Holy Week celebrations represents a large source of income.

Music accompanies the dead throughout all the stages. Musicians come to play or sing familiar songs such as "Dios nunca muere," "La Martiniana," or "La última palabra" during the wake. They play outside where the men are sitting; at some point, they will come in and play for the body in front of the altar. If the departed had a favorite musician or favorite songs, that person may be encouraged to come and sing. In the case of Ta Chu's wake, César Lopez came, and sang for hours because Chu loved the way he sang and had a collection of his recordings. In such cases, the musician is there as a mourner and friend rather than as someone paid to play. Hebert Rasgado sang frequently for friends who had died. He sang at the first memorial for poet Enedino Jiménez. He said to me that singing at wakes and funerals required him to honor Zapotec traditions and hold people together in their grief at the same time that he sang his dead friend on his journey. Many singers came to accompany him when he died in December 2007.[6] In addition to solo singers such as César Lopez or Hebert Rasgado, trios of singers and guitarists often provide music at various events, the newest of which, Binnisa, was formed by Feliciano Marín, Hebert's good friend, precisely for the purpose of safeguarding traditions of repertory and of singing for particular occasions.

For the procession to the cemetery, a band is normally required. In its absence, a rezadora accompanies the body. The musicians come to the house, play outside, and then lead the procession to the cemetery. At the cemetery, they may play some sones, especially ones that the departed particularly liked, often finishing with "Dios nunca muere."

For Masses—forty days, one year, and seven years—for the dead, musicians wait outside the church, and then walk in front of the procession to the home

---

6. Hebert was a good friend, and we had talked on several occasions about the documentary I was planning to make. He brought his friend and fellow musician, Feliciano Marín, and I filmed the two of them talking about music and singing. At the end, and quite spontaneously, the two sang "La última palabra" (in Zapotec, "Guenda nabani"), two voices, one guitar. The three of us sat in silence at the end, stunned, I think, by the way the two voices came together in that powerful and tender performance. It is, of course, a song about death and the continuation of relationships after death—a well-known song in Juchitán and much beloved. We had no idea that one year later Hebert would die, still young. When I got the news, grief sat on me like a huge weight. I was here far away from all the rituals and all the people who were mourning him. I got out the videotape I had shot thinking to find some comfort in it. I took it and wove it into a short film, *Homenaje a Hebert Rasgado*, realizing that this was a way to sing him along his journey and to help mend the tear his death had made in the community of family and friends. I have visited since sending copies to his family and to Feliciano and know that they too found comfort in it.

Plate 11. Hebert Rasgado, musician and composer. 2006. Photograph by Anya Peterson Royce.

Plate 12. Feliciano Marín, musician and composer. 2008. Photograph by Anya Peterson Royce.

of the departed's family.[7] When Jesús Urbieta, the well-known Juchiteco painter, died and was brought back to Juchitán, his coffin was accompanied by musicians from his home to the Casa de la Cultura, where he lay so that people could come and pay their respects. From there, the band went with the procession to the cemetery, Panteón Domingo de Ramos, where he was laid to rest. Urbieta's burial music and the joyful Palm Sunday music, at one point simultaneously played, was a vivid instance of the sensory and symbolic import of music in Zapotec ritual. With music such a central ingredient in rituals of all kinds, having celebratory and mourning music at the same time is not uncommon.

As we will see in chapter 9, musicians play a critical part in the Holy Week observances, especially but not exclusively during the Holy Tuesday services.[8] They adopt a more festive role on Palm Sunday and during and after the Mass of the Resurrection. They are hired by families for their observances at the three cemeteries. They play somber music for the very recently dead and happier music at the tombs of the long departed. They also accompany the mayordomos or sponsors of all the Holy Week societies on their many processions to and from chapels and churches.

Musicians as a class range from those who are self-taught to those who compose their own music and texts, and who make recordings of their repertory. Some, such as Hebert Rasgado, have translated well-known songs into Zapotec, such as the Beatles' "Yesterday." Others have made arrangements of music such as Burt Bacharach's "Raindrops Keep Falling on My Head" for their own bands. In 2006 musicians collaborated with poets on a CD titled *El señor de los sueños*, an homage to local poet Enedino Jiménez. As with the other crafts, accomplishment is recognized creating a hierarchy of talent that is agreed-upon by most Juchitecos. There is enough work for local musicians for them to consider it a full-time occupation. Some of these musicians offer their services to the Casa de la Cultura teaching aspiring youngsters so that traditions are not lost. Two children's groups now give performances. One, La Cigarra (Bigarii, in Zapotec), describes its music as "prehispánico," its flutes and drums familiar to most Juchitecos. It has a CD out published by DIF in 2005. The other, Badu Naxhi, is newer, founded in 2006 by a local music teacher. It is a full brass band with brand new instruments purchased through a generous gift from a local patron. In its short history, it has become the band of the

---

7. The use of the band for the forty-day Mass is a recent innovation, according to Delia Ramírez Fuentes.

8. The services that occur on Holy Tuesday are not part of the Roman Catholic Holy Week liturgies, which begin on Holy Thursday. They are only nominally presided over by the priest, and after his departure, the Zapotec continue with prayers, music, and other observances. Tuesday is interesting because Christ's image is put in his glass coffin and displayed in front of the altar. I have not been able to find an explanation for the adoration of the crucified Christ three days before his Good Friday crucifixion. There are societies in charge of the care of the images of Holy Tuesday, and they drive the observances.

pueblo, most recently playing for a delegation of people from Spain who had given a statue of San Vicente Ferrer to the parish of San Vicente in recognition of their community's allegiance to San Vicente. They also played as part of the celebrations surrounding Juchitán being named a "heroic city of Mexico."

Hired Help

This category, like that of musicians, is almost completely dominated by men. It includes skilled and semiskilled laborers who can do several of the short-term jobs required to meet one's obligations to the dead. Cleaning and repairing tombs may require masons, carpenters, and painters. The cemeteries hum with this kind of activity just before Palm Sunday with families making repairs or new additions to the tombs of their loved ones. Constructing *biguié'* or even the newer forms of altars rely on manual labor, if not of the men in one's household, then of men hired for the occasion. Men who own teams of oxen also find extra employment during the communitywide observances of death. They load and carry the heavy bundles of banana stalks and green cocos used in the altars of Day of the Dead. They also carry palm and willow branches to the various cemeteries during Holy Week that are used to repair and build temporary "houses" for the dead.

Throughout the year, people may hire men to dig graves or to open up the floor of established tombs for a resting place for a newly departed. More skilled men are employed to craft crosses of wood or stone for the tombs, the concrete or stone plaques with names carved in them, and stone flower vases. Both active cemeteries employ *panteoneros* who can direct people to particular tombs and who supervise the digging of new graves and the building of new tombs.

Businesses

Finally, there are the local mortuaries. Embalming is a recent and not widely used practice.[9] Burial ideally happens quickly after death, within twenty-four

---

9. Anything that requires opening the body, observing or removing organs, or adding anything (for example, embalming fluid) runs counter to deeply held notions about the human body. Zapotec has three terms that refer to the body: *guidi ladi* refers to the outside of the body; *la'dxi'* refers to the inside of the body, specifically, the internal organs. It also refers to the pulp of fruit. *Ladxidó'* is used today to mean "heart" or "stomach," but it literally means "the center of the inside body." The place where the spirit resides would be another meaning. Cutting into a deceased body (*ba'* or the body prepared for burial) would release the spirit in an untimely manner and in an unfamiliar place causing it to lose its way. In 2004, the state, with the approval of Juchitán's municipal president, began construction of a facility for performing autopsies. It was to serve all the communities nearby, including Ixtepec, Espinal, Tehuantepec, and Ixtaltepec. Juchitán was chosen because of its

hours. If a person dies in the early morning, he or she will be buried in the late afternoon. If a person dies during the day, then the wake goes on for the remainder of the day and throughout the night. Burial takes place the following morning. Embalming may be used if a person dies away from Juchitán and has to be brought back, a five-hour journey from Oaxaca City and twelve hours from Mexico City. Sometimes a vigil may be extended to give people time to arrive, which necessitates embalming. Lastly, if the person died in an accident and is disfigured, the body is taken to the mortuary, embalmed, and made presentable for the wake.

The funeral homes are the most common providers of coffins, both metal and wooden. A large cross, candlesticks, and chairs come with the purchase of a coffin, and families may keep them for the nine days of prayers. I know of no instances where a vigil or viewing has been held at the mortuary. This would be a serious break with the tradition of sending the departed on their journey from the homes they knew in life, especially their natal home.[10] Included in the services for those who have purchased coffins is someone to dig or open the grave. The funeral homes are all owned by local families who tailor their offerings to local sensibilities.

As with other innovations, funeral homes provide services that relieve people from what would be burdensome work if they had to do it themselves. But Juchitecos use those services to the extent that they help ease the burden, not as a service that would make all the family preparations and rituals superfluous. Death is too important for both the dead and the living communities to

---

central location. They began building on empty land to the east of the Panteón Miércoles Santo, the cemetery in Cheguigo. The people, especially those from Cheguigo, objected vociferously. The authorities sent more police to patrol the site. Finally, the crowd outnumbered the police in increasingly greater numbers. The police put up a token show but soon faded away. All the construction was leveled to the ground. As with all differences of opinion in Juchitán, there are multiple underlying causes. In this case, ownership of the land was one of those as well as antipathy toward the tactics of the municipal president, but the long-held aversion to autopsies, to opening up the body in such an intrusive way, was a major factor in the protests.

10. In August 2008, Manuel Pineda died. He died in Huatulco, a community on the Pacific coast about four hours from Juchitán where he lived with his son. Although he had lived there for many years, his family wanted him to be remembered and reconnected to his birthplace in Juchitán. He was cremated and his ashes brought to the family residence in Juchitán where all his family and friends observed the nine days of prayers and grieving. They laid out a ba' yaa in front of the altar even though the urn with his ashes was visible on the altar. He subsequently returned to Huatulco to be laid to rest there. He honored both homes and his family and friends who did everything to make his journey to the land of the dead a proper one. People were willing to accept the fact that his ashes and the ba' yaa were in front of the altar at the same time because reconnecting him to his birthplace and to his Juchitán relatives was paramount. His closest family in the city will not attend this year's Vela Pineda because they are observing the prescribed period of mourning.

give it over to the sterile, nonfamily ministrations of a mortuary. It is the work by family and community that restores and maintains family and community.

Conclusion

Death requires the craft and services of many people while still remaining a family affair. In Juchitán, one cannot die without prayers, flowers, candles, bread, food, and music. These proclaim the communal import of death at the same time that they serve as the transformative forces that move the recently departed to the community of the dead. The focal point for all the rituals surrounding the newly dead is the house in which that person lived and the earth on which the house is built. Perhaps this has always been so. Pre-Columbian Zapotec housed the dead in their compounds. In the case of nobility who were laid to rest in the great cities of the dead such as Mitla, Liobá, and Stibaa, they were taken from the residences where they had lain to their new home. It is before the home altar that the body lies, first on the floor where it is closest to the earth, then on a cot, and finally in a coffin. It may leave in its physical manifestation within a day of death, but the spirit remains for the forty days of prayers, housed in each of the successive "bodies," readying itself for departure. It does this surrounded by loved ones, by flowers of the wild and music that give it sustenance, and by the prayers that gently move it on its journey. And all are held together by the daily gifts of bread, food, flowers, and companionship.

4

Tending to the Dead

Home Altars and Cemeteries

Rosa and I went to her brother's tomb in the Panteón Miércoles Santo. It was a Sunday in March, still Lent but before Holy Week. She carried a pail of water and flowers laid over her arm. It was a largish tomb with a dirt floor, thatched palm roof, and cement block walls. The morning was hot; the sun's glare enough to make you squint your eyes, but inside the tomb it was cool and dark. Rosa stepped inside, scooped handfuls of water from the pail and watered down the dirt. You could feel the damp rise, making a healing earth bed for her flower offerings. She kept the cordoncillo out but put the rest of the flowers in the pail to keep them cool and wet. Bending forward, she wound a circle of cordoncillo on the ground. As she shaped the long stems, the peculiar sweet-pungent smell signaled green, nayaa. Working quickly, she filled the circle with hibiscus, all red save for one yellow bloom that she placed at the top. She put two sprigs of white reunión de señoritas (clusters of small fragrant blossoms) at the bottom. She splashed more water on the finished corona then reached across it to hang wreathes of cream-yellow frangipani round the cross. Standing up and backing out, Rosa knuckled the sore muscles from her back. "Ma'" she said, "Already." Her obligation was met.

—Field notes, March 12, 2006

Introduction

Dying transforms the relationship to the living, and with that it changes the ways and times in which that relationship must be recognized both by large, communal commemorations and by daily acts. Among members of the community of the living, these relationships are acknowledged communally in rites of passage such as birth, coming of age (for girls), weddings, graduations, and birthdays. They are acknowledged daily within the family in meals, seeking and giving counsel, conversation, decision-making, and argument.

The same is true of the relationship between the dead and the living. Communally, the two citywide commemorations are the Day of the Dead prayers and visits and the Holy Week cemetery visits. Within families, daily acts serve as reminders of the ongoing relationship. These include the series of rituals that begin with the death and burial, the first nine days of prayer, the forty-day cycle of visits and prayers, and the Masses at the end of the first and seventh years. In addition, the living have the responsibility of maintaining the home altar with fresh flowers and candles, as well as cleaning and decorating tombs in the cemetery.

The individual is situated within a family and an extended family. No matter where the individual might go, the locus of family is the household, the home. In the past, when a person was born, his umbilical cord and placenta were buried in a pot in the earth of the compound. The Zapotec word for the umbilical cord is *doo yoo*, "house cord." When a person dies, he remains within the family, but also becomes part of the community of the dead. The locus then shifts to the cemetery home. In their physical manifestations, the home inhabited by the living and the cemetery home are remarkably alike. Tombs are, in fact, little houses, and cemeteries are laid out with wide streets and narrow alleys just like the city. Just as people's homes have four walls, a roof and a floor, so do tombs. The passage from life to death transports the dead from the family home to the cemetery home occupied by departed family members. The daily, weekly, and other rituals that attend to the dead take place within these two homes.

Home Altars

Every home has an altar. Minimally, the altar might be a small table covered with a cloth on which are a saint's image, photographs of dead family members, votive candles, and flowers. More elaborate ones may have several images of saints, prayer cards of different saints, and flowers in vases as well as loose flowers on the tabletop. The altar may also be a stepped arrangement with items at different levels, with photographs placed on the table but also on the wall. Regardless of the size and complexity of the altar, family members will keep a glass of fresh water on it for the dead, especially for those who have died within the past two years.

The altar takes its most extravagant form for the recently deceased and is open to friends who come to visit. In old, large families, recent deaths are common so the altar is often used in this way, but regardless, it remains the altar for the all ancestors, both recent and long departed.

Na Rosinda inherited a beautifully carved Christ crucified that dates to the mid-eighteenth century. This is the Christ who broods over the family altar, which is upstairs and away from the more public areas. In addition, on the table are several saints' images, as well as photographs of deceased relatives related both by blood and marriage. Two large vases are replenished once or twice a week with fresh flowers; candles remain lit; a variety of prayer cards lie on the white cloth or are put in the frames of pictures; flowers of the wild (jasmine, hibiscus, and frangipani) are scattered across the cloth. This is the altar where family members go to pray each morning, interceding for the souls of their relatives and asking that the dead intercede for them. Because of its location in a small room on the second floor, this altar cannot be used for occasions such as wakes, nine or forty days, or the one- and seven-year Masses. There is simply no room to accommodate all the people who come. Downstairs, in the back of the compound, is a large room with an altar that can be used for these more public commemorations. This is the altar that was used for Na Berta, Rosinda's mother, and for Ta Chu, Rosinda's husband. Berta and Chu were laid out in front of it; their flower-body replaced the physical bodies after burial; and the altar held their photos or lu bidó' (image) after the nine days. It was the *xandu' yaa* (fresh altar) in year one, the *xandu' guiropa* (second year altar) in year two for Day of the Dead, and the focal point for the prayers leading up to the first- and seventh-year Masses. It is small now, but still has photos, candles, and vases of flowers.

As discussed in chapter 1, there is some evidence for an early Zapotec origin for home altars, given the practice of burying family members in the patio of the household compound. It is intriguing to imagine that the change to burials away from family households necessitated spring (now coincident with Holy Week) visits to the cemeteries to honor the ancestors. It might be that daily devotions in the homes continued, even in the absence of burials, and that when the Day of the Dead became a major holiday under the Spanish, the Zapotec simply elaborated the worship they were already doing. Day of the Dead celebrations in other parts of Mexico occur in the cemeteries, rather than in the house. This makes the Isthmus Zapotec practice worthy of careful scrutiny.

Cemeteries

Burial places in the two cemeteries currently in use, Panteón Domingo de Ramos and Panteón Miércoles Santo, range from small dirt-covered plots to very large family mausoleums. Space is at a premium now and will become even more so as the city continues to expand past its current population of more than 100,000. Occasionally, where one is buried becomes a political issue. Populist parties have, in the past, wanted to democratize the cemeteries, making everyone equal in death. They have run into the fierce opposition of families who have owned large tombs for several generations. It is a sensitive subject because no one wants to be buried away from those with whom the ties in life were the closest. Being buried in a family tomb ensures the continuing attentions of the living as well as the comforting companionship of relatives who have gone before. Family members who have gone to live outside Juchitán maintain their ties to the city while they live. Most hope to return at their death.

The larger family tombs are constructed with an eye to accommodating as many family members as might come along. There is always extended discussion about who will be buried there. It seems to be the accepted practice that a nuclear family—parents and their children, occupy or have a right to occupy a common tomb. But they may represent several generations of family. The decisions become more problematic if family members are buried in different cemeteries because that precludes expanding into contiguous plots. For example, Rosinda's parents, Na Berta and José Fuentes, are buried in the Panteón Domingo de Ramos as are two of her siblings and several aunts and uncles. Other siblings have made their plans for burial in that cemetery as well. Ta Chu, Rosinda's husband, however, is buried in the Panteón Miércoles Santo in Cheguigo, so that is where she will go to rest.

The floors of tombs are concrete slabs, and when a new death occurs, the concrete is raised, the body interred, and the floor returned to its place. People's names are inscribed, either in a set-in plaque on the back wall or on a cross of marble or granite placed against the wall. In the case of tombs without doors or in the interval between a death and the completion of the permanent plaque or cross, a small wooden cross with the deceased's name painted on it serves to identify the occupant. Granite vases on the floor or set on pedestals represent what most people hope to have, but numerous acceptable alternatives exist depending on the status of the family and the finished state of the tomb. Ideally, tombs are closed on all four sides as well as on the top and bottom. In their enclosing form, they are functionally identical to the biguié' ("spirit flower" altar). Being enclosed creates a comfortable home for the dead at the same time that it contains spirits who otherwise might be inclined to wander. One recent tomb in the Panteón Miércoles Santo tried to achieve this ideal with readily available materials that could be assembled by a few men. They constructed a lattice-structure of light poles, such as those used to build temporary enramadas, enclosed on all sides and the top.

After the funeral, during the forty days of prayers, family members, with the exception of the chief mourner, visit the cemetery daily. It is a way of respecting the deceased as well as encouraging her or him to be comfortable in the new home. At this stage, coronas of flowers of the wild are laid out on the floor of the tomb directly in front of the cross or plaque. Votive candles are tended to so that one is always burning. There is always a glass of fresh water from which the spirit may drink.

After the forty days, the chief mourner will join other family members in tending the tomb. They may visit more often, but visits are expected every Thursday and Sunday. No one visits on Saturdays is because this is the day that the Blessed Virgin visits the cemetery, taking the souls who reside there to the river to bathe. In the sixteenth century, the Augustinians established confraternities of Our Lady in honor of the Virgin. They celebrated a Mass for the Living every Saturday because that was the day of prayer especially consecrated to the Virgin (Ricard 1966:182). It is very likely that there is a connection between these two traditions.

Commemorations Whose Center Is the Home

Juchiteco homes buzz with activity day and night. People come and go, gather around meals; children of the extended family are welcomed in any number of homes, doing their homework, playing with cousins, eating meals; the home is often the site of crafts or other kinds of work; women vendors, especially of tortillas, cheese, fish, and pan dulce (sweetened bread), bring their wares to the homes of their steady customers; in the evenings, people settle down to talk or to watch television, and are still talking or doing chores until late into the night. Homes are the place one spends the most time—the opposite of our North American tradition. Within the home, doors are never shut, and people are seldom still. Most families have lived in the same place, usually the same house, for generations, and each young generation regards that place as home. They may travel or study outside of Juchitán but clearly their natal home is always an emotional center to which they return on holidays, for commemorations, and for vacations.

It is not surprising, then, that the home functions as the center of much of the extraordinarily diverse and frequent ritual. It is the center of most rituals having to do with death and the dead. And the focal point for those is the home altar or altars.

Funeral and Nine Days

A person's death mobilizes the household and extended family. On July 28, 1978, Ta Porfirio Pineda died in the morning. His wife was in Mexico City and his daughter and her husband had left before dawn to go to the Guelaguetza in Oaxaca. Ta Porfirio was alone with one of his sons. In the absence of the close female relatives, Na Rosinda, Porfirio's niece, arranged for a Mass at 5:00 that afternoon in the home and for another the following morning at 10:00. By the afternoon, the eldest daughter had returned and was receiving family members and friends who came to mourn. Women would come, arms laden with votive candles and white flowers, greet the eldest daughter who received their offerings and condolences. The men arrived, passed briefly through the altar room, acknowledging Ta Porfirio, and then sat in the patio where they smoked and drank with the male relatives. At 4:00 p.m. women helpers passed bowls of chicken soup to the women seated in the altar room. Father Zanella arrived at 5:00 p.m. and said Mass on an improvised altar in the room where Ta Porfirio was laid out in front of his *santo* (altar). By the time Father Zanella said his second Mass the following morning at 10:00, most of the absent relatives had returned, some from as far away as the northern city of Monterrey. His burial was at 4:00 p.m., accompanied by music and about eighty mourners. The nine days of the rosario began immediately after the burial. The ba' yaa had taken the place of Ta Porfirio's body and would be replenished with fresh flowers each of the remaining nine days.

Whatever the specific arrangements with funeral homes or the complications caused by a person dying away from home or by absent relatives, the ideal is that the body, washed and dressed in the person's best or favorite clothes, be placed on the floor in front of the home altar, which is the locus of all the ritual to come. The body may be placed directly on the floor or on a mat (*daa* in Zapotec, *petate* in Spanish). What is of critical importance is that it rest on the floor or ground, even if for a very short period of time. This practice is consonant with other behaviors that follow from being an autochthonous people. One comes up from the earth, and one returns to it. Ideally, these two occur in the same place; hence the importance of one's natal home. Birth is marked as local and earth-connected by the practice of burying the cord and placenta in the home compound. Death observances repeat that connection by placing the body on that same ground, in one sense beginning the journey of the dead to a new home, like the old gods. The earth also carries important healing properties—it is moist, fresh, and fertile. It gives life and receives it; it ensures that the journey of the dead is measured and calm, giving the spirit time to adjust, and to become a strong and beneficent ancestor. Through the offerings of water and flowers, which are mediated through earth, individuals are able to make the journey from the home of the living to the home of the dead.

In the midst of the grieving, the family of the deceased must meet its responsibilities to those who show their solidarity by coming to the house. Pan dulce and coffee are given to the women, cigarettes and mezcal or brandy to the men who may also get pan dulce and coffee. If people stay the duration of the wake, they must be fed (chicken soup in the case of Ta Porfirio). Similarly, if friends dig the grave, they must also be fed. In the past, it was more common for a priest to celebrate a Mass at the home. Now a priest may come to the house to do the Celebration of the Word rather than a Mass but it is more common for a priest to come at the last set of prayers commemorating the nine days. The rezadora may come at any time, but she must be there at night for the prayers or just before the funeral procession leaves the house.

The altar provides an anchor point where the living and the dead come together. It is especially important after the body has been taken to the cemetery and while the spirit is still reluctant to leave the house. It provides a safe "home." It is offered as a home again on the occasion of the xandu' yaa when the spirit is invited back. The petate spread on the floor in front of the altar or which becomes the floor of the biguié' is heaped with flowers and fruit suitable for the dead—fresh, moist, green. And it is there that the primary place of healing resides—on the ground in the natal home in front of the altar. It is where the living and the spirit of the dead may come together in harmony.

The body remains in front of the altar for the duration of the wake, moved from the floor to a cot, and finally to a coffin. It is surrounded by flowers and large candles, and the prayers of the rezadora. When the body leaves the house, it is immediately replaced by a "flower" or "fresh" body (ba' yaa). This is laid down on a cross of sand in exactly the same place where the coffin stood. The sand is covered with flowers of the wild and cordoncillo, evergreen branches, or basil, all of which have healing properties. Incense now burns, its clouds of white smoke rise with the voices of women, marking each evening with prayers. The women who come to pray are given two pieces of bread and a tablet of chocolate for each set of prayers. Every other day they are given a small bucket of atole (*nisiaabala'dxi*), which they take home with them, returning the bucket on the next day of prayers. On the ninth day, there is one set of prayers at nine in the evening, then a second set at 5:00 a.m. After the second set of prayers, the ba' yaa with all its sand, is lifted up by the men of the household and their male friends, placed in a *xiga gueta* (painted and lacquered half gourd), and taken to the chapel nearest to the house of the deceased. When the people return, they are given tamales of *mole rojo con res* (beef with a sauce made from red chiles, sesame, nuts, tomatoes, and bread for thickening), bread, and coffee. The ba' yaa is replaced by the third "body," a photograph of the deceased placed on the altar.

From the Ba' yaa to the Forty-Day Mass

The remaining days, until forty are reached, are filled with activity whose center is the altar room. The altar is filled with flowers, constantly replenished by the stream of visitors who come to express their sympathy. A single row of blossoms—hibiscus, frangipani, sweetheart roses, and gardenias—runs perpendicular to the altar. The end farthest from the altar is marked by a votive candle and the ever-present incense burner. The prayers now occur each Friday evening. The rezadora leads the women of the household and their close female friends and relatives in prayers for the soul of the departed. On the afternoon of the fortieth day, Mass for the dead is said in the church, and everyone returns to the house for tamales de mole negro, bread, soft drinks for the women, and beer or a shot glass of brandy or mescal for the men. The procession from the church to the house is led by musicians, a relatively new innovation that has replaced the rezadora. The photograph of the deceased is carried by a young family member, usually a girl, women carry the large vases of flowers, and men carry the candles. A final set of prayers takes place at 10:00 p.m. The small flower "body" is gathered up to be taken to the cemetery in the morning or to some place with a cross.

First-Year Mass for the Dead

The whole year after someone's death is a period of mourning. Normal fiesta activities are curtailed radically, especially for the surviving spouse, daughter, or other chief mourner. Their time is spent taking care of the deceased. The activities center on the home altar, the one that becomes the public altar during the wake, nine days and forty days, but also include twice-weekly or more frequent visits to the cemetery. The home and its altar once again are the site of commemoration extending beyond family when the first year anniversary is celebrated.

Preparations begin many months in advance with conversations among the family about how many people can be expected, who should be contracted to make the mole, who should provide the bread, and what band might be available. The women are also readying what they will wear. This is still a time of mourning but the appropriate dress is *enagua de olán* and huipil in a somber color. These include purple, brown, deep green, or blue, as well as black or black and white. Because the mole with its *relleno de puerco o pollo* ("stuffing" of pork or chicken) is taken home by women guests,[1] the family must buy containers. Traditionally, these were pottery bowls that one bought in bulk in the market. Today, plastic containers with lids are preferred. They are lighter, easier to carry, and the lid prevents mole from spilling and staining clothes. Juchitán has several stores that sell plastic ware in bulk, and people usually make several trips to look at containers before they settle on one model as the right

---

1. Women take home the food they are given whenever they attend an observance, unless they go as helpers and are fed throughout the duration or in the case of *velas* where the dance or fiesta lasts all night or most of the day. The food they carry home is then redistributed or eaten later by the family. Men who attend observances consume the food at the host's house.

size. Delia and I made these rounds of stores six months before the seven-year Mass for Ta Chu, finally settling on a design and size. Even with all the planning, we ran out of containers on the day of the Mass.

The week before the Mass, the compound is alive with activity. All the women relatives, both local and those who live elsewhere, arrive to help with the preparations. Men bring in rented chairs and flats of soft drinks and beer. Women put the bread into individual plastic bags. Trays are stacked and ready for serving. The altar is refreshed with flowers, candles, and incense. Everything is ready the night before. Mass is in the morning, and all the family attend as well as close and distant relatives and friends. Helpers remain in the compound to make the final preparations—filling containers with mole relleno, stacking bags of bread on trays, receiving the gladiolas that are sent by those close to the family, putting the soft drinks and beer into coolers, and setting the tables where the men will sit with plates, cutlery, and beer at each place. At the end of the Mass, the family take the vases of flowers and the large, ribbon-wrapped candles and the photograph of the deceased from the chancel of the church, and organize themselves into the proper procession form. They are followed by everyone who attended the Mass. The musicians who have been waiting outside the church approach, ready to lead. When the procession arrives at the house, the family go to the altar room with the flowers, candles, and photograph, which they arrange on and around the altar. The chief mourner sits ready to receive her guests who come to acknowledge her and the deceased, leaving a small monetary offering. The guests who do so are women (with rare exceptions), and after greeting the mourner, they find a seat. Helpers and family members serve them the container of mole, the bag with bread, and a cold soft drink. They may drink the refresco, but they take the food home. The male guests, in the meantime, have found their way to the tables and are being served plates or bowls of mole relleno, which they wash down with beer.

Felix López Jiménez

Ta Feli died on March 11, 2004, after a brief illness. He was the healer who brought comfort to so many, the one whose prayers kept the world from spinning out of control from its own excesses. He was my friend. Delia called to tell me about his death, and I asked her to take flowers to the house. Throughout the year, I felt his absence, sometimes a dull ache, sometimes as if my heart had disappeared to be replaced by a cold windy space. In March 2005, I was back in Juchitán, and I asked Delia if she knew where his tomb was so I could visit. She asked his niece, Minerva, who said she would go with me because I would not find it on my own. The next morning, Irma bought flowers for me on one of her trips to the market—guie' biuxhe, simple flowers—frangipani blossoms and

Plate 13. Leaving the church after the Mass for Jesús Ramírez Escudero, "Ta Chu." 2004. Photograph by Cristina de la Cruz Pineda.

Plate 14. Returning from the Mass for Ta Chu to the Pineda compound to receive the guests. 2004. Photograph by Cristina de la Cruz Pineda.

frangipani wreathes, flor de china petals, which are used for the floors of recent tombs. Minerva came for me in the late morning. We stood in the middle of La Esmeralda holding each other and crying as we remembered Ta Feli. "Why have you left us, my little father," Mine repeated through her tears. Her husband drove us to the cemetery, the Panteón Domingo de Ramos, filled a bucket with fresh water, and then joined us as we snaked our way through the little paths off the main street through the cemetery. It was a hot, cloudless day, and we spoke little. "Turn left at this blue curbstone; that's the only way to find him," Mine said. We plunged into even more narrow paths, up and down over uneven stones discarded from old tombs. Then we were there. "The ground is so rocky here that we haven't had time yet to dig the tomb out completely," Mine gestured toward Feli's new home. It had a dirt floor and stone walls reaching up midway to the thatched palm roof that shaded it. Because it was a small space, but also out of a sense of respecting each other's privacy, we took turns crouching in the cool hollow of the tomb, talking with Feli. After a year of feeling his absence, I suddenly felt surrounded by him, welcomed home just as I always felt when I would turn into his compound and he would greet me. "I knew you would be here today; I dreamed it last night," he would say as a smile slowly spread across his face. Did you know, I wonder, that I would come here today—the day before the first anniversary of your death?

Mine crouched next to me and we began making his corona (a circle of flowers). Her husband handed us the branches of cordoncillo used for the base so that its freshness and life-giving properties can mediate between the grave below and the flowers above, magnifying the power inherent in the flowers themselves. On top we then spread the loose red-pink petals of the flor de china, smelling vaguely of roses. We patted them smooth, formed a perfect circle, then scattered the loose guie' chaachi blossoms. A few stubborn stems of cordoncillo stuck through the blanket of flowers, and we tucked them back into place. The garlands I had brought we hung around the wooden cross that bore Ta Feli's name. "O, Virgen Maria, madre de Dios, bendita eres," Mine began the prayers and I joined her. I remembered Feli's first vision when the Virgin Mary was his guide through a palace of flowers and told him that he was called to be a healer. She sent him out, and now he was back in the safety of her arms. It seemed to me then that Feli had drawn the two of us together with him and, for that moment, there in the fragrant shade of his tomb, we were a trinity. The water we scattered over the flowers, the stones of the sides, the dirt of the floor, the cross with its frangipani garlands, the palm-thatched roof became the blessing that Juchitecos believe it to be—cool, moist, able to draw forth the sweet fragrance and wetness of the flowers.

As we walked back through the cemetery, our hands were cool and fragrant even as our heads were bowed under the white glare of the sun. Death has not diminished his power, I thought.

The next morning, the first anniversary prayers began at 10:00 a.m. in his home next to his temple. The prayer leader arrived promptly, accompanied by four old men, their voices guiding the gathered women through the prayers. I took my votive candle to the altar, lighting it and placing it among the scattered blossoms so that its light and heat would raise our prayers more quickly to the saints who would intercede for us. Ta Feli's photograph, his lu bidó', was the one I had taken of him a few years earlier. He had just showered when I arrived that day and was cool in his Calvin Klein T-shirt. He graciously granted my request to photograph him, and then told me that Graciela Iturbide had also taken his picture. Iturbide is a very famous Mexican photographer who has stunning albums of photos including several from the Isthmus. I have not seen her photo of him, and she did not send him a copy. Minerva said that she appreciated my photo because it was the only good one they had of him. I began to appreciate the importance and power of the images that are chosen for the altars for the dead. This one held so many memories of my friend, and it seemed to speak to others who knew and loved him.

Images of saints, flowers, and candles filled all the space on top the table that served as the altar. In the center at the back was a large image of the Virgen de Guadalupe; just below her was a photograph of Ta Feli's sister who had preceded him in death, and then came his photo. Garlands of creamy yellow frangipani were draped over the two photos and around the crucified Christ. Facing the altar, I could see another row of images to the left of center: St. George and the dragon, Mary and the Christ child, and on the bottom a female saint. Just to the right of these framed images, there was a carved Virgin Mary dressed in red and below her another carved Mary, this one in white. On the right side, there was a large figure of the crucified Cristo de Esquipulas (the Black Christ). The Tibetan sandlewood prayer beads I had given Feli a few years ago hung around the cross. Behind the Christ was an image of San Vicente Ferrer (San Vicente *dxu*—the "foreign" Saint Vincent) and another female saint. Flanking all the images and photos were two large vases filled with white gladiolas and lavender chrysanthemums. Inside those were two smaller vases with yellow roses. A small vase of gardenias released its fragrance in the heat of the candles. Twenty or so votive candles, primarily white, filled most of the space in front of the images and flowers. They had been placed there and lit by the women attending the prayers. Finally, frangipani blossoms, jasmine, and hibiscus carpeted the spaces in between. The table was covered by a white lace cloth that reached all the way to the floor in front. Two large white candles in their tin holders sat on the floor in front of the altar and in the center was an incense burner.

Altars accumulate images and photographs reflecting the particular devotions of household members as well as providing a kind of photographic genealogy of the ancestors, both recent and distant. From the visions and stories that Ta Feli recounted to me, I know that the Virgin in all her aspects was especially

Plate 15. Felix López Jiménez, "Ta Feli." 2001. Photograph by Anya Peterson Royce.

important for him. I was touched and surprised to see the Tibetan beads in such a prominent place but Feli always delighted in those gifts that I brought him, chosen because they had spiritual resonance from various traditions.[2]

The prayers for the dead, based primarily on the rosary and the Our Father, caught us all up, the steady voices of the prayer leader and his colleagues keeping the rhythm and pace. Minerva was the chief mourner, and from time to time she would be overcome by loss, weeping and again asking her uncle why he had abandoned her.

2. Sending young healers off to be apprentices to practitioners of different cultures has been a long Mesoamerican tradition. Ta Feli told me about his time spent in Guatemala working with a healer there. The gifts I brought him fit into that tradition.

Toward the end of the prayers, one of the old men who had come with the prayer leader rose from his seat, moved to the front, and picked up the incense burner. He blew the coals into life, put more incense on them, and began to cense the altar and everything on it. Shortly afterward, the prayers were completed. We greeted each other and began to talk. Minerva's helpers served each of us soft drinks. Those were soon followed by bowls of chicken mole and bags of bread (pan bollo) that we took with us. We left a few at a time, feeling the bond between us strengthened and the bond between us and Ta Feli, indeed, all the dead, renewed.

Up to this point, the observance for Feli corresponded closely to what normally happens around the first anniversary. Because he had been a healer with his own temple, however, there were some additional observances. On the stepped altar in his temple, many of the images had been cleared away, some finding their way to the altar for the dead in the house. On the first step of the temple altar was a smaller version of my photograph of Feli, flanked by two vases of red roses. Red hibiscus hung atop the photo and rested at its base. On the step above, stood a carved image of the Virgen de Juquila—a nearby shrine to this Virgin promises miraculous cures and many homes have her image. Three steps above that were two footed glass bowls with floating candles. On the top step was another bowl in front of a cross. On either side of the altar were very large vases in white wrought iron stands with red Asiatic lilies and yellow chrysanthemums. On the flat space in front of the lowest step of the altar, lighted votive candles sat in a sea of red hibiscus. Three large beeswax candles stood in wooden candlestands in front of the altar. To the left of the altar against the wall, Feli's followers had placed the chair on which he always sat to conduct his healing sessions. An old wooden straight-backed chair, it was now covered with a skirted white cloth. On its seat was a vase of white daisy mums, a glass of water, and scattered frangipani and red hibiscus. Seeing that was the most difficult for me because it brought memories of all the times I had sat opposite him listening and being restored to myself.

Other departures from death observances may have been occasioned by Ta Feli himself. "He told me that he did not want me to mourn," his niece said to me. "Don't wear black and weep," he said. I know that he believed absolutely in his calling, knowing who had called him, and he was not worried about leaving this existence for the next. Those of us still here had a harder time letting him go.

Seven-Year Mass for the Dead

The Mass that is offered on the seventh anniversary of the death follows the same format as the first year. November 15, 2004, marked the seven-year anniversary of the death of Ta Chu, Jesús Ramírez Escudero, husband of Na Rosinda Fuentes, father of Delia Ramírez Fuentes, and my "adopted" father. I arrived in Juchitán on the morning of November 10 to help with the preparations and to participate in the observance. My participation had actually begun six months earlier when Delia and I went shopping for the plastic containers for mole and discussed what I would wear for the Mass.

On that first day, Na Rosinda and Na Lidia, the cook in charge of the mole,[3] began the process by removing the seeds from seven kilos of chile ancho, a large, mild, full-flavored red chile. They sat in the back of the compound under the wide roof of the porch, enjoying the shade and conversation as they worked. The passageway from the street into the compound itself was lined with bags of onions and garlic. Elsewhere in the compound were the twelve liters of sesame oil, almonds and raisins, twenty-eight kilos of sugar, potatoes, and bread that would go into the mole. The 400 plastic containers awaiting the mole relleno were stored in Berta's (Rosinda's sister) part of the compound. The heavy pewter candleholders and the tall beeswax candles were stacked in Rosinda's dining room. Delia had ordered twenty-eight pans of the bread, which is required for such commemorations. She had also ordered the flowers to be sure that we have enough of the right colors and kind.

Na Rosinda and Na Lidia deseeded another seven kilos of chile ancho the next morning. The big bags of onions and garlic, together with the sacks of raisins and almonds, had migrated to the back of the compound awaiting the rest of the helpers. Na Lidia is a valued cook who learned her business from her mother-in-law. Her grown son, Antonio, comes to help with some of the preparation.

On Friday, three days before the Mass, Na Rosalia, the breadmaker, sent her daughter-in-law to our house with three tortas, large round breads, for the family to sample and, where desirable, to suggest any changes. The samples were hot and fragrant, straight from the ovens, and we were soon seated around the table, breaking off and eating big chunks and commenting on taste and texture. Soon Delia, Rosinda, the daughter-in-law, and I were joined by Rosinda's siblings Na Irma and Vicente, and José (Vicente's son). Rosinda and Delia thought it could use more sugar; Rosinda also thought it could use a little more fat. José, Vicente, and I thought it was fine. Irma said perhaps a little more sugar. We had by now eaten almost all the bread, and we sent the daughter-in-law off with instruction to add a little more sugar to the batch of 240 tortas. We had also ordered enough of the small, round individual breads (pan bollo) to feed the cooks and the helpers. They would also be fed venison stew (*cheguiiña*).

---

3. Na Lidia is one of the most talented cooks in the city and much in demand. In 2006 she also took on the *mayordomía* of the eighteenth-century Christ that belongs to Gonzalo Jiménez López' family.

Any sort of hot meat dish is appropriate, but a man and his wife had come by the house that day with two big basins of cut-up venison. We bought three kilos, the wife cutting chunks off to order.

The large order of bread requires big containers to transport it from the baker to the house so we bought boxes and plastic sheeting to line them. A friend with a sport utility vehicle (SUV) drove Delia, me, and the boxes to Na Rosalia's house. On the way home, we bought three kilos of plastic bags into which we would put each portion of bread. The worry is always there about whether we will have enough bread, enough containers, enough mole relleno. We did, in fact, add to the bread order and on the day of the Mass, we had to use every extra container we had left in storage from earlier Masses.

I was awakened Saturday at 4:45 a.m. by the sound of someone practicing the tuba, a deep bass thump like a heartbeat. Then San Vicente's sacristan began sweeping the churchyard, finally ringing the bells at 5:30 a.m. for the 6:00. Mass. Na Mavis, Na Rosinda's sister living in Mexico City, had arrived on the early morning bus, and the women began to gather at the back under the porch roof to help Na Lidia and her son peel and chop onions and garlic, green tomatoes, and macho bananas for the mole.

Men delivered the rental chairs from the Corona franchise, hauling them off the truck and into the compound passageway and patios, large stacks of wooden folding chairs lining the walk. After the big midday meal, Na Rosinda, Delia, and I sat at the dining room table wrapping the deep purple ribbon around the thick beeswax candles, seven turns around and up the candle starting from the base. A small cluster of purple artificial flowers hid the end of the ribbon at the top. We then wrapped paper around the fat end to make it fit the candleholders. We put each one into its holder, making sure it did not wobble or tilt by sliding a heavy old peso piece between the candle and the holder.

Two of the family's paid helpers, Chave and Moises, went to get the 270 tortas and the 100 pan bollo from Na Rosalia. They are all in the plastic-lined boxes in the front of the family jewelry store because everyone thought they would be safe there from potential insect or animal pests attracted by the smell of food. My cousin Gloria and I went to get a light dinner for everyone, and when we returned, Chave was polishing the tall wooden stands for the biggest flower arrangements. My cousin Rosi was arriving even later from Oaxaca—all the family gathering for the celebration.

Sunday was going to be busy and long. Some of us—Delia, Tomasa, Vicente, and I—went to the cemetery in Cheguigo to change the flowers in Ta Chu's tomb. We brought big bunches of purple, yellow, and white chrysanthemums and arranged them in two vases, put a fresh votive candle in the center, and stood the image of Saint Teresa upright. She had mysteriously fallen over between visits. When we returned, Na Lidia and her son had just arrived. Ramiro, our friend with the SUV, took her to get the firewood and the huge galvanized tin basins in which everything would be cooked. "The best mole is cooked over a fire made of mesquite," I remember Orfia saying years before when we celebrated Na Berta's seven-year Mass. Enrique, Irma's husband, helped build the fire, arranging large bricks in a circle, then placing the mesquite branches and logs inside the ring. Na Lidia cleaned the basins, and the helpers chopped and peeled more ingredients. In the jewelry store, Mayella's daughter, Dani, and Vicente's daughter, Rosi, helped by two-year-old Monserrat, and later joined by Sugey, Monse's older sister, began stuffing the tortas into the plastic bags, readying them to be given out to guests. Na Rosinda and Chave were cleaning the public altar room. I arranged two big vases of gladiolas. Just before 11:00 a.m., the first of the day's visitors arrived bearing gladiolas. She sat to talk with Na Rosinda, and when she left, was given a bag of pan bollo.

People were coming and going, each with separate tasks and inclinations. The entire patio began to smell like frying chile and mesquite smoke. Na Lidia poured liter after liter of sesame oil into the basins and stirred the chiles into the hot oil. More people arrived to help Na Lidia with the cooking. Emma, family friend and rezadora, came to help stir the chile, and then the onions and garlic. Enrique came and went making sure that the fire was burning well and helping Na Lidia. Na Rosinda was now receiving a steady stream of visitors, all of whom brought the big bunches of gladiolas that are required for Masses for the dead. Each woman would stay for a short time, then leave taking her bread with her. Just before noon, Chave and Tomasa, one of Chu's sisters, began serving cooks and helpers horchata, a cold sweetened drink made of rice and cinnamon, and *nisiaaba'* (atole).

Delia took charge of the flower arranging. All of us retired to the altar room carrying the heavy bundles of flowers, the vases, scissors, and the bleach we put in the water to keep the flower stems from rotting. Mavis, Emma, Gloria, Irma, Delia, and I arranged eight large vases for the home altar—yellow and white lilies and purple wild asters. We also made six very large arrangements of yellow and white lilies and spider mums. We carried four of those to the church, along with twenty dozen gladiolas that had been brought to the house. The gladiolas filled every available container in the church. Guillermina, the other sacristan, took charge of arranging the gladiolas, counting the blooms so that each vase had the same number.

When we returned to the house, the cooks and their helpers were eating the venison stew. The rest of us chose between the stew and barbecued chicken that we had bought earlier from a chicken franchise. Feeding all the helpers takes increasingly more time as their numbers grow.

By 2:30 p.m. all the ingredients had been cooked in the hot oil, removed, drained, and put in separate containers. Ramiro and the cooks loaded all the cooked ingredients into the SUV, and we drove to the Molino Nixtamal where the miller awaited us. The grinder sat in the front room, a storefront business with the family occupying the rest of the compound and patio. The mill itself had been built by ingenuity out of parts that themselves came from many places. The grinding mechanism, like a very large meat grinder, was run by an air compressor and a belt. A large tank filled with water sat on top of the grinder to keep it cool and to provide liquid to facilitate the grinding. The women kept the ingredients separate and gave them to the miller in the following order: cooked nuts and raisins; onions, green tomatoes, and garlic; the potatoes and bananas; all the chile ancho; and, finally, the bread. The bread goes last to clean the chile and garlic from the grinder because much of the miller's business is grinding corn for tortillas. As a container would fill up, two women would whisk it away while a third slid an empty container under the grinder. The miller made sure that all flowed the way it should, and there was good-humored bantering among the women, the miller, and Ramiro.

Forty minutes after we arrived, all the ingredients had been reduced to a smooth thick sauce. We packed all the containers back in the SUV and drove very carefully, avoiding potholes, back to the compound. The containers were emptied once again, all save the bread; this time the contents were strained into the large basins. While we had been at the mill, Enrique got the fires going again. At this point, the mole had to be stirred constantly so that it would not scorch. It is hot and smoky work so several women took turns stirring. When the mole reached a slow boil, more bread was added a bit at a time, just enough to thicken, but not so fast that it made lumps. It simmered and was stirred for another hour before the fire was put out. Now the mole would sit, covered, overnight, to be heated once again just before the Mass in the morning.

While we were making the mole, another cook and her helpers in another part of the city were busy making the relleno. We had contracted for three pigs and several containers of chicken relleno. The result is like slow-baked pork and chicken flanked by a kind of "stuffing." Na Rosalia was also baking an extra two bolsas (a unit of measurement) of bread that arrived about 8:30 p.m.

We served dinner to all who were still there helping. We then assigned ourselves the various tasks that remained for the day of the Mass itself: Na Rosinda would sit just outside the door to the back room and receive guests; Delia would be inside the room with the altar; Emma (Ramiro's wife and a close friend) and I would give out the soft drinks; Rosi and Dani the bread; Mavis and Irma the containers of mole relleno; and Antonia and the helpers would serve the men in Antonia's patio. The helpers would have filled the containers while the family was at the Mass. I had already arranged to have a friend who is a local photographer use my camera because I knew I could not both participate and take photographs. Late in the afternoon, when there was nothing left to do, we all had hot chocolate and torta. It was somehow just what we needed, despite the Juchitán heat and the fact that we were all exhausted and nervous about the next day. Our clothes and hair were redolent of mesquite smoke and the spiciness of the chile ancho.

At 5:30 a.m., the day of the Mass, we were all up and busy. The men of the household took the folding chairs from their stacks and placed them in a single row all along the two sides of the passageway and along the walls of the porch in the back next to the altar room. Na Lidia and Vicki arrived early to begin heating the mole. Chave, Ermelinda, and Moises, who had come a little after 7:00 a.m., helped with the fire. At 7:30, ten big clay casseroles of the relleno were unloaded from the cook's truck and carried in one at a time on the shoulders of the men. Under Na Lidia's direction, they arranged them in the little alcove off the passageway just across from the steaming pots of mole.

All of us who were going to the Mass were dressed and ready by 8:30 a.m. After group photos of the women were taken, we all started to the church next door. We took our time, matching our pace to that of Na Rosinda who walks slowly and Sugey who was carrying the large picture of Chu. We filled the front four rows of pews on the Epistle side, with Na Rosinda on the aisle of the first pew, Delia next to her, I next to Delia, and then Tomasa and Antonia, Chu's two sisters. Behind us sat Dani; America and her two daughters, Monserrat and Sugey; and Rosinda's sister Mavis. Alma Delia (Mayella) sat in the nearest side pew perpendicular to the others. Irma had stationed herself at the front of the church to give out the beautiful memorial crucifixes that Mavis brought to give to those who came to the Mass. Since Irma knows everyone, she would know which woman was the head of each family. Tomasa had gone ahead of us and censed the entire church, every saint in its niche, and everything in the sanctuary. She used the incense sent by Father Nicholas Radelmiller, a friend of mine who had visited Juchitán several years earlier. The whole church was filled with the combined fragrance of flowers and incense.

The church was filling rapidly but it was still too early for the priest. Some of the women came up to greet Na Rosinda, and then found places. We sat with our thoughts, looking critically but ultimately with a sense of satisfaction at the flowers and the candles. Suddenly someone noticed that one of the four big candles was burning. Tonio, the sacristan, swore he had not lit it and neither had we. Ta Chu! He is letting us know that he is there. I had known him in the days when he was a powerful man, full of life and energy, so I was not surprised. Neither was I surprised by the consensus among all the women that he had worked this particular miracle.

We had another surprise awaiting us. When the priest, Father Pancho, the rector of the parish church, finally appeared, he was accompanied by Father Poncho. Poncho is an old, old friend of the family, and now the priest in Ixtepec, a city across the highway. He had spoken with Delia about the time of the Mass but never said that he was coming to concelebrate it with Father Pancho.

At the end of the Mass, everyone who had a crucifix came up to the altar rail to have it blessed with the holy water Father Pancho was dispensing over the crowd. Women and some men came to greet Rosinda and extended their greetings to all of us in the front pew. It touched me deeply to be there and to be greeted by people who have been a part of my life for so long a time.

With the priests gone, the rezador and his four colleagues led the congregation in prayers for almost half an hour. Then the procession began to form. Tonio gave each of the four men a candle, taking them out of their holders. Some of the old peso coins we had used to ensure a tight fit clinked to the marble floor and rolled a ways before settling. Sugey went up to get Ta Chu's photo. We formed ourselves into the proper order: the rezador; Sugey preceded by Vicki with the incense; the four men with candles walking two-by-two; Na Rosinda, Delia, and me; four women carrying jars of flowers; women carrying the candlesticks; and finally the rest of the participants, men making two lines on the sides and women in the center. The four singers and the guitarist played and sang only during the Mass, not being part of the procession. If we lived further from the church, they might have been but we are just next door.

There was already a huge crowd when we arrived. Na Rosinda went to the back, sitting just outside the altar room to receive people's greetings and limosna. Delia went to sit inside the room. Since the distribution of refrescos seemed to be well in hand, I greeted people, all of them friends. Tía Urania had died just six days earlier but her daughter came, honoring the family obligation. Women came, greeted Na Rosinda, went into the altar room briefly, came out, and sat along the passageway where they were given bread, refrescos, and mole relleno. After a few minutes, they left. The men arrived and went to Antonia's patio where they sat down at tables and were served plates of mole relleno with tortillas and beer. The men also give a donation, although it is usually less than that of the women.

By noon most people had come and gone. Father Emilio arrived and led about fourteen of us, all women of the close family, in prayers in the altar room. Father Nick's incense was a huge success there just as it had been in the parish church. Then the family had lunch—what else?—mole relleno, which was superb as only the Pinedas can make it. Dani, Mayella, Delia, and I sat with Father Emilio. Enrique brought us icy Coronitas and shots of mescal. It was good to sit down and realize that we had, in fact, honored Ta Chu in a way that would have pleased him greatly.

Na Rosinda stayed in the altar room most of the remainder of the day, an obligation to keep watch. The leftover mole was spooned into plastic bags for women to take with them. Mavis would take several bags back to Mexico City with her. People came and went through the rest of the day, bringing flowers, leaving limosna, visiting, sharing memories.

In all the acts from the moment of death to the end of seven years, two characteristics are striking. The first is that, while Masses may be said in the church, the locus of the real intercession and healing is the home altar. It reflects the way in which the Zapotec of the Isthmus have adapted to and adopted external influences while remaining faithful to those values that sustain them.[4] Clues to which are the important Zapotec values being acted on can be found in language. One clear instance is the difference in the Spanish "raising the cross" and the Zapotec "raising the body." Adopting Roman Catholic practice, especially intercessory prayer and liturgy, increases the likelihood of positive results, in the same way that the use of some Western medicine increases the chance that a sick person will recover. In the case of all of the practices that surround the dead, however, what is irreplaceable is the complex of observances centered on the altar in the home, and, as we shall see, those that are practiced in the cemeteries.

The second characteristic is the reciprocal giving—of hospitality, food, flowers, candles, money, and expressions of condolence, which creates and sustains relationships. With regard to death, reciprocity reminds everyone of the ties that bind the living because of their relationship to the departed. Furthermore, it acknowledges the change of status between the living and the departed while creating a new kind of relationship, one marked by reciprocal giving. The family and friends create a pattern of intercession, and provide the necessities that the departed needs in the transition—water, flowers, incense, prayers. They make a temporary place for the spirit around the altar in the home, and then make a pleasant home in the cemetery so that the spirit will feel comfortable in a new setting. They maintain the former relationship by remembering the departed's favorite food and drink, music, saints' images,

---

4. Western ways of thinking that allow for either-or responses or for the creation of a new hybrid underlie much of the theory of syncretism in social anthropology. This is especially true in the descriptions of Western, colonial religions and their encounter with indigenous religious traditions. Victor de la Cruz, an eminent Isthmus Zapotec scholar as well as poet, has written clearly and compellingly about indigenous Zapotec beliefs in his 2002 essay found in the volume he edited with Marcus Winter. Two scholars of Fijian philosophy, spirituality, and religious beliefs offer a radically different way to approach this challenge. It is one that seems to explain the Isthmus Zapotec case. Christina Toren (1988) addresses the mutability of tradition in Fiji. In constructing the present, she says, "people may also be constructing a past with which it is continuous and in whose terms it is explicable. . . . What constitutes a living tradition may reveal an extra dimension to the past—one whose validity is not a matter of 'what happened' but of how it may be understood" (p. 696). Hirokazu Miyazaki (2004), in his examination of Christian and Fijian rituals, insists that they should be regarded as two versions of a single form, which unfolds in time, and he goes further to explain that the common Fijian claim that the two ritual processes are at once the same and profoundly separate is based on the aesthetic experience of ritual participants (p. 99). Marilyn Strathern (2006), in an article on new knowledge, uses Toren and Miyazaki as examples of new ways of thinking and analysis: "He [Miyazaki] follows Toren's argument that the Fijian church is not simply a ' local' rendering of Christianity but institutes ritual processes through which Fijian chiefship ('the land') is also made visible. Toren explores parallels in Fijian meals, including the way in which the chiefs dispense kava and the ubiquitous imagery of 'the Last Supper' " (p. 206).

flowers, and name day. The departed reciprocate in one very vital way—they intercede for the living with Christ and the Virgin and with the ancestors who are the community of the dead. In times of stress, illness, or misfortune, they can provide support and counsel.

Commemorations at the Cemetery

Just as the activities around the altar in the home involve the family daily and reaching out to the community on certain occasions, so, too, do the activities that take place in the cemetery. The family tomb, in fact, is an extension of the family home. Similar activities characterize both places. People sweep and clean the tomb just as they do their home; they make sure that there are fresh flowers, a glass of water, and a votive candle in the tomb just as they place all those items on the home altar. They visit with the dead, have conversations, and pray. As we shall see in chapter 9, the tomb becomes the site of a celebration with music, food, drink, and guests during Holy Week when the departed invite the living to visit them.

The Burial

The first observance is the burial. The procession arrives, having wound its way through the streets led by a rezadora or a band of musicians. Close female relatives dress entirely in black, hair covered by a black scarf, and wear no jewelry. Other women wear black or other dark colors but do not cover their heads. Men have more latitude about color; they may wear white guayaberas and black pants, a black band around their arm, but they may also choose other subdued colors. It is a long walk to any of the cemeteries if one lives in the center of the city. From October through February, the nortes pummel the processions with fierce winds and clouds of dust and grit. In the rest of the year, blazing sun and temperatures in the 90s mark the passage to the cemeteries. The grave has already been dug or opened in the case of a family tomb with multiple burials beneath a concrete slab floor. The coffin is lowered into place and covered, either with dirt or the concrete slab. White flowers are mounded on the grave. If musicians have accompanied the body, they may play *son gue'tu'* (music for the dead) during the burial.

In July 1998, the father of Lucila, a valued helper in Doña Tonia's household, died. He was ninety-two, and after making his confession, he stopped talking and eating. He decided that it was time to go on to a new life. Several people came to visit him and to pray—"*se lo ayuda para descansar*" ("it helps him to rest, to let go"). His wake and funeral were attended by 160 people. His coffin left the house accompanied by a band. They carried him a block to the house of one of his sons-in-law where they set the coffin down and stood there talking and crying. After five minutes, the procession turned around and went slowly through the streets to the church. The pallbearers set the coffin down in front of the altar and Father Saul said Mass. No collection was taken but at the end of the Mass, everyone went up to the altar and placed a donation in a basket resting on top the coffin. The pallbearers shouldered their burden once again, and, preceded by the band, the procession made its way to the cemetery in Cheguigo. At the place of the three crosses in Cheguigo, the coffin rested again while the band played a son. At the entrance to the cemetery, the procession broke up as everyone took the easiest route through the cemetery to the gravesite. There the men gathered around the coffin, expressing their sense of loss and praising the deceased. Many of the women were crying as well. After the coffin was lowered and the men threw handfuls of dirt on it, the mourners began to disperse. They gathered again at the entrance to the cemetery where the band was waiting. The music led the procession, now reduced to about fifty people, including the pallbearers carrying the trestle on which the coffin had been carried.

While the general outlines of funeral processions remain the same, variations are made that have to do with the deceased's preferences for music or a particular sacred place. There may be more stops along the way to accommodate relatives who live nearby or to give an opportunity to play more than one son. It is less common today to celebrate Mass en route to the burial.

Visits to the Tomb

Each morning of the nine days following a death, members of the household visit the tomb. For the remainder of the forty days, someone will go every Thursday and Sunday. The chief mourner remains in the altar room at home so others in the immediate family carry out this obligation. They make sure that the grave has fresh flowers, that it is swept clean of dust and debris, that the votive candle burns continuously, and that the water in the drinking glass is changed daily. While one family member removes the wilted flowers, handing them to another who decides whether they can be cleaned and used again, someone else is sweeping the floor of the tomb, then mopping it. When everything is clean, the flowers are arranged, and the leftover bits are gathered up and carried away from the tomb. When the door is locked once more until the next visit, the tomb is spotless and fresh as is the immediately surrounding area.

The flowers during the nine and then the remainder of the forty days include coronas of loose flowers on the floor of the tomb. The flowers are spread in patterns that are pleasing to the eye, usually concentric circles of alternating colors—the cream of frangipani and the red of hibiscus, white gardenias, deep pink sweetheart roses, white jasmine, and purple bougainvillea. Sometimes people will make a cross of contrasting color flowers in the center of the circle. I have seen these offerings in the shape of hearts, and, less frequently, in the shape of a cross. Just as it is important that the deceased be placed on the ground or floor in the beginning of the wake leading up to the funeral and that the ba' yaa be laid out on the ground, so these healing flowers must be on the floor of the tomb. It is a tender time for the spirits of the departed, and the flowers both heal and connect them.

In the larger, enclosed tombs, flowers of another sort are arranged in large vases that sit permanently on the floor or slightly smaller vases that are placed on ledges that stand in place of an altar in some tombs. These are always guie' guidxi, cultivated flowers, that include chrysanthemums, asters, carnations, lilies, roses, alstroemeria, and others. While such flowers delight the eye, they have no curative powers. If there is a cross or image or anything from which something can be hung, there will be frangipani leis, lending their fragrance, color, and healing power.

Smaller tombs or ones that have no doors will use the flowers of the wild on the ground or hanging from a cross or nail. Sometimes they will use a paint can or its equivalent as a vase, usually filling it with yet other flowers of the wild. The offerings in many of these tombs are laid out with loving care

Plate 16. Arranging flowers of the wild in a tomb in the Panteón Miércoles Santo, also called Panteón Cheguigo. 2007. Photograph by Anya Peterson Royce.

and a fine artistic eye. Those tombs with earthen rather than concrete floors are cleaned of debris that accumulated in the day or days since the last visit, and then sprinkled with water. In a climate with an average temperature of 88°F, and one four-month season in which the winds whip through streets and across fields in billowing clouds of dust, this treatment of earthen-floored tombs makes sense. They are transformed into fresh, moist, and cool spaces. It is precisely the same way that people cultivate the small areas of plants in their compounds. The earth is swept clean each morning and sprinkled down with water. Individual plants are surrounded by bare ground—any weeds or grass are pulled up. Sometimes the plants are in ceramic pots either on the earth or set into it. Trees large enough to provide shade are valued too. All the plants in home gardens have some purpose. They include healing herbs, flowers of the wild that can be gathered to take to the cemeteries or placed on home altars, fruit trees, and shade or flowering trees.

After the forty days, visits to the tomb settle into a routine of Sunday mornings. It is appropriate to stop laying out the coronas, but some families continue arranging flowers on the floor. People make special visits on the name days of the departed. They may also visit on the day of a saint to whom the departed was especially attached or on a day with some other special significance. Na Rosinda and her siblings go to the tomb of their father, José Fuentes, on the feast day of San José. Na Rosinda's youngest brother, José, is buried nearby, and also gets a visit on this day as well as on January 4, his birthday. And finally on these visits, leis of frangipani are hung on the crosses.

The most important communal remembrance occurs during Holy Week, on Palm Sunday, Holy Monday, Holy Tuesday, and Holy Wednesday. This is the time when all families answer the invitation of their departed members and visit them in their tombs. While the preparations are made by individual families, the commemoration at the cemeteries involves extended family and friends in a continuous round of visits. Relationships are cemented again through the person of the departed.

Conclusions

All of the daily and weekly activities that center around home altars and tombs arise from the firm belief in the continuing relationship between the living and the dead. Moreover, they reflect the underlying value of reciprocity that characterizes all of Zapotec belief and behavior. Tending to both home altars and tombs is the responsibility of the living to the dead. Creating a "home" for the departed in the form of a tomb that is, in fact, a house in miniature, involves all the normal activities that happen among the living—cleaning the home, providing food and drink (in this case, flowers and water), praying for family members, and talking. The obligation of the departed is to intercede for the still living family with Christ, the Virgin, and the other ancestors. In addition, the departed may be asked for counsel when the family members encounter difficult problems. The mutual reciprocity is most visibly demonstrated in the two large, communal celebrations that revolve around home and tomb. Day of the Dead invites the departed back to the homes they occupied in their lifetimes. Holy Week observances invite the living to the tombs of their departed.

In all these activities and the spaces in which they occur, the vital role of the earth is unmistakable. Placing the recently deceased body on the ground in front of the altar connects the spirit with his home, the earth, so that he may take leave of the home of the living to begin his journey to his new home among the dead. At the same time, that contact gives the spirit sustenance and comfort, bringing to a close the cycle that began with birth and the burial of the umbilical cord in the household compound. Flowers and greenery that have the properties of freshness, moistness, coolness, and fragrance are essential to the well-being of the departed, guaranteeing that the journey will take its allotted time, and not be rushed or abrupt. They symbolize the body for nine days, lying on the floor in front of the home altar, a time in which the spirit remains in the home. Arranged for forty days on the floor of the tomb, they continue to provide sustenance. They provide a safe place again during Day of the Dead when they are placed on the petate in front of the Xandu'. Thus is reinforced in each venue the trinity of water, flowers, and earth that is essential for the passage from life to death.

Flowers of the wild, home altars, and homelike tombs create places of comfort for spirits. It is especially so for the newly departed whose spirits are tender and in the process of transformation, but the crucial importance of home for the Zapotec applies to the long-departed too, those who have become ancestors. It is in those places, mediated by flowers and incense, that all the significant observances for the dead occur. The living and the dead are drawn together in mutual responsibility through the rituals that they share.

5

Flowers

The Water of Life and of Death

Guendaxheela' ndaani' Guidxiguie'

Guendaxheela' ndaani' Guidxiguie'
Laa nga duuza' gundani
ra ruchaagaxla'dxi'
Ba'dunguiiu na ba'dudxaapa'
xquichu guendanayeche' zeeda
xa baca'nda' xti' ziñayaa,
bacaandaguie' biele' lu ca duubanuí
neza ridi' di' guendarannaxhii

—Maestro Enedino Jiménez

Wedding in Juchitán

A wedding in Juchitán
is a field born where the hearts
of a man and a woman come together.
Your people are happy
under the shade of a thatched roof.
A flowery dream flourishes
in the purity of the roads
where love travels.

—Translated by Anya Peterson Royce with
Delia Ramírez Fuentes and Isabel Luis López

Introduction

This is the first stanza of a poem by Zapotec poet Enedino Jiménez. It is a particularly powerful example of the flower and countryside imagery that abounds in the poetic literature of Juchitán. Indeed, the Zapotec word for poetry is *diidxa' guie'*, or "flowery speech." The word Jiménez uses for Juchitán, *Guidxiguie'*, can be glossed as "town of flowers." Hearts coming together in love creates a field, a place of calm and enchantment. The thatched roof is the enramada under whose green branches rituals are celebrated. Flowery dreams are those that take one away to a place of sweet-smelling flowers. Flowers, fragrance, cool green shade, fields—all these are repeated again and again across quite different domains of Zapotec life and appear especially clear in the domain of death.

In Nahuatl, Xochitlán means the "place of flowers." This was the name given to Juchitán; indeed, Juchitán is a corruption of the Nahuatl. From its beginnings in the mid-fifteenth century, *Juchitán* has been associated with flowers. Today, the highly educated as well as the campesinos often refer to their city as Juchitán de las flores, Juchitán of the flowers.

What strikes the visitor to Juchitán is the abundance of flowers and flower imagery. The flower market dominates the central plaza even during ordinary times, becoming an explosion of scent and color during Day of the Dead and Holy Week. Juchitecos carefully nurture plants in their patios—jasmine, hibiscus, siempreviva (*Sedum dendroideum*), bougainvillea, frangipani, among others, as well as flowering trees—lluvia de oro (golden rain tree, *Galfimia glauca*), jacaranda (*Jacaranda acutifolia*), flamboyán (flame tree, *Delonix regia*), and clavellina (Bombax or shaving brush tree). Small shrines and crosses on street corners always have garlands of frangipani or the stray blossom. I was enjoying the cool greenness of the Foro on a hot day in May when I watched an old woman approach the Santa Cruz 3 de mayo there by the river. She took single blossoms—frangipani and hibiscus—out of a plastic bag and laid them carefully along the arms of the cross, praying softly all the while. She bent down even further to lay the remaining flowers at the foot of the cross. She stood back up, erect, took the last blossom, touched the cross with it, pressed it to her forehead, and turned to go.

The Centro de Acopio (recycling center), founded fifteen years ago, has a large nursery dedicated to propagating regional plants, which they sell to Juchitecos to help support the center. In 2001 the center broke ground for the Foro Ecológico (Ecological Forum) in an adjacent lot (formerly a school run by an order of nuns) to realize the dream of Julio Bustillo Cacho. It is truly visionary in its goals and its design. Walking through the construction site, I came across one tree or shrub after another that had been integrated into the design so that virtually none were uprooted. One tree rises through the three stories of the structure, and spreads its branches like a canopy over the roof.

Native flowers are everywhere, many in large, locally made ceramic pots that may have a turtle head peering out from the bottom or an iguana climbing up the rounded swell of the pot, or the webbed feet and wide mouth of a frog forming bottom and top of yet another.

Frangipani, as single blossoms or in garlands to hang, appear everywhere in rituals, and as adornments, on the traditional dress of Zapotec women. On Good Friday, Juchitecos bring basins of water filled with frangipani blossoms to the churches to be blessed. Frangipani fill the water glasses at each of the Apostles' places for the reenactment of the Last Supper. Frangipani blossoms are whipped into the chocolate froth that tops bupu, a local drink the origins of which may be found in pre-Columbian rituals of marriage and death.

Many flowers are used in healing. Flowers also figure significantly in the visions of healers. The first vision of Ta Feli, Félix López Jiménez, begins quite vividly with flowers: "I was taken to a beautiful palace with many rooms. There were flowers everywhere of every kind and every color. Their perfume filled the soft breezes." Following a young woman, the Virgin Mary, he comes to a river of blood. "As we came closer, I could see that it was blood. I could not smell the perfume anymore, only the darkness of the blood." The Virgin tells him that the blood was the shame of humans, and then makes it disappear. He finds himself in a bright room and she tells him that he has been given

Plate 17. Frangipani, *guie' chaachi,* one of the most important flowers of the wild. 2007. Photograph by Anya Peterson Royce.

the power to heal. This vision came when Ta Feli was fourteen and seriously ill with a high fever. When he suddenly recovered, everyone knew it was a sign that he was to be a healer.

The presence of flowers and their perfume is associated here, as it is throughout Zapotec culture with well-being, health, and happiness. Their fragrance is explicitly a protection against evil. Bad smells, on the other hand, like the river of blood, are associated with the work of the devil (see footnote 1, chapter 8). Feli and other healers use flowers and herbs in their curing practices. The small-leaved basil indigenous to Mexico, *guie' stia* in Zapotec, *albahaca* in Spanish, is used in bunches to cleanse a patient. Rubbed over arms, legs, face, and neck, it has the power to cool the person, restoring the balance between hot and cold, dryness and wetness. Red hibiscus in water is prescribed as a cooling, cleansing bath. Indeed, much of the healing arts rely on plants that cool and that provide moisture.

When I visited a healer who had been apprenticed to Feli, one of his adepts reported the vision that came to her while she was "curing" me with basil. She had seen a white flower dropped into a glass of deep purple liquid; the flower rose immediately to the surface. The white flower was my gift, the gift of light; the purple liquid the envy of others (Royce 2004:211). The association of flowers, especially white flowers, with light gives them the power to transform, to enlighten.

Zapotec women, dressed for a celebration, are a flower garden in themselves. The traditional dress of long, full, gathered skirt, and short-sleeved blouse (*traje*), in its most elegant manifestation, is heavy with embroidered flowers, vines, and leaves. The kinds and colors are limited only by the imagination of the embroiderers. Photographs of turn of the twentieth-century dress (Kamar Al-Shimas 1922) show the varieties of jasmine common to the Isthmus, frangipani, guie' bi'chi', and other of the small flowers of the wild. The flowers on the blouse are arranged in rows following the shape of the blouse. One photograph shows a young woman holding a bunch of tuberose, and yet another shows the woman posed against a wooden stand that has the big, flaring white flowers of toloache or datura.

Today, almost every kind of flower, both "of the wild" and cultivated, is incorporated into the dress. Much depends on the taste of the individual women. One pattern that has great appeal to some is made solely of frangipani. Some want to go back to the earlier pattern of very small flowers in single rows. A few years ago, calla lilies appeared on many dresses, white with yellow stamens on green backgrounds. Calla lilies became an emblem of Mexico through the paintings of Diego Rivera who also painted scenes from the Isthmus. Whatever the desire of the woman, the process is a very long one, from sitting with the people who own the patterns or who will create to order, to choosing the material and thread, commissioning the embroidering itself, and then checking on the progress. There are individuals whose expertise lies in the pattern making, and among them are individuals very knowledgeable about the flora of the Isthmus and the history of how it has been incorporated into festive dress. They also are keen observers of the importation of flowers from outside the region and are prepared to design patterns using those as well. Of the three kinds of traje—traje bordado (embroidered), traje tejido (woven), and traje de cadenilla (chain-stitched by machine), the bordado is usually the choice for important occasions like a woman's vela because its design uses flowers exclusively and because it is the most striking in its lush use of color. Tejido may mix woven geometric patterns with flowers but the patterns, not the flowers, are what draw attention. Cadenilla displays geometric patterns created by a machine-made chain-stitch.

Young women are likened to flowers, both in their freshness and in their fragrance. Local poet and writer Gabriel López Chiñas (1975) uses this image explicitly in his poem, "Guie' ro'," "Parade of Flowers" (p. 77):

> Badudxaapa sicaru
> ca ti' xhica gui' ri yu' du'
> ruaaca' nuu bidaniro'
> ruluica' guie' zeru' iruugu

> Beautiful young women
> support heavy church candles at their waists;
> their faces framed by the splendor of the *huipil grande*,
> they seem like flowers that soon will be gathered.

> —Translated by Anya Peterson Royce

López Chiñas refers here to the young women's role in the *vela* parades called *regada de frutas* (throwing of fruit) even though today's *regadas* throw neither fruit nor flowers. The parade of López Chiñas's poem is most likely the last parade of the May *vela* season, the Vela San Vicente (personal communication, Delia Ramírez Fuentes). The young women are members of the *vela* society, and they walk in the procession wearing their *huipil grandes (bidaani quichi')* in the manner for church, their faces tightly framed by the white lace of the headdress. Their participation is guaranteed by the gift of bread that is sent to them by way of invitation. In another part of the parade, more young women ride in ox carts, painted and decorated with willow branches and banana fronds woven with flowers. Willow and banana are also "of the wild," displaying all those qualities of freshness and health that characterize the flowers of the wild, the same characteristics that describe young women. The flora themselves are the same used for rituals of death.

In addition to their appearance in the poetry of local poets and in the lyrics of songs by local composers, flowers, often in association with women, are also depicted in the paintings and mural art of the many young local painters. One of the first paintings to greet visitors to Juchitán hangs in the bus station at the entrance of the city. By Jesús David García, it shows a Juchiteca in full traje, flanked by two mudubina, a kind of water lily that young women make into a cooling necklace for themselves or their friends.

In a recent competition for children and teenagers, each was asked to paint a mural that showed something typical of Juchitán on a wall whitewashed for that purpose. One young girl painted a large guie' xhuuba' (jasmine of the Isthmus). Paintings that decorate the interior of the indoor market abound with flowers. Other murals that appear on walls of houses and compounds feature the face of a woman in a mature corn plant, an image that derives from the myth of the young Corn God who was sacrificed and comes back through the medium of a growing corn plant. The plant is watered by his blood and when it matures, he is reborn from it. Both plant and god follow the cycle of death and rebirth.

Categories of Flowers

By examining the qualities people attach to flowers and the use made of them, we can sort them into several broad categories. The first and most important for their transforming role in life and death is the category of guie' gui'xhi' or "flowers of the wild." The qualities that empower them are that of moistness, coolness, and freshness or nayaa in Zapotec, and the quality of being sweetly scented or nanaxhi. Flowers in this category of "flowers of the wild" may also be further defined by use. For example, guie' biuxhe or "simple flowers" refers to those appropriate for the ba' yaa. These are single blooms of jasmine, frangipani, copa de oro, hibiscus, small roses, and, more recently, gardenias. They also serve as the flowers thrown at the feet of Christ during the Stations of the Cross procession. Here, the Zapotec is aptly descriptive where *biuxhe* refers to the act of tearing into pieces, the way in which the loose petals are created. Guie' ndase or "scattered flowers" are those one sees being thrown over the heads of the images of saints being carried on litters, especially over the coffin of Christ as it is carried from the parish church to a nearby chapel. Again the Zapotec is highly evocative—*ndase* describes the quality of lightness or softness, as in the soft rain of the south wind falling. Guie' ndase include petals of flor de china (similar to impatiens) and roses, jasmine, and often, healing herbs such as basil and dill. All are fragrant and colorful.

Quite apart from this large category, which is characterized by the use of Zapotec rather than Spanish terms, is that of the guie' guidxi or cultivated flowers, "flowers of the town." There are no Zapotec terms for the individual flowers within this category. Most are imported from Puebla or Mexico City. Guie' guidxi seem to be exclusively decorative and without any healing or protecting powers. We might lay out these categories in the following manner:

guie' gui'xhi' (wild)	*guie' guidxi* (town)
guie' biuxhe (simple)	*guie' ndase* (scattered)

The flowers that fall into the category "wild" include those flowers, many of them highly aromatic, indigenous to the region of the Isthmus:[1] tuberose (guie' stiya), frangipani (guie' chaachii), jasmine (guie' xhuuba'), dragon's blood (guie' bi'chi'), marigold (guie' biguá), palm flower (guie' bigaragu), cordoncillo (guie' daana'), flor de china, hibiscus (biruba gui'ña'), madrecacao (guie' nisa), rosa de Castilla (guie' bicohua), palillo or Croton morifolius (nenda xunaxhii), water lily (mudubina in Zapotec; nenúfar in Spanish), and a second kind of water lily (stagabe'ñe'). To these, we must add the nonflowering trees and shrubs whose foliage is believed to be *nayaa* or fresh, green, and moist: banana stalks and leaves (biduaa, "banana"; bandaga, "big leaf"), cocotero (coconut palm), willow (yaga gueza), basil (guie' stia), dill (eneldo), and cordoncillo (guie' daana'). In the last five years, people have begun including evergreens such as cedar, pine, and fir in this category.

PROPERTIES OF FLOWERS OF THE WILD

The most important functions that these flowers of the wild play in rituals having to do with death are mediation and transformation. They mediate between the living and the dead, the wet and the dry. The living who still have the quality of freshness offer flowers with that same quality to the dead whose transformation from freshness to dryness has been made irreversible by death. The living who may suffer drying illnesses have recourse to cures that can restore them

---

1. My identification and categorization of these plants is based on a variety of sources. First, I have interviewed Juchitecos whose work involves a knowledge of flowering plants—persons connected with the greenhouse at the recycling center and Foro, healers, flower vendors, and people who know the traditional culture of the area. I have also photographed many of the plants for identification purposes. Written sources have also provided important data: Fray Juan de Córdoba's *Vocabulario en Lengua Zapoteca*, dating from 1578; Eustaquio Jiménez Girón's *Guía Gráfico-Fonémica para la Escritura y Lectura del Zapoteco* (1979); Velma Pickett's *Vocabulario Zapoteco del Istmo* (1971); and Blas Pablo Reko's *Mitobotánica Zapoteca* (1945). Although her work centers around Mitla, Ellen Messer's article "Present and Future Prospects of Herbal Medicine in a Mexican Community" (1978) provided useful comparisons. Two of the Zapotec terms I list are no longer in use in Juchitán—*guie' stiya* for tuberose and *yerua* for dill. Their appearance in Jiménez Girón and Córdoba respectively may mean that they were Valley Zapotec terms rather than terms in Isthmus Zapotec.

to a balanced state between wet and dry, while the dead are set on the path to ultimate dryness when they become the ancestors.

As we will see in chapter 7, frangipani hung deep around the large crucifix that the Christ impersonator carries in the Stations of the Cross quite literally protect him from the attacks of the Centurion. The latter is stopped by the flowery barrier, indeed, on his third and last approach, he is drawn by the sweetness to kiss the flowers. It is such a powerful force for life that the menace of death cannot touch the one it protects.

Another instance of mediation lies in the use of flowers that have been in contact with images of the saints. Visitors to the churches and chapels will leave flowers on the bodies of the images or at their feet; in return, they take a flower or two already there. They rub it lightly over their face or head or any part of their body that is ill, and its holy freshness and fragrance works to alleviate the pain or illness. They may also take flowers home for children or relatives who might benefit from the healthful contact. Even people who are not ill will take a flower because its very presence comforts and protects. The sweetness and freshness of those flowers is extraordinarily affecting. One contributing factor has to be the contrast between the relative darkness of the church interior compared to the almost white light of the sun outside and the cool softness of the petals in contrast to the exterior heat. Placing the flowers in a basin of water restores them to their fresh state, and one feels soothed simply through contact with them.[2]

In all of these instances, flowers are a force for life. In their use as a trans-forming agent, they gently move the just deceased to a new state and a new place. They begin with the incontrovertible fact of death and give it a pace and a trajectory. As I said earlier, one of the reasons for the antipathy toward cremation is that it causes the most abrupt disjuncture possible between the living and the dead. In the norms for celebrating the first Day of the Dead, if a person has died within forty days of the dates for Day of the Dead, then the observance must be postponed until the following year. This is, I have heard many say, to give the spirit time to complete its journey, or as I would phrase it, the first important stage of transformation. The rituals of the forty days after death complete the move of the spirit to its new cemetery home, a journey that began with death and burial and continued through the nine days of prayers.

---

2. A similar response to the year-round high temperatures can be found in the manner in which women wash clothes or even dishes. Clothes are washed by hand in outdoor concrete basins shaded from the sun. The water is cold and rinsing the clothes is accomplished by filling a half gourd (or now frequently a small plastic bowl) with clean water and pouring it over the clothes. In the pouring, the hand holding the bowl is turned back toward the body, and tilts the bowl allowing the water to run across the wrist before it gets to the clothes. It is very refreshing to have the water bathing one's pulse point when otherwise unrelieved heat is all around. When healers are curing with basil, they concentrate on applying it to the inside of wrists, throat, and ankles, again all pulse points.

Elsewhere I have described how flowers are used in these transformations. They both surround the body, protecting it and connecting it with the earth from whence it came, as well as comforting the spirit that now has to leave the home it has known to take up a new residence. Flowers fill dozens of vases, blossoms are laid on the altar, and they are often placed in the coffin. Flowers keep the spirit company in the altar room; on the floor of the tomb, they are a fresh, healing blanket for the deceased. The flower-body that has been refreshed for nine days in front of the altar is taken to the nearest chapel on the ninth day, the spirit accompanying it. A single file of blossoms remains, together with the healing white smoke and fragrance of incense. It is a faint memory of the body now transformed and transported to the new cemetery home.

In all of these observances, the flowers with the power to transform, mediate, and transport are the flowers of the wild (guie' gui'xhi'), simple flowers (guie' biuzhe), and flowers that are scattered (guie' ndase). With one exception, none are flowers that can be arranged in vases, rather they find their place close to the earth or scattered on the altar. The one exception is the tuberose, *guie' stiya*, whose tall spiked stems loaded with sweet-scented white blossoms suit the large vases that flank the coffin, the ba' yaa, and then the single row of flowers. One can see this striking use in a photograph of a home altar dating to the 1940s. All the vases are filled with tuberose. The flowers heaped around the

Plate 18. Flowers of the wild: tuberose and *guie' biuxhe* (scattering flowers). 2006. Photograph by Anya Peterson Royce.

base of the vases are bougainvillea. The ba' yaa appears to be made of individual tuberose blossoms, guie' bi'chi', and bougainvillea with a foundation of basil. Today's vases are filled with white gladiolas rather than tuberose, a flower of South African and Mediterranean origin, as opposed to the indigenous tuberose. Yet the local flower vendors often have tuberose. Indeed, they also sell calla lilies from time to time, a flower that Messer (1975) tells us was one of the favorites for altars (p. 405). One striking difference between tuberose and gladiolas lies in their scent. Tuberose have a very heavy, sweet aroma; gladiolas have no scent. So why have gladiolas replaced tuberose or calla lilies? The white color and the spiky nature of the gladiola make it an appropriate choice; it also lasts longer, which may cause people to prefer it. Calla lilies need a more temperate climate than that of the Isthmus, and even in their more northern habitat, they are seasonal. Gladiolas can be had year-round and are relatively inexpensive. In very recent years, highly scented Asiatic lilies have made their way into the local market. People like them very much, especially the white varieties, but they are quite expensive in contrast to other options, and they do not last long in the Isthmus heat.

It is interesting to speculate about the flowers that might have been placed in the Zapotec tombs at Monte Albán. The large anthropomorphic funerary urns of the Classic Period (200 bce–700 ce) suggest a kind of deification of important personages (Flannery and Marcus 1976). Tomb 104 has one very large funerary urn with four smaller accompanying urns, representing companions perhaps of the deceased. The tomb also has a huge inventory of pottery offerings of all kinds, including vases. Ancestors who were treated in such an extraordinary way were precisely the ones whom one would approach for intercessions. Steps leading down into tombs indicate that people visited after the burial, adding to or repainting murals on the tomb walls, asking the ancestors for advice and intercession, and possibly leaving offerings of flowers, incense, or prayers. There are flowers native to Oaxaca that would have had the desired qualities of wetness and fragrance—tuberose and a wild marigold, for example.

Wet and Dry

The qualities of wetness and dryness were very likely to have been significant ways of explaining domains of illness and healing and life and death in pre-Columbian Mesoamerican civilizations. They certainly appear in iconography beginning with the Early Classic Period in Central Mexico, the Maya area, and the tombs of Monte Albán. Symbols of these qualities also appear in the Nuttall Codex, a Post-Classic Period Mixtec text depicting the life of Eight-Deer Tiger-Claw, a Mixtec ruler. George Foster agrees that this dichotomy, wet and dry, preceded that of hot and cold, which became more important because it shared fundamental characteristics with the Spanish-imported beliefs about causes of illness and ways to heal.[3] What is clear for the Isthmus Zapotec of Juchitán is that wet and dry as principles that organize several domains including illness and health, dying, and aesthetic values are fundamental in contemporary thought and usage, and are embedded in the language. Hot and cold, on the other hand, much more prevalent throughout Mexico and Latin America, appear to be less significant for the Isthmus Zapotec.

The continuum between wet and dry as an organizing principle may be more widespread in Mexico than we had previously thought. For the Zapotec, it lies both in the language and in activities that cut across many domains of culture and society. Only through gradually working through the language and after many years of field study did I realize its importance. Its significance for peoples such as the Isthmus Zapotec whose sense of origins refers to an autochthonous emergence is even greater and more likely to still be an active principle. Associated with an emergence from the earth origin are creatures such as turtles, snakes, lizards, iguanas—animals of the wild whose primary quality is wetness.

Geographic and climatological factors also contribute to basic organizing principles. Water is essential to human survival, but water that is predictable and balanced. Areas that swing between drought and flooding may likely have more concern about a stable source of water. Juchitán's climate suffers an excess of rain in the wet season and drought in the dry. It also suffers the desiccating force of the north winds, the bi yooxho, whose season can be as long as four months between November and February. For the Juchitecos, then, maintaining a healthy balance between wet and dry is essential.

---

3. George Foster (1960) was one of the first anthropologists to address the process of resistance, change, and synthesis begun after the arrival of the Spanish in Mesoamerica. Foster kindly read parts of this manuscript as well as a manuscript on Zapotec notions of illness and healing. He agreed with my argument for an indigenous origin for wet and dry: "I am inclined to believe that the wet-dry dichotomy that you describe is *not* a part of Gallenic humoral medicine but rather is an indigenous development" (letter, October 7, 2001). The basis for this pre-Columbian origin lies in the indigenous language. Continuing with the centrality of water in Zapotec belief as a cleansing, healing, and transformative substance, I find it intriguing that water in Roman Catholic belief and liturgy parallels its centrality for the Isthmus Zapotec although notions about instrumentality differ. Baptism, from the Greek *baptizein*, "to dip in water," is the fundamental rite of admission to any of the Christian denominations. For Catholics, both Roman and Anglican, baptism means that the baptized dies and is reborn with Christ. It is a rebirth, a cleansing regeneration by means of water. Water is also the source of life and fecundity. Life is born out of God's breathing over the waters. This is embodied in the consecration of the baptismal water in the prayer that asks God, through His Son, to cause the Holy Spirit to descend on the water so that the baptized are born of both the water and the Holy Spirit. Water, in its uncontrolled form as in the torrential waters of the Flood, destroys old ways creating the possibility of new life. Finally, both water and blood pour from the side of the crucified Christ, symbolizing Baptism and Communion, water and blood, the two fundamental sacraments of the Church.

Imagery

The first stanza of this song written and composed by Zapotec musician Hebert Rasgado combines powerful flower images with those of water.

Bixidu'

Me gusta rodear tu talle
como un bejuco
para ofrendar un beso de tulipan
a tu boca;
desprender el pétalo de guie' xhuuba'
que me toca
y esperar
el bi nisa de tu aurora.

Kiss
I want to encircle your body
like a vine
to present a hibiscus kiss
on your mouth;
to loosen the petal of the jasmine
that touches me
and await
the water-wind of your dawn.

—Translated by Anya Peterson Royce

The water-wind or bi nisa in the song is the same wind off the Pacific Ocean that brings the gentle rain that is necessary for crops to thrive and that made it possible for the early Zapotec to cultivate two or three crops a years without irrigation. That, in turn, was the basis for their thriving economy of long-distance trading. The rain that comes off the Gulf of Mexico drenching the states of Veracruz and Tabasco turns, as it crosses the Isthmus, into the fierce, dry bi yooxho that plagues Juchitán four months of the year. Sometimes, however, hurricanes blow up from the south and flood the city. The story told by Ta Feli (see chapter 1) about the water and the wind reflects the deep concern with the cycle of flooding and drought that characterizes the southern portion of the Isthmus.

Forces out of their proper place and power need to be restored so that they might be harnessed for the good of the community. Water and the properties of wetness and dryness are no exception. In balance, they sustain life. They also work to restore the balance that death disrupts. This poem by Pancho Nácar (1973:14) speaks both to death and to water.

Bacaanda'

Nuchi' guniéxcaanda'
zúbanu xa ñee ti yaga,
caguiñe ti bi nanda
ne cusaba stale bandaga.

Ne gaxha neza ra nuunu
cuxooñe' ti nisa ya,
sicagá dxa nisa ruunu'
ni rusa'bu' lu dxa ba'.

My Dream

It is night and I am dreaming,
seated beneath a tree.
A wind beats down
and the leaves fall before its force.

The path is dark where I sit;
water flows.
I am water, just like the rain,
the rain that falls as water
into my tomb.

—Translated by Anya Peterson Royce

Pancho Nácar was born Francisco Javier Sánchez Valdivieso on December 3, 1909, in Juchitán. When he died in Mexico City on November 14, 1963, his family brought him home to be buried among his friends and family. He wrote poetry his entire life, most of it in Zapotec, and all of it deeply emblematic of what Zapotec hold most central. This poem, "My Dream," illustrates the complex association of water with death and life. One of the essential rituals at both the tomb and the home altar is to maintain a glass of fresh water—"water into my tomb." Death means that restoring life-giving wetness is no longer possible, but it does not mean that the dead do not need infusions of moistness. As we saw in chapter 2, when the spirits of the recently dead return and speak through one of the adepts, they ask for a glass of water because their "journey" has made them thirsty. This is perhaps the spiritual parallel to the gradual drying of the physical body. The journey or transformation is long, and it is made easier, perhaps even possible at all, by the rituals of flowers of the wild and water. These function here, as they do in life, to keep a person healthy. They keep her moist and connected to the old earth home until she reaches her new earth home.

Excess, Lack, and Vulnerability

Wetness or freshness (nayaa) is preferable to dryness but too much makes one vulnerable to illness. Babies are quite vulnerable because their recent birth makes them as wet as they will ever be. Much care is taken to protect them from *aire* or *bi* (wind) because this acts on their wetness to cause illness. They are kept swaddled to protect orifices such as eyes, nose, and mouth, and they are never taken out uncovered when the wind is blowing. Among other illnesses, *susto* or fright (*dxiibi*) is caused by aire entering the body of someone who is fresh. The dryness and cold of the *aire* interacts with the wetness and heat of the baby causing illness. Young girls, who are described by poets, composers, and the community as fresh, sweet-smelling, and green like flowers of the wild, are vulnerable for the same reason. At the same time that they themselves are "green," they need the protection of life-giving green plants. The green willow branches and banana stalks that adorn the ox carts in which the young women traditionally rode serve this function. Youth signifies an imbalance—too much wetness and very little dryness. This creates a very fluid state with little "structure" of the sort that comes with the gradual dryness of maturity. Perhaps this is another message we can see in Ta Feli's story about Sea and Wind, the impetuousness of the young girl and the restraining and drying influence of Wind.

Certain illnesses are recognized as manifesting extremes of dryness. Tuberculosis, for example, is referred to either as *rubidxi*, literally dry cough, or *guendahuara' bidxi*, "dry sickness." Wasting diseases also fall into the dry category with sufferers being described as *naguundu'* or "wasted," "dried out." This is the more general experience of aging—people lose the fluidity and resiliency of that wet state as they become more inflexible. Then they are like the tree Pancho Nácar describes—it loses its leaves to the force of the wind because it refuses to bend. This state makes them just as vulnerable as children and youth. Again, the being out of balance is the problem.

Water by itself, the moistness of flowers of the wild, and the combination of flowers and water as in the blossoms of frangipani in water about to be blessed—in all its forms, water is essential to the unhurried transformation from living to dead. It sustains the newly dead, softening the shock of the separation of spirit from body; it surrounds the spirit with a womblike cradle as it finds its way; it offers protection from extremes, ensuring a safe journey.

Conclusion

Water and flowers of the wild both transform and protect the dead, reestablishing the connection with the earth from which all life comes. They do this through their life-giving properties of moistness and their scent. Their placement on the ground—flowers and sand sprinkled with water—for the first stages of the death rituals emphasizes the regenerative power inherent in them. Never absent from human death and all its accompanying rituals, they are even more extravagantly present in the death of Christ as we will see in all the observances of Lent and Holy Week described in the coming chapters. Here they become the means through which the entire community reaffirms its common belief, and in so doing, heals itself by restoring the balance.

6

The Day of the Dead—*Xandu'*

Che Conra and Na Mari were sitting on one of the cement benches in the municipal park when Irma and I passed by, arms loaded with flowers. "You may as well save time and just give those to me," Che Conra quipped, "and if you take my picture, I will have everything I need for my xandu' yaa."

Che Conra, Ta Conrado De Gyves Pineda, was known for his quick wit, but for the last fifteen years or so, many others have teased me for my picture taking. Whenever I bring a particularly evocative portrait of someone, they refer to it as a lu bidó', literally, "face of the altar." Several family and friends have asked that I take their portraits and will dress in both festive attire as well as mourning clothes for the pictures. Lu bidó' are placed on the altar during the prayers and commemorations of the Day of the Dead. So the teasing has a serious side to it because people want to have images of their loved ones that capture some quality that made them special. The image is ultimately the choice of the chief mourner but is almost always the result of a strong consensus. In the case of Na Berta, the choice was unanimous and immediate—a photograph of her dancing at her vela, wearing a purple and white traje de cadenilla, the one, in fact, in which she was buried. She would have been in her late sixties when the photograph was taken. And now each of her children has a copy of this photograph somewhere in their home. In later altars, when she is not the one being commemorated, that photo has been replaced by one that taken of her as she was dressed in mourning colors to go to a Mass.

The number of years a family will continue building an altar varies. Two years after a family member's death is obligatory, and most continue for a third year while commemorations beyond that time depend on the desires of the family. If a person dies within forty days of October 31, then the xandu' yaa (fresh altar) must wait until the following year since the family will still be observing the forty-day mourning period and the spirit is too unsettled. The face that occupies the focal point of the altar is always that of the most recently dead; other photos find their place according to the desires of individuals, supported by the consensus of the women who are creating the altar. When I came to Juchitán for the xandu' yaa of Ta Chu, I brought with me three photographs of close friends who had died within that year. In this case, the notion of family was extended to include my friends. That they were included also changed the ways in which I was expected to participate. I had brought big, fat white candles and large glass containers for them to place for Chu. For my friends, I brought things that were associated with them—fudge for my friend with a sweet tooth, a rosary for the priest, and a flute for the musician. I was clearly not a guest but rather a member of the family in its narrow sense. Like Delia, I too was a "daughter" of Chu and Rosinda. Because I was not in my home to commemorate my friends, I was in some ways a sponsor of them with this altar, so I was doubly responsible.

Xandu' for Jesús Ramírez Escudero

Jesús Ramírez Escudero, Ta Chu, died in November 1997. He was a large, outgoing man when I first met him in 1971, a much respected goldsmith, husband to Rosinda, father to Delia. He contracted adult-onset diabetes, losing a leg and then his eyesight to it. He continued to dominate the household by his presence but, eventually, even though the family did everything possible to take care of him, with specialists coming regularly from Oaxaca City and Salina Cruz, he slipped away. I remember how stunned I was to get the news. I put the phone down and sat, my legs suddenly too weak to support me. Chu had been part of my life in Juchitán from the beginning. It was hard to imagine him gone.

Chu's death came just after Todos Santos that year, so his xandu' yaa came in the following year, after he had settled into his new state. In the first two years especially, the soul of the departed is still tender or nayaa—fresh, green, and wet. That state of tenderness springs from the transformations it undergoes, especially from the community of the living to the community of the dead but also to a dryness that, unhealthy in life, is normal in the long dead. Dying accelerates the process, begun at birth, of drying out. The soul gradually becomes increasingly more dry until it becomes like the binni gula'sa', the ancestors, the old ones whose likeness is caught in the pre-Classic Period figurines excavated in many Isthmus sites. It becomes as dry as that centuries-old clay. In the still tender years, the soul craves water and fresh flowers, also categorized as nayaa. Flowers of the wild are especially desirable.

Preparations for Chu's xandu' yaa began on Tuesday, October 26, when Delia and I went to our flower vendor in the main plaza and ordered flowers for Saturday, October 30. In the division of tasks that acknowledges particular abilities, I was nominally in charge of the flowers. It became clear, however, that there were canons of appropriateness of which I had been unaware. For example, all the big vases had to be the same. We decided on enough white spider mums and yellow gladiolas to fill four tall vases. We also ordered enough purple and white mums, white wild asters, and white daisies to fill ten smaller vases. I bought some purple carnations and yellow daisies, which I took with me to refresh the flowers then on Chu's altar. While we were at the flower market, the men in the family set up the altar proper. It is a seven-step affair with boards set across a frame of graduated blocks. Because it involves carrying heavy boards and the frame, it falls to the men of the household. They can sometimes be convinced to drape the white sheets over the steps, but refuse to tack the cutout colored paper to the white background.

We began the prayers for the dead that afternoon at 5:00 p.m., led by Emma, the rezadora who is always the household's first choice to lead prayers. One of my duties in these evening prayers, in addition to praying, is to count the participants and make sure that we have enough bags of chocolate and bread for each woman who comes to pray. At the end, I distributed them, beginning with the rezadora, and then to all the women who had joined in the prayers with the exception of immediate family members—Rosinda, Delia, and me. Rosinda's sisters and their children received the little gifts. On the first evening when I went from the altar room to the kitchen to get the bags, I discovered that one was missing—somebody's sweet tooth, no doubt. I frantically searched for the reserves of chocolate and bread, finally finding them in the microwave, which has come to serve as a very effective storage cabinet.

Celebrating one's own Xandu' does not relieve one of all other obligations, especially those having to do with death, which impinge on everyone's daily life. So immediately following the prayers for Chu, Delia, Mayella, Irma, and I went to a seven-year Mass for Tía Bernarda at the Capilla del Calvario. The chapel was filled with family—Pinedas de la vela (Pinedas of the Vela Society),[1] aunts of the older generation, and women of the neighborhood. After the Mass said by Father Martín, we followed the Banda Santa Cecilia to Bernarda's house. We left our wrapped donation of money, and in exchange were given two chicken mole tamales, bread, and a soft drink. After a brief round of greetings, we took our leave and went home. I remember visiting Bernarda with Mayella. Like all the Pineda women of that generation, she commanded respect and had a steady stream of visitors. She also had a lively wit and a wondrous supply of gossip. When her old dog growled at me from its place under her hammock, she silenced it with the same voice that brought the humans around her to attention.

On Saturday, October 30, we spent the entire day building the altar and tending to preparations. Several trips to the market were necessary. We retrieved the flowers we had ordered on Tuesday. We also stopped by the mounds of globe amaranths, marigolds, and scarlet cockscomb so big that they nearly dwarfed

---

1. Being "of the *vela*" means that one honors one's responsibilities—giving the donations of money, bread, and time. If one "carries a stand," one is a member of an even more exclusive group—those whose donations are expected to support part of the costs of the vela itself and those who will have a stand of chairs under the *vela* tent to which their invited guests come and are received with food, drink, and small gifts. These categories of *vela* participants are one way of deciding who is family.

their sellers. We bought huge armloads of the orange and crimson blooms, enveloped in that pungent marigold scent. We could not carry more so we returned to the house, dropped them off, and returned to choose the woven palm decorations, green cocos, marquesote with its sugary white decorations, little candy skulls, and a Day of the Dead confection that showed a skeleton lying on a bed holding a bottle of tequila.

By now, it was time for the midday meal, a hurried affair because we still had much to do. We arranged the four large vases that would go on their own separate stands, two on loan from the parish church next door. Rosinda brought all the materials for preparing the incense, so we sat to keep her company as she tried to get the incense to burn. We used up nearly an entire box of the tiny, wax matches before we were successful, but it was good to sit and laugh. Emma arrived just before 5:00 p.m., followed by the other women who had

Plate 19. Marigolds and cockscomb in the market for Day of the Dead. 1999. Photo by Anya Peterson Royce.

Plate 20. Banana stalks and green coconuts for Day of the Dead. 1999. Photograph by Anya Peterson Royce.

Plate 21. Interior house decoration for Day of the Dead. 1999. Photo by Anya Peterson Royce.

Plate 22. Isabel Luis López helping with Day of the Dead decorating. 1999. Photograph by Anya Peterson Royce.

come each evening. After the prayers, which include a quiet time for chatting afterward, during which people comment about the progression of work on the altar and how we might want to arrange it, it was time for serious flower arranging. Gloria and I filled the remaining ten vases and placed them on the steps of the altar. The top step held the vases with the calla lilies, bought as a special touch. Rosinda already had placed the Pineda photographs, leaving space to accommodate the ones I had brought. Other women of the households in the compound and those who had traveled to be here, had gradually been filling the altar room. Once all the vases were placed on the steps, they began putting the fruit, sweets, candles, bread, drink, and other special things on the altar. What goes on the altar is determined by the tastes of the departed who are given food and drink they were especially fond of in life. Tamales are unwrapped and put on a plate with a fork. Bottles of rum, tequila, or soft drinks are opened—everything must be ready for the spirits to consume. People who had a special relationship with the dead use this as an opportunity to bring something fitting. I brought four glass candleholders and ivory star-encrusted candles as a gift for Chu. Karime brought special multicolored candles from Puebla. Tía Mavis was sending flowers by bus from Mexico City. Little Rosinda had found unusual candy skulls in the market. We finished the altar by 7:30 p.m. and stood back to admire it.

Plate 23. Day of the Dead altar for Jesús Ramírez Escudero, "Ta Chu." 2000. Photograph by Anya Peterson Royce.

Plate 24. Doorway decorated for the Day of the Dead. 2001. Photo by Anya Peterson Royce.

With no one totally recovered from the previous day's demands, the next day nonetheless began early. The first task was to frame the inner and outer doorways with arches of decorated banana stalks so that both the living and the dead would know that there was a xandu' yaa. As good Zapotec, they would respond to the invitation and visit the altar. Walking through the streets of the city on these two days, one's eyes are drawn to the huge green arches decorated with bright orange marigolds, green bananas, cocos, and small loaves of marquesote. Because the banana stalks are heavy and unwieldy, this is work that normally falls to the men of the household. No men appeared, however, and so the women pressed the one acquiescent man into service and worked alongside him to construct these green invitations. The presence or absence of men and the unpredictability of their willingness to work is one of the major factors determining whether a household celebrates with a xandu' (altar) or a biguié' ("spirit house"). An altar can be put together by women if necessary while the biguié' relies both on the strength and knowledge of men in placing the thick stalks to form a house and creating the lattice framework for all the decorations. When Delia and I visited the biguié' of one of Rosinda's uncles two years later, I saw why the participation of men is so important. This biguié' reached all the way to the huge crossbeams of the twenty-foot-high ceiling. The lattice backdrop descended from the crossbeams and was stuffed with loaves of marquesote, oranges, marigolds, and bananas. That structure rested on a table decorated with candles, the photographs of the dead, and fruit. Below that was the "floor," a mat heaped with nayaa fruits and flowers. Without the work of the men, constructing a biguié' of this size would have been impossible.

The remaining chore before we were ready for guests was to get the tamales we had ordered. Again, there was no man with both a car and a driver's license, so Gloria was dispatched to retrieve the tamales. We were barely ready with decorated doorways, altar, and basins of tamales and bread by the time the first guests started arriving midmorning. Na Rosinda sat in the altar room in a comfortable chair near the doorway so that she could receive people. Delia and I were there to take the contributions of flowers and candles and to return with bags of tamales and bread. Women would come, give Rosinda a monetary donation, candle, and a big bunch of flowers, almost always marigolds, cockscombs, or amaranths. If the latter (guie' gui'xhi'), we would place them on the mat in front of the altar, and take the candles back to a large box in an adjoining room. If the flowers were of the guidxi (cultivated), we would arrange them in vases and return them to the altar. In the press of guests, we were often reduced to dropping them into one of the laundry basins to deal with later. Returning, we would give the guest a plastic bag with two tamales and two pieces of bread (pan bollo). The women would sit and chat for a few minutes with Rosinda and among themselves. Most would comment on the attractiveness of the altar and say something about Ta Chu. Then they would stand, throw the ends of their shawls over their shoulders, and make their fare-wells. If they were visiting several altars—almost always the case—they might have a helper with them to carry things or a bag into which they could put the tamales and bread. Brightly colored tin trays are quite popular as a way of carrying the flowers and the candles because they can then serve to carry away the food. When several women all carrying trays arrive at the same time, the household helpers are expected to remember which tray belongs to whom.

As the hour of the final round of prayers approached, the altar room began to fill, the rezadora arrived, the incense cooperated, and we began. It felt very comfortable in the call and response of the prayers, the pungent smoke of the incense, the intimacy of the women, and the spirits of the dead. People were reluctant to leave the warmth and the light, the beauty of the massed flowers and their fragrance, and the pictures of their loved ones. Indeed, after the prayers concluded around 6:15 p.m., people continued to come, and at the time when people would normally be eating cena (about 8:30 p.m.), we served coffee and opened tamales for everyone. We finally left the altar room at 9:45 p.m.), using a marigold to snuff out all but one candle, and shutting the door behind us.

Being a Guest

What is it like to be one of the visitors to the Day of the Dead altars? Fami-lies who celebrate Todos Santos for two years after the death of a loved one are thoroughly occupied constructing the altar or biguié', holding the cycle of prayers, and receiving all the guests. Although this prevents them from visiting the altars of their relatives or friends, it does not cancel the obligation. People understand the constraints, but they do expect an eventual accounting. In the interim, one can send votive candles and a monetary donation by way of another family member or a household helper. The third year after Chu's death, all our obligations came due. His altar was much smaller that year, and we expected few visitors except for those who came for the prayers each evening. Delia and I were expected to visit every altar of relatives marking either their first- or second-year commemorations. On October 30 and 31, we took candles, flowers, and donations to twenty-five altars. What we took to individual houses depended on the closeness of the relationship—the more distant ones did not require flowers, although donations and candles went to all.

When we entered a house, we would seek out the chief mourner, in all cases, a woman. She would be sitting usually off to one side of the altar in a comfortable chair. Each of us (unless I did not know the household) would give her our donation in a folded paper tissue, say the few words of condolence, and offer the votive candle and the flowers (for those households to which we gave all three). Usually there would be a helper or a relative by her side to take the candles and the flowers. On our way to the chairs, we would pass by the altar or biguié', pause and cross ourselves, and then sit down. We would talk with others who had come, usually about the deceased being honored or the beauty of the display. Helpers or family members would bring us the bag of tamales and the two small square loaves of bread. A minimum visit would be ten or fifteen minutes while some would stretch into half an hour or more. Leaving required a round of goodbyes, crossing oneself again in front of the altar, and taking leave of the chief mourner.

By the time of the midday meal on the first day, we had been to seven houses. When we returned after the visits, we sorted out the tamales and the bread. The gueta guu beela za (a particularly rich beef tamale made with lots of lard) we ate right away, putting the rest in the freezer for me to take to Mavis on my return through Mexico City. A quick visit to the market to buy more marigolds and cockscombs was on the afternoon's agenda.

The city seemed awash in images, sounds, and smells of the Day of the Dead. Double rockets punctuated the ordinary sound of the city, going off at intervals for the souls of those who died unmarried. The whole central part of the city smelled of marigolds and everywhere on the main plaza were bundles of the bright orange flowers alongside purple amaranths and red cockscombs. Banana stalks, cocos, woven palm stars, sugar skulls, and skeletons were hawked in every space. There was a cacophony of gossip, bargaining, buying, and selling. Trucks and ox carts came and went, carrying the essentials of Xandu'—all saints and all souls coming to visit on their appointed days.

We awoke the next morning stiff from so much walking the day before, but we were visiting even more altars today. I would have liked to get an early start before the day's heat settled in, but because these visits involve many of the residents of the compound, that proved to be impossible. Chu's sister Tomasa had to go to the market to buy more flowers, and she stopped to visit and chat with friends and merchants. When she returned, we began getting together the candles, the big shopping bag for bread, two black plastic bags for tamales, and the painted tray, which always seems to disappear from one day to the next. Finally ready, we had to wait for our driver who had come, eaten breakfast, and then left again on another errand. In the meantime and not to waste time, we went to Lourdes Ferra's house, just around the corner, with flowers, candles, and donations. She had built a huge, elaborate altar in honor of her mother and had stacked willow branches all around the edges of the room. Three large images of saints, including a Mary and a Christ, comprised the backdrop for the altar. Because we were in the neighborhood, we walked to two more houses before returning to the compound. The car and driver were waiting. We loaded ourselves, all the flowers, candles, bags, and the flowered tray into the car and drove across the river to Cheguigo. By now, it was 11:15 a.m. and hot. After visiting all the houses on our list in Cheguigo, our driver and cousin, Vicente, had to pick up his daughter from school so he dropped us off in the center of the city, and we walked to four more houses. We staggered back home with both tamale bags bulging, and bread flowing over the top of the shopping bag.

After the meal, Delia went out again with Vicente to the remaining houses while I stayed to help Rosinda prepare for the 5:00 p.m. prayers for Chu. We packed the bags for the women who came to pray—two yemitas and a tablet of chocolate inside each one. Then we spent an hour in the back of the compound once again trying to light the charcoal for the incense. At one point, after one of the lit wax matches caught under my fingernail, Rosinda, Irma, and I laughed so hard we could scarcely stand. Just in time, the charcoal caught, Emma arrived, and we began the prayers. When we finished this last time for the third year, I passed out the bread and chocolate; Delia served the soft drinks, and we chatted. The candles stay lit as long as the chief mourner wishes, and while they are lit, someone has to remain in the room. People came and went. Father Hector came to visit. Finally at 9:00 p.m., Rosinda stood. We put out the candles and left the room, our obligations met for another year.

Tradition of Altars and Biguié'

Like every other community in Mexico, Juchitán gives itself over to commemorations of its departed those last days of October and the first of November. The unmistakable pungency of marigolds, the ancient flower of the dead, permeates the main plaza, the Parque Benito Juárez, and the blocks surrounding it. Even though the municipal officials try valiantly to collect use fees from vendors for space, their numbers continue to crowd into every corner of the plaza, filling it with the flowers and greenery of death. Trucks come and go, dropping their loads of flowers, tied up in rope and canvas, which disappear in a flash as shoppers search for the freshest buy. On the first day, when people are beginning to build the base of their biguié', women arrive before dawn to wait for the trucks with the banana stalks and leaves. They surround each truck as it arrives, bartering for the best stalks, motioning the horse cart drivers to load their purchases, and take it to their homes. Unlike the marigolds, amaranths, and cockscombs, the banana stalks are always in short supply, and, without them, you cannot build a biguié' or frame your doorway. The green cocos also disappear, though not as rapidly as the banana stalks. October 29 is the busiest day for building and decorating altars since October 30 is the first day of visits to the altars of family and friends. The actual days when the souls visit include October 30 and 31 and November 1. Which of those days is determined by the place of burial (there are two active cemeteries and two not used) supported by family custom. Counting back nine days from the day of the visit gives one the day on which the prayers for the departed begin.

Whether the family chooses to welcome the departed back with a biguié' or an altar[2] is a matter of family tradition and the availability of help. Both were documented as being in use by Gabriel López Chiñas in his 1969 book *El concepto de la muerte entre los zapotecas*. People do have some notion that the biguié' is older. Several years ago, in fact, the Casa de la Cultura sponsored a contest for the best biguié', sending judges out to view and photograph them. Whatever the form, the connection with the departed is very old, predating the Spanish invasion of the New World. Mortuary practices of the pre-Columbian Zapotec include subterranean burials, the use of funerary urns depicting important personages, reentry into the tombs, and the continuing relationship between the living and the dead as shown by the repainting of murals and the practice of petitioning ancestors to intercede for the living with the gods. The most well-known pre-Columbian rituals that pertain here are those that recognize the dead. The Aztec celebration when people went to the tombs of their relatives occurred in the fourteenth month, *quecholli*, which now coincides with the Roman Catholic celebration of All Saints' Day and All Souls' Day (Weckmann 1992:200–201). But the Aztec honored their ancestors in virtually every month because different modes of death—dying in first childbirth, men dying in war, women dying in war, dying a violent or unexpected death, dying in childhood, those struck by lightning, those who drowned, and a general honoring the dead during the fiesta for Xochipilli, the God of Flowers—required distinct observances.

With the exception of royalty who were buried at Mitla, Stibaa, or Zaachila, most pre-Columbian Zapotec probably buried their dead beneath the floor of the patio of the compound of the living relatives. Evidence of this comes from larger sites where the patios were frequently paved. The practice also lends support to the early origins of shrines and altars within family compounds to provide focal points for the rituals surrounding the dead originating with family and closely related kin. Contemporary cemeteries are usually located on the edges of the town, although in some cases, as with Cheguigo and Saltillo, the town has grown around them. At first glance, these cemeteries appear to be extensions in miniature of the town. Laid out with streets and avenues, their older, more substantial tombs resemble small houses with roofs, floors, walls, often of glass, and a door through which one enters. Each cemetery has its

---

2. There is no Zapotec word for this. *Bidó'* is *el santo*, the saint, and when people speak in Spanish, they will refer to the small home altar as *"el santo."* All home altars have at least one saint's image in addition to the photographs of the departed. The expression, *lu bidó'*, "face of the altar," uses the term in its extrapolated sense. Pre-Columbian Zapotec households were defined in part by household shrines, so this word probably comes from that early usage. *Xandu'* in its primary usage refers to All Saints' Day and All Souls' Day. *Xandu' yaa*, or fresh *xandu'*, designates the first year celebration; *xandu' guiropa*, or second *xandu'*, refers to the second year. *Xandu'* is more than likely a corruption of the Spanish "santo." Simply in linguistic terms, we can say that the *biguié'* is the older form of shrine, but we shall see other evidence to support this.

own chapel as well. On the Holy Week visits to the cemeteries, whole families crowd into these tombs, celebrating with food, drink, and music. Many but not all new tombs, "fresh" tombs, are made of earth and palm, gradually becoming more permanent structures. In terms of the physical landscape then, the term "community of the dead" has great legitimacy. These house-tombs are cleaned just as is the departed's former house. Families come at least weekly to sweep, mop, change the water glass, clean the vases, replace old candles with new ones, and bring new flowers. The tomb itself has small chairs so that people can sit and visit, as well as a stock of cleaning supplies—broom, mop, bucket, bleach for the flower vases. Once a year, during *Nabaana Ro* (Time of Great Grieving, referring to Holy Week), the tombs are cleaned from top to bottom. They are often repainted, any crumbling concrete walls are rebuilt, and masses of flowers are brought in to adorn them. The living come to be with the dead in their community, reciprocating the visit of the dead during Xandu'.

López Chiñas suggests that there may have been a multiday celebration at this time of year at the sites of Mitla (Liobá) and the secondary site of Stibaa or Ceetoba. Mitla was not only the central site of living royalty but also the cemetery for the highest nobility (see Mendieta y Núñez 1949). Stibaa, in Zapotec, literally means "another cemetery." This explanation is consonant with the association of different cemeteries in Juchitán with different days of Holy Week. The first observance, on Palm Sunday, is celebrated at the Panteón Municipal or Panteón Domingo de Ramos (Palm Sunday cemetery). Holy Monday was the day for the families of those buried in the cemetery of Cheguigo Saltillo (mostly families of the Revolutionary party of Che Gómez) to celebrate. There are very few living family members to carry on this tradition, but I did see a new tomb here of an infant who died in 1988. The old chapel has been replaced by a larger, new chapel. Holy Tuesday recognized the former cemetery associated with the chapel of Calvario, in the fourth section of the city. Now not in use as a cemetery, people of the neighborhood still gather there on that day, and there is an hermandad (church group) that cleans and decorates the chapel and provides the musicians for the evening visits. On Holy Wednesday, there is a large celebration for the dead at the Panteón de Miércoles Santo (Holy Wednesday Cemetery) in Cheguigo. As I mentioned earlier, where one is buried will determine the date on which one returns to the altar in the family home. This cycle of visiting is examined in chapter 9.

Communal Celebrations

Structurally, Day of the Dead and Holy Week represent reciprocal celebrations. On the first, the spirits of the dead are called back to their homes among the community of the living. They are called to a specific place and for a specific time, and these are framed by the use of "fresh" plants and "homes." In that first year, the spirit is still fresh, nayaa, and longs for the company of the living. To ensure that it does not wander or overstay its time, the home and the altar are closed off by plants considered "fresh" (green bananas, cocos, and marigolds) as is the route into the compound. These might well be the modern equivalent of pre-Columbian household rites for the dead buried in the patio[3] where there might have been a prayer leader, a minor religious functionary with a set of memorized rituals and responses who was hired to help families through the appropriate rituals. Holy Week rituals today might be the modern equivalent of celebrating the dead in a place where the dead reside, as would have been the case in Mitla. But the argument for structural reciprocity is more compelling in light of Isthmus Zapotec values and practices, which are consistent across several domains, some of which we shall discuss in subsequent chapters. What is significant is that these Holy Week visitations at the cemeteries are unique within Mexico.

Moist and Dry, Wild and Town

The association of "fresh" plants and water with the recently dead is striking. Whether altar or biguié', the altar and doorways of houses commemorating recent deaths are decorated with "fresh" fruit and branches. Banana stalks, woven green palm decorations, and green coconuts frame the doorways, both showing the spirit the way back home and drawing it by the freshness. Marigolds are woven into the greenery and heaped on the mat in front of the altar. Marigolds, purple globe amaranth, cockscomb, and green cocos, and oranges form pyramids on the mat (*daa*), the "floor" of the little house within the house.

The flowers and the greenery that decorate altars and biguié' include the two categories of wild and cultivated. During the Day of the Dead festivities and Holy Week, huge truckloads come and go daily from as far as Mexico City and Puebla. The commercial flowers include chrysanthemums (of all varieties— pompon, spider, button, daisy), lilies (Asiatic and San José), carnations, daisies, roses, bird-of-paradise, tuberose, baby's breath, stocks, gladiolas, calla lilies, wild asters, and more. "Wild" includes anything found or grown locally on the outskirts of the city—five or six kinds of jasmine, globe amaranth, cordoncillo, ilán, frangipani, coyol (palm flower), hibiscus, albahaca (basil), dill, cocos, green bananas, banana foliage, palm, a local orange with a green skin, willow branches,

---

3. Until the advent of births in hospitals and clinics, the common Zapotec practice was to bury the umbilical cord of the infant in a pot in the patio of the compound. The Zapotec term is significant, *doo yoo*, literally "house cord." That act was one of the things that defined one as family, as Zapotec, as a Juchiteco. Perhaps there is a relationship between that and burying the dead to keep them close.

and guie' bíchí. Marigolds, *cempasuchitl* in Nahuatl, and called by the Zapotec guie' biguá, also belong to the "wild" even though they are trucked in for Day of the Dead. While native to Mexico, they are seen at no other time in Juchitán, and are used exclusively in conjunction with this celebration.[4]

Oppositions in the Altars

Field notes and photographs of altars and biguié' make clear the distinction between town and wild. That the spaces are clearly marked off for the two kinds and that one is considered to be older is seen most clearly in photographs and descriptions of the altars. Spatially, the town flowers are arranged in the many vases that sit on the sides of the steps of the altar. If visitors bring arrangements that cannot be accommodated in the vases on the altar, then the mourners will put them in a vase on the floor in front of the mat, and never on the mat itself. The flowers and fruit of the wild lie on the woven palm mat laid on the floor in front of the altar. This is usually a sleeping mat measuring about 4-foot by 7-foot. Cockscomb may sometimes be put in vases and set on the mat, but all the others are simply stacked on the mat itself as they are brought in armfuls by the visitors. The cocos and green bananas are arranged on the mat by members of the household. Being wild, their place is on the mat, while cultivated, usually non-local fruit, adorns the altar—apples, pears, grapes, and hothouse oranges.

Of all the altars I have seen and photographed as well as those that appear in López Chiñas (1969), only one violates this distinction. This was the altar in the home of Señora Emma Musalem in honor of her mother on the Day of the Dead, 2000. The only flowers used were of the wild—marigolds, cockscomb, globe amaranth—and they were in vases along the sides of the altar steps as well as on the mat in front. Even the large candles were decorated with marigolds and orange ribbons. Emma's use of banana stalks to the sides of the altar suggests that she was recreating as closely as she could the older type of altar. And her household is similar to ours in that she cannot count on the labor of men to construct a biguié'. Emma also uses flowers of the wild in her family's tomb in the cemetery in Cheguigo. This is a common practice for many families but town flowers are regarded by some as showing more respect and affection for the deceased. The tombs in the Panteón Miércoles Santo in Cheguigo are more likely to be filled with flowers of the wild than those in

---

4. *Tagetes erecta* decorates the Day of the Dead altars in Juchitán, but a wild variety, *Tagetes* spp. *(T. lucida, T. micrantha)* is native to the state of Oaxaca. All these have a very pungent smell, which is valued for this purpose of greeting the dead.

the cemetery in the central sections of the city. Everyone, however, uses flowers of the wild in the tombs in the first days and weeks after a death because the spirit needs their freshness.

Biguié'

I have described the biguié' as being a house-within-a-house, and one can see this notion embodied in the structure itself. Four large banana stalks are the pillars of the house. A lattice of woven palm and banana fronds makes the ceiling and the back of the house. That back "wall" is decorated thickly with oranges, bananas, marigolds, fruit tied on with a string, and loaves of marquesote with the deceased's name written in sugar and egg frosting. The "ceiling" is also decorated with these same objects hanging down. The "floor" of the house is the mat, either a very large petate or several smaller ones that overlap

Plate 25. Day of the Dead altar for the mother of Na Emma Musalem. 2000. Photograph by Anya Peterson Royce.

so that no space is left open. Four large beeswax candles sit two on a side at the edges of the mat, further protection against a spirit wandering away out of its house. The lower part of the back wall is made of a table with two steps on top, the whole covered with a white sheet. Photographs of the deceased rest on the steps and on the mat in front of the table. Food, drink, bread, votive candles, and fruit fill up the steps and the table top. A ba' yaa is often laid out on the mat—a sprinkling of loose petals in the shape of a body, which then has marigolds or hibiscuses or frangipani placed on top. There will be votive candles at both ends and surrounding the whole will be green bananas (the large cooking variety), marigolds, and local oranges. Other permissible additions would be cocos, amaranth, and cockscomb. Rarely one might see town flowers as part of a biguié', but this is not regarded as appropriate and is usually because an individual family member wants to include them or a guest has brought them. The whole structure is built so that it has boundaries—top, sides, back, and floor—that mark it off from the room in which it sits. The spirit it honors and summons enters through the outside portal of the house with its banana stalk and marigold arch, and then into the biguié' through the open front. In this way, the spirit is both invited and constrained.

Plate 26. Biguié'—older style of altar for the Day of the Dead. 2000. Photograph by Anya Peterson Royce.

Plate 27. Biguié'—older style of altar. Note the ba' yaa shape of marigolds and cockscomb. 2000. Photograph by Anya Peterson Royce.

Communal Altars

Various constituencies of the city also construct altars, more rarely biguié', at this time of year. The municipal government built one, all in purple and orange, under the portals of the Municipal Palace. Pimpollo, the orphanage attached to the parish church of San Vicente, had one the children built. This one had names of children who had died while resident in Pimpollo. The churches constructed altars in front of the main altar, while those with images of the Virgen de Guadalupe had two—one in front of the main altar and a second in front of the Guadalupe. These all had bread or paper with names on them, some the names of members of the parish, others with names of Zapotec heroes such as Che Gómez or Charis or Binu Gada. The Capilla de Miércoles Santo in Cheguigo built a biguié' that took up the whole space between the altar and the front pews. The priest of this church (who is not from the Isthmus) wants to remind people that Cheguigo is home to farmers, craftsmen, and fishermen, not the white-collar workers and professionals who inhabit the center of the city. He thinks that biguié' are more traditional and so more appropriate for that church. Some of the vendors with stalls in the big market made small altars in them decorated with Day of the Dead flowers, candy, and fruit.

The Required and the Optional

As I wrote in the introduction, the continued success of the Zapotec of Juchitán in charting their future springs from their commitment to community and the considered response to external forces which that dictates, coupled with their willingness to step boldly into the unknown, transforming themselves and their traditions. It is a useful exercise then, to examine Day of the Dead practices in terms of what Zapotec believe is essential and those items and practices that are optional or acceptable. Certainly, the increasing importance of Halloween and its assorted rituals falls into the category of acceptable innovation from the outside. Small and not-so-small children dress up in the same sorts of costumes you find in the United States—the media heroes and heroines of the moment, witches and ghosts, all manner of animals, including lots of purple Barneys, fairy princesses, and butterflies—and beg treats from family, friends, and occasionally strangers. Unlike their neighbors to the north, these children, knowing a good thing when they see it, begin three days before Halloween. Kindergartens and elementary schools allow pupils to come to school in costume and, indeed, sponsor parades so that everyone can enjoy the masquerade. It is a community affair, and like many of those, it indulges the children.

In terms of Day of the Dead observances, however, which are those elements that are required, that are not negotiable? Most important, whatever the economic state of the family, a xandu' yaa and a xandu' guiropa are required. If these rituals pose a hardship for financial reasons or if the remaining relatives are few or ill, help is extended by more distant relatives or fictive kin. In some rare cases, the first commemoration can be postponed. An altar or biguié' is necessary whether it is large or small, elaborate or simple. An image of the deceased has to be displayed. I have seen old paintings and hand-colored photographs on altars as well as recent photos. In pre-Hispanic times, small clay figurines, anthropomorphic funerary urns, and tomb murals served this purpose. Flowers of the wild and willow, palm, banana stalks or cocos in some combination are essential as are marigolds. Votive candles, large candles in silver or tin candlesticks, and incense must be in evidence. Food and drink, including the decorated breads—marquesote and roscas—have to be part of the altar. Mandatory rounds of prayers each evening lead up to the day on which the spirits return. Families hosting an altar must provide tamales and pan bollo for guests who arrive with condolences and limosna, in addition to the bread and chocolate they give to the women who come to the prayers. Guests must come minimally with a votive candle and a gift of money, even if a token amount. The rules of communal obligation require a person to attend the observances of kin and close friends. Both hosts and guests wear some variant of mourning, depending on the relationship to the deceased.

Having listed all those required items or behaviors, I have to say that there is much room for individual choice and much latitude for aesthetic preferences. These choices begin with whether one builds an altar or a biguié'. Decisions are made by some families depending on available labor. But which to build is ultimately a choice reached consensually, based on a number of factors. Families may be honoring past traditions. Aesthetic preferences enter the mix as well. If one likes cultivated flowers, then one will most likely have an altar because it is appropriate to have vases of store flowers on the steps of the altar. Such flowers are rare in biguié', usually there because a guest has brought them. Earlier, I mentioned the exception to the general understanding about which flowers belong to which kind of altar. When Emma Musalem used all flowers of the wild on her mother's altar, guests were tolerant, remarking that she also took those kinds of flowers to the tomb as well. It could certainly have been an aesthetic choice because the altar was visually striking. Certain kinds of flowers might appear because the deceased liked them. Na Berta, for example, loved hibiscuses, so her altar always had them. Even more serendipitous, in Berta's case, was the use of agapandos (agapanthus). One of the first arrivals when Berta was laid out in front of the altar brought big bunches of the purple flowers, which happened to match Berta's traje. After that, the family intentionally bought these for the altar. In terms of the greenery that represents moistness and the wild, willow is not as common as banana stalks but is an acceptable alternative. Willow is not commonly for sale in the market so perhaps the people who have access to it help gather it so it may be used rather than other options.

What and how much one puts on these altars, given the requirements outlined previously, depends on the number of participants, the amount of money available, and personal preference. No one who wants to participate is excluded, and people will bring items for the altar that they think will please the spirits or remind them of some happy time. Younger members of the family, in particular, are encouraged to bring something for the altar. The chief mourner and closest family will have the ultimate authority about where these special offerings will go on the altar, but I have never seen any rejected completely.

Very little latitude is available about the food that is given to guests and participants in the prayers. Certain kinds of tamales are expected and the kind of bread is even more closely prescribed. The bread given to people who come to pray can be either pan bollo or yemitas. The chocolate is the standard tablet form sold in the market. For prayers, one can pass out other things—soft drinks, candies—after the prayers are concluded. Because I was assigned the job of making sure we had enough for the number of women attending, I was curious about what would happen if we ran out of something. One can make up for a lack of chocolate by adding another piece of bread or vice versa. In the case of visitors to the altar during the day, particular women may be given more tamales or more bread or both, depending on the decision of the chief mourner, however one cannot change the minimum expectation of two tamales and two breads. Sometimes this means that someone will be sent out to buy additional portions of whatever is needed—the guests simply wait until they are given their portion. No one would ever comment on any delay.

Clearly, there is a certain flexibility of choice. It is not so much that something new or different takes the place of a more traditional item; it is, rather, that new things or practices are added to the repertory. At some point, there may be a shift but Zapotec are quite content to keep old and new, more rather than less. This has proven to be an effective strategy for maintaining certain fundamental cultural elements while allowing incorporation of items and practices that are appealing on several grounds—they are interesting in themselves; they are part of a larger global culture; they are pleasing to the eye (and the Zapotec are very much concerned with this dimension of their lives); they have properties that make life easier. Thus far, none of these innovations—ranging from plastic containers to videos and VCRs to computers and Internet cafes to fast-food barbecued chicken have threatened the integrity of Zapotec culture. It is unlikely that Halloween or cultivated flowers will dismantle the communal celebration of the Day of the Dead, which is uniquely Zapotec in both form and purpose.

7

The Way of the Cross

Beginning with the first Friday after Ash Wednesday, Juchitecos of all ages and backgrounds walk the Way of the Cross every Friday in Lent. The last Friday, the Friday before Holy Week, is in honor of the Virgen Dolorosa, the mother of Christ, in anticipation of the impending death of her Son. On Good Friday, the stops during the noon procession of Christ, the Dolorosa, and Saint John represent the Stations. Finally, after the Good Friday liturgy, when the crucified Christ in his coffin is taken from the parish in procession, those faithful who are not able to walk the distance involved remain and walk the Stations that are set high on the walls inside the church.

These pilgrimages, for such they are, are known as the Way of the Cross, the Stations of the Cross, Via Crucis, or the Via Dolorosa. Throughout their history, they have taken many forms, have been walked for long distances in the open air, and have been walked around the interior perimeter of churches. Stories of origins and number have varied widely, but today in most of the Roman Catholic world and in Juchitán, fourteen stations represent the Passion and death of Christ.

The Thirteenth Station

My family has, for a long time, hosted the thirteenth station on the first and the fifth Friday in Lent. They have a station because they are devout; they have the thirteenth because the house is next to the parish church of San Vicente, indeed, shares a wall with it. On March 14, 1997, we began our work early in the morning, sending Tomasa to the market to buy flowers. She returned with frangipani—both loose blossoms and blooms woven into leis—stalks of dill already in flower, basil, and deep pink sweetheart roses. To keep them from wilting in the heat, we put them into buckets of water in what had been Ta Chu's workshop. When Rosinda and I got to them in the late afternoon, we carried them out into the corridor of the compound so that we could work more comfortably. We talked as we reduced them to small bits of greenery and flowers, cutting the dill and basil into half-inch pieces, tossing them into three buckets and mixing in the loose frangipani blossoms (the guie' biuxhe mentioned in chapter 5). Rosinda then turned to the tin incense burner, wrapping it carefully in foil. Setting it aside, she sat in the doorway, and took up the incense, pounding the big lumps into pieces that would catch fire and produce billows of white, fragrant smoke.

Other chores occupied us until 5:00 p.m. Then José, Vicente's son, carried the small metal table with a wooden cross lashed to it out to the street in front of the family business, the Joyería La Esmeralda (jewelry, gold coins, and watches). Rosinda and I covered the table with a white cloth and arranged the flowers and votive candle. We hung leis of frangipani from the cross and arranged the sweetheart roses in two ceramic vases flanking it. The candle sat directly in front of the cross, and we scattered single blossoms on the cloth. The three buckets with their healing mixture of flowers and herbs were ready, standing in the shade of the corridor leading into the compound.

Gauging the arrival of the procession is nearly impossible because it leaves from one of the outlying chapels—in 1999, the Capilla Ique Guidxi (chapel at the entrance to the city), in other years from even more remote chapels in the colonias across the highway—and winds its way through the city, stopping at each of twelve preceding stations. I went around the corner to the eleventh sta-

Plate 28. Garlands of frangipani for Stations of the Cross. 2004. Photograph by Anya Peterson Royce.

tion in front of Chu's sister Tomasa's house. No sign of the pilgrims! Returning, I stopped briefly at the twelfth station in front of the Casa Ferra department store. Still no procession. Returning to our station, I joined the women of the family who were enjoying the afternoon sitting on the cement benches in front of the house and talking. While we were thus engaged, first a young boy, one of a group of teenagers on bicycles, stopped briefly in front of our station to cross himself. A few minutes later, an older campesino pushing a barrow stopped, wiped his forehead, and then crossed himself. The same acknowledgment of the cross takes place regardless how informal or humble the setting.

At 6:15 p.m., the procession turned into our street. Delia, Delia's friend Tere, and I went to the corner to escort the pilgrims to our station. Tere and I had the buckets, and waiting until the Centurion and his keeper had passed, began throwing the flowers at the feet of the young man who had taken a vow to represent Christ for that Via Crucis. He was dressed in a brown cassock, belted with rope, had a white head cloth held by brown cord, and walked barefooted. He carried a large wooden crucifix in front of him, almost hidden beneath its burden of frangipani wreaths. Delia censed both the Christ and his crucifix as we walked backward, making his way sweet with life-giving flowers and clouds of pungent incense. The Centurion, being a Roman soldier, walked

Plate 29. Stations of the Cross, station of Señorita Tomasa Ramírez Escudero. 2004. Photograph by Anya Peterson Royce.

Plate 30. Na Rosinda, Delia, and Anya at their Station of the Cross. 2004. Photograph by José Fuentes Ramírez.

without either fragrance or flowers. He was dressed in dark shirt and pants with leather leggings and sandals. His face was covered with a cloth that hung from a helmet of leather with a little bird on top and ribbons that hung down the back. He had a sword-belt and a sword.

At our station, a cantor prayed the readings for that station and the accompanying prayers in Spanish. A young woman then took the microphone, and read the same in Zapotec. A brief drama between the Centurion and Christ followed. The masked Centurion advanced menacingly toward the Christ, three long steps punctuated by the slash of his sword through the air on the third. At the end of the third set, he was close enough to the Christ to bury his face in the frangipani. The flowers, more than the crucifix that bore them, protected Christ, and turned the Centurion repentant. The crowd was silent during the drama—no children talked or played; no dogs barked. Everyone's attention was on what transpired before them—this encounter that moved everyone's hearts. When the keeper led the Centurion back to his place, the crowd began its prayers. This is a drama that does not change, and I have seen it four times within the last twelve years.[1] The drama and the prayers completed, the procession began moving once again, this time to the last station in the parish church courtyard.

---

1. The first time I went to the origin point of the procession, I had walked just three Stations with the crowd before the intense emotion of what I was seeing and participating in overwhelmed me, and I returned to the house to gather myself together and wait for the procession to get to our Station. While I have not had that profound a reaction in subsequent years, it is still a deeply moving ritual.

We moved with them, scattering flowers and herbs, and censing the Christ. The drama enacted in the churchyard was longer than at any of the other stations, but we finally moved into the church making a carpet of flowers all down the center aisle. The Centurion was not allowed to enter, being led instead by his keeper into the church offices where he could take off the heavy costume and rest. He only enters the church on Good Friday during the Descent from the Cross. The young Christ impersonator stood the frangipani-laden cross in front of the altar, and Delia knelt in front of it on the marble chancel steps, tending to the incense. The prayers lasted another twenty minutes, and when they were over, perhaps forty people descended on the cross, taking frangipani away with them for their home altars. The flowers were now holy, invested with healing power by their contact with the image of Christ.

Participants

For five consecutive Fridays, Juchitecos enact this drama of Christ's Passion and crucifixion. They walk through the dusty streets in the heat of the day, stopping fourteen times along the way. As a crow flies, the distance from the farthest chapel to San Vicente is one and a quarter miles, but the route is not a straight line. It winds through the streets to stop at stations, some humble, some elaborate, offered in the name of Christ by the faithful. The actors in the drama participate as a result of vows they have made, usually promising their services for three years. The prayer leaders for the Spanish and the Zapotec liturgies are chosen by their churches and church societies. For several years, all the readers of Spanish were men while the readers of Zapotec were uniformly women. The role of the Centurion is especially fraught with danger, given his enmity toward Christ. No flowers are strewn in his path; he is guarded by a keeper; he may not enter the church. On Good Friday, he menaces the crucified Christ for the last time inside the church of San Vicente, and then is forgiven. He follows Christ's coffin from that church to the Capilla de la Misericordia, one of the beneficiaries of Christ's sacrifice.

The people who walk the Way of the Cross come from those who belong to the numerous societies associated with the churches and chapels, those persons who feel a special piety or who have taken a Lenten vow of discipline, and others caught up in the drama. They include people of all ages and social standing. The majority walk each of the five Via Crucis. Many of the people who have stations in front of their homes have done so for many years; many of them host a station for more than one Via Crucis. Again, it is motivated by piety first and foremost, but also a sense of communal obligation.

The pilgrimages along the way of the cross are composed of lay people and conducted in the absence of clergy. Even the last entry into the parish church

and the prayers that are prayed there are done without clergy. This is quite typical of the different responsibilities that dictate the actions of clergy and laity.[2]

History of the Way of the Cross

As an established liturgical practice in the Roman Catholic Church, the Via
Crucis arose from the desire of the devout to reproduce the important places
of the Holy Land in other countries, originally to identify themselves with the
places even though they could not visit the Holy Land. The Via Crucis became
a particular devotion in the fifteenth century, allowing lay people to experience
the Passion and crucifixion of Christ as a kind of penitential pilgrimage. It was
particularly practiced by the Franciscans and carried with it the granting of
indulgences. The Franciscans were given the guardianship of the holy places in
Jerusalem in 1342. Christ's way, or the Via Sacra, grew to be a devotion by itself
as rituals and liturgies proliferated. Chapels or stations were erected in various
parts of Europe, including Spain, Greece, Germany, and France. The writers of
the devotional manuals associated with each of these places probably dictated
what has come down to us as the liturgy of Stations of the Cross. Until the
seventeenth century, the Via Crucis was a pilgrimage in the open air, with some
being set up to approximate the actual distances a pilgrim to Jerusalem might

2. Two processional occasions call for the presence of a priest. One is the Palm Sunday procession,
which makes its way from the chapel in the Panteón Domingo de Ramos (Palm Sunday cemetery)
to the parish church of San Vicente. It is a joyous procession with the priest leading the women
and men of the Palm Sunday *hermandad* (society), the orphans of Pimpollo (a church-sponsored
orphanage), and any women, men, and children who wish to join (see the description at the beginning of chapter 1). The second is the procession with the Blessed Sacrament. The exposition of the
Blessed Sacrament to the faithful is part of the feast of Corpus Christi, a movable feast established
toward the end of the thirteenth century. In defense of the feast, Pope Urban IV wrote that just
as there was a day for every saint, so too Christ's body deserved one. In Juchitán, Corpus Christi
(sometimes combined with the Feast of the Sacred Heart, a nineteenth-century feast), involves a
special liturgy, most likely the one composed by Saint Thomas Aquinas. In it the priest carries the
monstrance containing the Blessed Sacrament (the consecrated host), priest and monstrance both
draped in garlands of frangipani, from one saint's image to another—the Virgin of the Sacred Heart,
the Christ of Good Friday, Saint John, the Virgin of the Ascension, followed by women belonging
to the associations of Corpus Christi and Sacred Heart, singing Aquinas's hymn. The priest carries
the Blessed Sacrament out from the church, through the churchyard to the open gates, and back.
Then he comes forth again, this time to make a procession through the streets, stopping at five
flower-decorated altars set up by families to receive the Blessed Sacrament (*El Santísimo*). Each altar
had a white cloth-covered table with a central circle of flowers on which the monstrance was placed
and a cushion on which the priest might kneel as he prayed. The procession followed the same
form as the Via Crucis, women scattering *guie' biuxhe* at the feet of the priest and the *Santísimo*,
another woman censing them, women and men following, standing silently through the prayers.
In this instance a priest was essential because of the holiness of the Blessed Sacrament.

have walked. Pope Innocent XI granted the Franciscans the right to establish the Stations in the churches under their jurisdiction in 1686 and granted them all the indulgences attached to the actual pilgrimage points in the Holy Land. In 1726, this privilege was extended to all the faithful by Pope Benedict XIII, and with that, the instances of the Via Crucis increased dramatically.

Two of the provisions attached to Stations of the Cross today are embodied in Zapotec practice. One dictates that the most efficacious element of the Stations is the wooden cross. Stations do not have to have pictures depicting the actions at each station, but they must have the wooden cross or an image of it. The presence of the wooden cross characterizes both the outdoor pilgrimages in Juchitán as well as the stations set inside the parish church. The second prescribes that any Way of the Cross that is outside the church should ideally begin and end in a church. In Juchitán, the processions always begin at a chapel or church and ends at the parish church.[3] Within the past ten years, some of the chapels have become full-fledged churches. Of them, the ones who have an image of the Santo Entierro (Christ after the crucifixion, reclining in a glass coffin) have instituted their own Via Crucis. Processions leave from one of the farther-flung chapels and end at the church. It does give more opportunities for participation to the newer colonias that have accommodated Juchitán's burgeoning population. It also means that the last procession on Good Friday that leaves from the parish church of San Vicente and takes Christ's body to the Capilla de la Misericordia has hundreds of onlookers rather than the thousands that used to line the streets, holding candles in silent witness.

Stations of the Cross Inside the Church

As I mentioned earlier, on Good Friday those devout who are unable to walk the procession following the crucified Christ remain in the parish church and walk the stations along the interior walls of San Vicente. These stations also draw people at odd times during the year. They walk them as personal devotions, often in times of stress or grief. Some who come to the church to pray make the rounds of all the images, including the Stations plaques. Unlike the other images, people do not bring flowers to leave at the plaques probably because they are set higher in the walls and have no ledge on which to place either flowers or candles. There seems to be no established Stations liturgy led by clergy inside the church just as clergy do not participate in the outside processions.

---

3. Another tradition of Stations has them erected in the open air, outside a church or on the grounds attached to a church or monastery. Typically, the distances would be shorter than Stations walked as a pilgrimage. The requirements that there be a cross and that they begin and end in a church are met in all the instances I have seen.

Zapotec Elements in the Via Crucis

Even though the Via Crucis offers individuals a penitential ritual, allowing them to walk with Christ, picking up their cross as the faithful are enjoined to do, the actions and symbols embody the elements of life as well as those of death. This dual embodiment permeates all of Zapotec belief and ritual surrounding death. The Via Crucis procession itself and the prayers are all about Christ's suffering and death. As with any dying and death, people are solemn and grieving. On the other hand, the use of the flowers of the wild and healing herbs as well as incense indicates the importance of life-giving elements. The young man impersonating Christ walks on cool, moist flowers and herbs. The frangipani wreaths cover the crucifix he holds so that he is nearly invisible beneath the blanket of fragrant, moist blossoms. They are the fragile barrier between Christ and the Centurion who threatens him with death. Fragile, yet each time the Centurion approaches, he is stopped by them. In the midst of the short journey that ends in crucifixion, Christ is protected by the flowers of life.

Their use here is similar to that of Palm Sunday when the image of Christ riding on the donkey into Jerusalem is covered in frangipani wreaths while the palms that have been blessed and distributed also fall into that category of flowers of the wild. The Palm Sunday Christ is not being threatened, rather he is being feted and hailed as the Messiah. Underneath that jubilation, however, he and the people know that he rides to his death when he enters Jerusalem, the city that kills prophets. The poem by Maestro Enedino Jiménez, "When Death Dies a Natural Life," at the beginning of this book seems to speak to the death in life and life in death nature of these two processions. The absence of boundaries between life and death or the fluidity of those states that is the heart of Zapotec attitudes about death are encapsulated in the Palm Sunday procession, the procession that is the Way of the Cross, and, finally, the midday procession of Christ, Mary, and St. John on Good Friday. Joy and sorrow, death and life, the transformation of the dead by virtue of a journey facilitated by powerful symbols of moistness and healing—all these are very old Zapotec notions that enfold the Roman Catholic institutions of Holy Week, transforming them and giving them transformative powers.

The flowers and herbs that are scattered under the feet of Christ in the Via Crucis are also an integral part of the other two processions that frame Holy Week (Palm Sunday and Good Friday). They are fragrant and cool, two of the most important qualities of healing and protection, associated with good as opposed to the qualities of stinking and hot and dry, which personify evil. The flowers and herbs are used in slightly different ways in these processions though they accomplish the same purpose. In Via Crucis, the single blossoms, petals, and torn-up dill and basil are scattered at the feet of Christ so that he walks on them, and his feet do not touch the bare ground. People explain this by saying, "*no se dejan pisar al suelo*" (they should not allow him to step on the ground). In the other two processions, blossoms and petals are thrown over the heads of the saints' images, falling around them like rain, bathing them, as it were, in coolness and sweet smells. In this case, the images are carried on their little tables, their feet touching the loose blossoms that heap ever higher on the tabletop. There is no sense at all that the men or women who carry the image stand for the saint and so might need to walk on flowers. They function like the black-garbed helpers in Japanese drama who help the actors change costume on stage, but who are "invisible" to the audience. Sprigs of basil find their way onto the images themselves or on the little tables on which they are carried, another instance of healing offerings.

The parallel with rituals that care for the dead is strong. But this is not surprising because the figures in the processions walk on their way to death. The observers, active and implicated, must help make their way sweet and transformative.

Processions and Pilgrimages

The Zapotec of Juchitán are a people dedicated to procession. Virtually every important occasion in the life of individuals or in the community life is marked by a procession. They are a way in which a person announces a change of status to the community at large, whether it is marriage, undertaking a sponsorship of a vela or a church society, the fifteenth birthday for girls, or every family-based observance that has to do with death—the funeral and Masses for forty days and one, seven, and twenty years. They are also ways in which the participants demonstrate their commitment to these important occasions as well as their ability to "perform" them well. Vela societies are a good example. They sponsor processions that leave from the mayordomo's house and go to the parish church. People crowd the route to see the floats, costumes, horseback riders, as well as to jostle for the little gifts that are thrown out to the crowd by the young women of the vela. Of course, politicians also choose parades as a way of either eliciting support in contested races or as a triumphal march to the municipal palace when they have succeeded. Nothing is celebrated in private; everything is held up to the community for its acknowledgment and commitment.

The tradition goes back to ancient Mesoamerica when the Zapotec at their great ceremonial sites would have processions in honor of the gods, for winning a battle, to celebrate a particular seasonal ritual, and to bury their leaders. These would be richly costumed, accompanied by music and priests, and the people would line the route waiting to see the status and fortunes of their countrymen portrayed in larger-than-life symbols and action. The site of Monte Albán is an excellent example. The ceremonial and political center of the vast region controlled by the Zapotec and, later, the Mixtec, inhabitants of Monte Albán occupied the top of a broad hill that reached above the level of the plateau. Those who belonged to this region and whose labor supported it lived in terraces down the sides of the hill. The layout of the civic center lent itself perfectly to processions and public ceremonies.

It is not surprising, then, that Stations of the Cross were adopted wholeheartedly by the Zapotec of Juchitán. In this case, the change of status being recognized is the impending death and resurrection of Christ. For the faithful who walk the Via Crucis and for those who sponsor Stations, the pilgrimage announces their willingness to take up the cross and follow Christ. They have made it their own by the very particular use of flowers of the wild, of incense, and of the healing power of the flowers that have hung on the crucifix carried by Christ. Given the importance of public witness and the pattern of adding new elements to the Zapotec cultural repertoire without abandoning the old, it seems very likely that these open-air pilgrimages will continue indefinitely. They are supplemented by the Via Crucis inside the church, but that will remain in the realm of private devotion until it becomes both public and communal.

8

Nabaana Ro

Roman Catholic Liturgy and Zapotec Practice

"In Holy Week, we savor death; we write it in colors and smells."[1]

—Hebert Rasgado, personal communication, March 2006

On the last Friday of Lent, the Friday of la Virgen de Dolores, the saints in the churches begin to get restless. Pilgrimages, processions, being out of their places of ordinary time will mark the next nine days. The saints will be taken out of niches, dressed in the attire of Holy Week, will accept the prayers and offerings of hundreds of Juchitecos, and be carried through the streets, main characters in the cast of the Passion. After their moment in the spotlight, they will return to their customary places, attended to, not by hundreds, but by the faithful few who belong to the religious societies. These nine days are a major disjuncture in the pattern of everyday life. They are appropriately named Nabaana Ro, a time of grieving, extending well beyond the Holy Week of Roman Catholic tradition, and including all the departed ancestors in the mourning.

Mention of Holy Week is almost nonexistent in the literature about the Isthmus Zapotec, with the notable exception of Gabriel López Chiñas (1969), a Juchiteco writer, and he writes almost exclusively about the unique custom of visiting the cemeteries (see chapter 9). Miguel Covarrubias (1946) reflects the views of most when he includes Easter as one of the major holidays and describes it as "the only important purely Catholic holiday" (p. 379). It may

---

1. In this conversation, Hebert was speaking Spanish and used the verb *escribir*, meaning "to write." The Isthmus Zapotec verb *rucaa*, which may be translated as "to write," has the additional meanings of "to fix" or "fasten." So we might well understand what he said as "we fix death in colors and smells." On December 4, 2007, Hebert died at age forty-six of a brain tumor. Even though he died in Mexico City, his body returned to Juchitán, greeted by music and the fragrance of jasmine and frangipani.

seem so if one focuses on the Great Vigil and the Easter Mass or if one accepts
the Roman Catholic liturgy of Holy Thursday, Friday, and Saturday as being
all that happens. In fact, that liturgy represents only a tiny fraction of the nine
days of observances and the beliefs that sustain them. This chapter describes
the events of these packed nine days, understanding that both Roman Catholic
liturgical practice and Zapotec observance are mutually interactive and vital to
the ritual health of the community. The ways in which they are interwoven
illustrate the steady flow of community and the moments of transformation
that have formed the core of Zapotec culture since their beginning. Juchitán's
Nabaana Ro presents all the symbols associated with beliefs about death in a
heightened and unmistakable fashion; furthermore, those beliefs and symbols
cut across every domain of Zapotec life. This display is unique in Mesoamerica,
pointing to the tenacity of Zapotec values and the value of a strategy of flexibility in the face of opposition. Thus far, all but Zapotec writers have missed

Plate 31. Parish Church of San Vicente Ferrer. 2004. Photograph by Anya Peterson Royce.

the significance of the Zapotec elements that characterize every observance, have missed even their existence.

Last Friday in Lent—La Virgen de Dolores

The Friday of the Virgen de Dolores is a busy time. It is the last Stations of the Cross procession. Inside the church of San Vicente, an hermandad of men are walking the stations that line the walls of the nave. From late morning on, the men and women of the societies of the Virgen de Dolores and of the Christ of San Salvador del Mundo have been working steadily, dressing these two images, and bringing them to their places, San Salvador in front of the communion rail on the Epistle side and the Virgen de Dolores on the Gospel side, behind the rail but in front of the altar. This week will be a busy time, a constant flow of images from their accustomed niches against the walls to places of prominence and display.

As the women and men work, others come in and out of the church not only to pray and petition those saints who have been helpful in the past, but also to pray particularly to these two because they have heightened powers during these days. A woman stands in front of the Virgin and prays "*Xunaxi yuuba'*" (Virgin of sorrows).[2] She has brought frangipani wreathes to offer the Virgin and scatters jasmine blossoms at her feet. When she moves on to another image, her place is quickly filled by women who have been waiting patiently to make their supplications. Those in charge of the images are remarkably gracious, stopping their work to let people approach the image, pray, and drape flowers over its head or lay them at its feet. Most of the flowers brought by supplicants are frangipani, jasmine, tuberose, flor de china petals, and sometimes hibiscus blossoms. They bring them in plastic bags, in buckets, hung over their arms and all are fresh, just out of the water. The image of San Salvador has three or four branches of albahaca (a small-leaved basil of the Isthmus) in his hand. Basil is used as the primary healing herb for those healers who diagnose and cure by reading the patient's body through touch and massage. This makes it a popular choice for offering to the saints.

---

2. *Xunaxi*, the Zapotec word for "virgin," carries with it the sense of sweet smell. *Nanaxhi* means sweet; *rindá' naxhi* means to smell sweet. Smell is a critical sense for the Zapotec in general and is prominent during Holy Week. All the flowers used to adorn the saints have powerful fragrances, very sweet, like jasmine and frangipani, *coyol* and *cordoncillo*. Incense, *guxhu bidó'* ("altar smoke"), is omnipresent. The fragrance of candles, added to flowers and incense, is essential for the efficacy of the rituals in which the saints figure just as they are during the wake and novena for the dead. Sweetness or sweet smell is linked with good and with purity. Bad smells are associated with evil and pollution. *Rindá' dxaba'* means "it stinks" or "stinking." The Devil is *binidxaba'*, literally "stinking person."

Santo Entierro

Another image which attracts particular attention on this day is the Santo Entierro (Buried Saint) or *Bixhoze enteru* (Buried Father). At this point, he is still in his glass-paned casket under the niche that normally holds the Virgen de Dolores. He is always on the circuit of prayers when people come to the church, but this day people have brought vases of white gladiolas and tuberose (funeral flowers) filled out with bunches of flowering dill, another of the healing herbs. In front of the flowers are ten to fifteen burning tapers set in their own wax on the marble floor. Women offer prayers, reaching out to touch the flowers. Sometimes they break one off, and rub it over their face and arms because its contact with the saint has given it powers to heal. All flowers that have been in contact with any of the images have similar powers. Mothers will rub them over their children; others will take them home to a sick relative. It is not simply the contact with the image, however, that makes them powerful, it is their inherent "fragrance," "freshness," "moistness," and "being of the wild" that makes them special.

Sweets and Sweetness

Sweetness is duplicated outside the church, in the courtyard and along Belisario Dominguez, the street that runs in front of San Vicente. Dozens of women vendors have set up their tables in the late afternoon and do a brisk business selling food and drink as well as the *cascarones* (emptied eggs refilled with flour or confetti), which send children shrieking after each other trying to leave their mark. Much of the food falls into the "sweet" (*nanaxhi* or *dxiña'*) category, and of that, most is made and sold primarily during the end of Lent and Holy Week—*regañadas* and *dxiña'*.[3]

López Chiñas (1969) writes about these sweets referring to them as *dxiña' ridaa' bladu*, or sweets served on plates. He is talking about the custom of women bringing their own containers for the sweets in their syrup. Women will still bring containers, especially if they live close to the vendors, but more often, vendors put the orders in plastic bags. The sweet drink sold on these occasions is a *raspado*—a glass filled with ice shavings over which is poured a

---

3. The fruits appropriate for this treatment fall into a category called *cuananaxhi* and include mango, papaya, plums, limes, sweet potato, jicaco, almonds (in their entire shell), guayaba, and nanche. Other sweet fruit such as tamarind, mamey, and chicozapote are not used, perhaps because the boiling process would destroy their integrity. In addition to selling at the *ermita*, women who make the sweets also go to the homes of good customers with their huge basins of syrupy fruit where they always find eager customers.

syrup, often with chunks of the particular fruit. Among the most popular are raspados of tamarind, mamey, cantaloupe, orange, or watermelon. Raspados can be had at other times but they are considered special treats during this season. It would be hard to overestimate the amount of dxiña' and regañadas consumed during this one week. People are constantly snacking on them, sending help-ers to buy more, and buying extra to pack in the care packages sent to those Juchitecos unfortunate enough to live outside the city.[4] While every Juchiteco seems to have a sweet tooth, the traditional diet does not contain refined sweets, although tropical fruits such as pineapple, mangos, papaya, mamey, and chico zapote are eaten both as snacks and at the end of meals. Stalks of sugar cane also remain a popular treat.

The other center of business in Holy Week is the flower market, normally at the north end of the main plaza in front of the municipal buildings but now spilling over into the interior, along all the radiating spokes of the park. The scent is overpowering from masses of frangipani, tuberose, sweetheart roses, gardenias, jasmine, and coyol still in its pods. Basil and dill are everywhere as are the loose petals of flor de china. There are also the cultivated flowers brought in from Oaxaca and elsewhere—lilies, carnations, baby's breath (called nube or cloud)—and all varieties of chrysanthemums.

Saturday—Procession of San Salvador

On Saturday, the images in the church receive visitors and gifts of flowers most of the day. The visits are punctuated by Masses, most of them Masses for the dead because more festive commemorations are regarded as inappropriate during Lent. Just after six in the evening, the procession of San Salvador to the Iglesia del Panteón Domingo de Ramos takes its leave of San Vicente. The men of the hermandad bring him to the central aisle where he rests during prayers led by a lay prayer leader. People approach and hang frangipani wreaths around his neck, and someone scatters flor de china petals at the donkey's feet (both

---

4. These care packages, or *cajas*, as in *voy a hacer una caja para* . . . ("I am going to make a box for . . ."), are prepared and sent any time someone is going anywhere where there is a relative. They contain food almost exclusively—fish, tamales (especially of iguana or the fat beef tamales made for Day of the Dead), shrimp, heavy cream, cheese, turtle eggs, *dxiña'*, sea salt, *curado*, totopos, and whatever food the recipient really craves. I always carry a *caja* with me for relatives in Mexico City when I leave Juchitán. On one trip, after the Day of the Dead celebrations in Juchitán, I carried a box full of the tamales one is given at visits to Day of the Dead altars. On the return in 2003 after Holy Week, I had, among other things, a pig's head, which was going to be made into *pozole*. Maintaining the connection between Juchitán and those living away from it is a fundamental value, and one at which people work very hard. Since they cannot send the fiesta or celebration, they send the foods associated with them.

the donkey and his rider, San Salvador, are on top of the little table platform). As the prayers are finished, men pick up the image on its platform, and carry it down the center aisle and out of the church. A young boy walks to one side carrying a lighted candle (veladora); men of the society walk in front, led by the prayer leader. The women walk behind, several with bags filled with magenta petals, which they throw over the image from time to time. Seen from the front, it appears as though San Salvador is walking through a shower of deep red petals. He is accompanied by members of the hermandad and by others who join them along the way, his way made sweet by flowers thrown at his feet and over his head. Arriving at the Panteón Domingo de Ramos, he is taken to the home of a family who live nearby. Those who accompanied him in procession are given tamales and *bupu*, the ritual chocolate drink so common in this season. Early the next morning, San Salvador is taken to the cemetery chapel where he awaits the blessing of the palms. At six in the morning of Palm Sunday (Domingo de Ramos), when I arrived with the family to clean the tombs of relatives and arrange the flowers, he was sitting on his donkey in the middle of the little church, bravely facing out, a palm branch in one hand. The rezador had come even earlier, and left two big bundles of palms at the donkey's feet and lit a candle before going off to take care of other business. The church had been swept, all the debris of the last year removed, and purple paper squares (*papel picado*) suspended across the ceiling.

In front of the church and all along the west-facing cemetery wall, the business side of Palm Sunday was getting into high gear. Oxcarts and trucks loaded with palm for building walls around recent tombs, little push-carts selling hot dogs and "*hamburguesas*," carts and stands offering tacos and garnachas, women everywhere with their tin tubs of regañadas, bullying the for-hire workers into carrying their tubs and chairs to the best places inside the cemetery, and, of course, the vendors of sweets sweeping through the gates, heavy basins on their heads.

Palm Sunday

When I returned at 9:00 a.m. with Mavis for the departure of the Palm Sunday procession, the sun was almost directly above the church and the heat was rising off the street. People of the hermandad were spilling out of the cool dark of the church, passing out palms to the members and to those, like us, who had come to accompany them. Somehow all was sorted out and the procession began to take shape—the orphans from Pimpollo marched in front in two lines separated by a space wide enough for the priest, Padre Pancho, to walk back and forth; a band of musicians paid for by the mayordomos followed; they in turn were followed by men and women, all carrying palms; the prayer leader

Plate 32. Profa. Delia Ramírez Fuentes buying sweets during Holy Week. 2003. Photograph by Anya Peterson Royce.

walked in front of the image of San Salvador, which was carried by four men. Behind the image came another large crowd of people, mostly women, who from time to time would throw handfuls of flower petals over the head of the saint. Despite the heat and the noise of vendors and people on their way to the cemetery, the children begging their parents for one of the many toys for sale along all the cemetery routes, taxis and oxcarts inching their way forward, Padre Pancho in constant motion, orchestrating everything, the procession had a power and a poignancy—the rain of petals flashing in the sunlight, the heavy scent of frangipani, the rhythm of the prayers interspersed with shouts of "Viva Cristo Rey!" (Long live Christ the King!), and the rustling clatter of palms.

In Juchitán, the sacred and the secular flow into each other. This is not to say that there is no cultural category that corresponds to what we might call "religious behavior," borrowing a term from Charles Frake (1964). Rather, it is that Zapotec religious behavior allows for or encompasses much of what Western society might see as secular. If we see a procession such as the one I have just described as sacred, then Juchitecos step in and out of this frame all the time—to attend to a small child, to buy a sweet, to chat with a friend. Behavior such as this does not lessen the power or the sacredness of the act. It is an acknowledgment that life must be attended to as part of one's "work," just as participation in processions, saints' observances, Masses, rituals around the home altar is part of one's "work." Neither is privileged; both are expected. There are times, however, during which individuals are expected to set aside ordinary obligations—the chief mourner for a death focuses all her energy on mourning for forty days during which time others take on her usual obligations; prayer leaders' work requires that kind of singular concentration; the twelve men who are the apostles on Thursday, Friday, and Saturday of Holy Week are relieved of all other obligations. In those moments, ordinary individuals become exemplars of communal values—a different sort of "work." And, while ever-present, that peculiarly Juchiteco aesthetic demands to be followed in all the actions of this week filled with ritual large and small.

With the image of San Salvador back in the church of San Vicente, the Palm Sunday Mass was celebrated. At its conclusion, members of the hermandad went to the house of the mayordomos. They continued their observance of the day in which this evocation of Christ reigns back at the chapel of the Panteón Domingo de Ramos. They had arranged themselves along the chapel's concrete apron as is appropriate for festivities. Men and women sat separated from each other, tables of botana (snacks that are given out to participants and guests) and beer behind the women. The band was alternating between sones (Zapotec music) and modern Latin-American dance tunes. Just outside the entrance to the church, men sat at two tables, one of which had bundles of palms, now blessed, and the other with brightly colored ribbons with the name of the her-mandad on them. You could buy either or both for a small contribution. The sale of ribbons characterizes the activities of all the hermandades during Holy Week, and the money they collect helps to buy new items of clothing for the saints or to make repairs to the chapels.

Regardless of whether they bought ribbons or palms, people entered the chapel and lit candles. They would make the round of the three crosses at the back of the chapel, touching them, leaving flowers, and also rubbing their faces and arms with flowers that were already there in contact with the crosses. While individuals move freely between the sacred and the secular—indeed, during this week, events in these two realms overlap or are happening at the same time—there is a peculiar sense of the sacred that confronts one when entering one of the chapels or churches pressed into service in these days. Walking into the Iglesia del Panteón Domingo de Ramos during the early evening of Palm Sunday, I left behind the sound of the band and people talking and the smell of beer and garnachas, and entered the quiet realm of murmured prayers and petitions, the scent of jasmine, the lingering smell of incense, and the glow of candles. That kind of experience was even more dramatic on the evening of Good Friday, moving from the sweltering heat and the smell of fish remnants on the street in front of the Capilla de la Misericordia to the inside of the chapel itself, which now held the body of the crucified Christ in his coffin. The hundreds of people who had accompanied him there in the silent procession had left mounds of sweet-smelling flowers everywhere; willow branches along the back of the benches gave off their coolness; and somewhere behind the chapel, the plaintive song of a bere lele[5] filled the air. The fragrance, the coolness, the prayers, and the song all made this seem as though I had stepped into another world.

Holy Monday

The day begins early on Holy Monday. The hermandad of Nuestro Padre Jesucristo (the society of Our Father Jesus Christ) comes early to San Vicente to prepare the image for the 10:00 a.m. Mass. They bring him from the narthex of the church, where he is normally the first image one sees to the left upon entering, to a position in front of the communion rail on the Gospel side. The image of San Salvador is opposite him, still receiving visits from petitioners. This image of Christ is carrying a large cross on his right shoulder. This morning he is dressed in white and gold, with frangipani and jasmine draped around his neck. Two large vases of white Asiatic lilies and gladiolas flank him, and, between them, on the floor, several large votive candles burn. The Virgin of Sorrows, whose place he has taken, is back in her niche over the Santo Entierro. The 10:00 a.m. Mass is a standard Roman Catholic Eucharist, brief and on the topic of the lectionary because Father Esau, who seldom strays from the lessons of the day, was the celebrant. Afterward, the prayer leaders of the hermandad took over, praying the rosary. When they had finished, everyone was given an opportunity to take their leave of Nuestro Padre, touching his clothes and the flowers. Those who were not going to the mayordomo's house approached and left their monetary donation. The rest gathered up the large candles and left in procession, women with candles, the mayordomo, the prayer leader, and the remaining members of the hermandad and their guests. This was the third and last Mass of that hermandad for the year. That morning's novena at the mayordomo's house was also the third and last. This Mass, like all the subsequent

---

5. Hearing the *bere lele* song accompanying the crucified Christ left an unforgettable impression. Vicente Fuentes told me that when the beloved writer Gabriel López Chiñas died and was brought back to the Casa de la Cultura to lie in state, a *bere lele* came into the room where the coffin was and began crying in that mournful cadence.

Plate 33. Image of Christ in his coffin on Tuesday of Holy Week. 2003. Photograph by Anya Peterson Royce.

ones of Holy Week, demonstrates the important, indeed, the dominant role of the laity in all the observances from Palm Sunday to the Great Vigil. The priest presided over the Eucharist, but the rest of the service was conducted by lay prayer leaders and members of the hermandad—this includes the prayers, the dress and care of the saint, the flowers used to smooth his passage. Not only does the laity determine all the ritual outside the church, they also take a direct hand in what happens inside the church before and after the Mass. As we shall see in the case of Holy Thursday and Good Friday, virtually every aspect of the church ritual is elaborated and shaped by the lay members of the societies.

Holy Tuesday—*Santo Entierro*

In what had become a rhythm for me, I went to San Vicente early on Tuesday morning to see the latest arrangement and dress of the saints. The end of each row of pews was decorated with arches of banana fronds for the morning Mass. Today, Holy Tuesday, was the Mass for the Santo Entierro,[6] and so, as

6. No one I questioned offered any explanation about why the crucified Christ would have a Mass in His honor on the Tuesday of Holy Week, nor can I find any parallel in the Roman Catholic liturgy. It simply has been the custom to do so. The liturgy for Good Friday remains the same so the Tuesday ritual does not replace the liturgy of the crucifixion.

I watched, members of the hermandad of the Santo Entierro, settled him into his coffin, which was placed on a long table in front of the communion rail on the Gospel Side. The coffin was parallel to the rail. Christ's head rested at the end away from the central aisle. What struck me about this scene and others that would be played out as the week progressed was how much it resembled the rituals surrounding the death, velorio, and novena of any Zapotec individual (see chapters 2 and 6). The dead Christ was laid out in his coffin, lined with white satin. At each of the four corners stood beeswax candles as large as Paschal candles. Giant vases of white flowers—gladiolas, lilies, chrysanthemums—marched down each long side of the coffin, and stood at both ends. Votive candles took up the remaining spaces. Around and in the coffin were all the flowers of the wild—jasmine, hibiscus, frangipani, and a sprig of basil. Christ's left hand held *lilias de San José* (Easter lilies), and his right was filled with jasmine blossoms and gardenias. When I had gone to the velorio of Don Rafael Saavedra the preceding week, his oldest daughter had sprinkled jasmine blossoms in his open coffin. The ba' yaa for his novena was one of the prettiest and most traditionally Zapotec I have seen—a base of cordoncillo (guie' daná), jasmine and cream and red frangipani, and red single hibiscus framing the white and cream flowers. This kind of ba' yaa would be echoed on Holy Thursday as part of the liturgy in San Vicente. Flanking the ba' yaa of Don Rafael just as they had flanked his coffin were vases of white gladiolas, lilies, baby's breath, and mums. Four large candles marked the corners of the flower body. Coming so closely one upon the other, I was struck by the parallels.

This Christ of the Santo Entierro has limbs that can be articulated so he can be positioned in the coffin, and, perhaps more important, so that he can be hung on the cross on Good Friday. In placing him in the coffin, the hermandad members make sure that his hands rest on the sides and that his head rises above the level of the coffin. In Juchitán, viewing the body of the dead is mandatory—no coffins are ever closed at Zapotec wakes. People need to take their leave, often leaving flowers and other small, precious items in the coffin. Because the coffin of the Santo Entierro is raised above eye level, viewing in the normal way is not possible, but one can touch his hands, placing flowers in them, and one can see his face.

The Santo Entierro looms over the scene. It is the most affecting presence in the Mass. The officiating priest was dwarfed by the coffin, and left by the side door off the chancel just as soon as the Mass concluded. Then the men of the hermandad all stood and approached the coffin; led by a rezador, they prayed a rosary. As the last prayers were uttered, six musicians entered the church; two saxophonists walked slowly down the aisle toward the coffin playing a very slow piece of sacred music chosen for this set of prayers. They were joined by another saxophone and a clarinet; finally two trumpets approached. The melancholy notes reverberated in the sanctuary, bouncing off the walls, amplified almost beyond bearing. After playing two pieces, the musicians left, retracing their steps down the central aisle. The men of the hermandad picked up four of the five candles and carried them out in procession followed by women carrying vases of flowers, two more smaller candles and two of the tin candleholders. The invited guests brought up the rear of the procession winding its way to the mayordomo's house. When they had gone, perhaps forty people who had been at the Mass approached the coffin to touch the flowers, asking for blessings, and carrying a few flowers with them for healing they said.

A similar ritual took place at the four other churches, which had images of the Santo Entierro. At the Church of Esquipulas, the 10:00 a.m. Mass was sponsored by a mayordoma who treated her guests to plates of breaded fish, a little salad of radishes and lettuce, a container of frijoles, and a small bowl of *dxiña' de camote* (sweet potato cooked in syrup). The Church of Esquipulas was decorated with willow branches rather than banana fronds, a matter of choice because both occupy the same functional category. The music was the same, however, and it is music played only during Holy Week.

Holy Wednesday—La Virgen de la Soledad

Holy Wednesday brought more changes in the saints on display. For the first time, the Virgen de la Soledad made her appearance outside her niche.[7] She is the patron saint of the state of Oaxaca, with her own cathedral in the capital city. Her hermandad has dressed her in a new black robe with gold trim down the front. Her crown is distinctive, a copy of the original in Oaxaca City. She sits on her low table in front of the communion rail on the Epistle Side. Frangipani wreaths hang two inches thick around her neck. Two large vases of white gladiolas flank her, and votive candles as well as two larger candles wrapped around with black ribbon sit on the floor in front of her. At her feet, on the little table, frangipani, jasmine, and hibiscus are evidence of a constant stream of petitioners.

---

7. La Virgen de la Soledad is another image of Mary, in some quarters the Mary whose son is crucified and lies in a tomb. She is totally alone, hence her name. For some in Juchitán, she represents the Magdalena, the one to whom the risen Christ first appears. For the people of Oaxaca, she is their Mary, their saint, the one who chose them and watches over them. She has the status in Oaxaca that the Virgen de Guadalupe has for the nation of Mexico. She has a crucial role in Juchitán's Holy Week, especially on Good Friday when she is the one to whom are presented all the implements of the crucifixion. Parsons (1936) documents la Soledad's part in rituals throughout the year in Mitla but there is no mention of her during Mitla Holy Week observances. In Spain, she is part of the Good Friday procession in many cities and villages, but this has not been the case in Juchitán.

Our Father Jesus (Nuestro Padre Jesús), now in black and silver, is back in his place in the narthex. There are two large, black wrapped candles on the floor at his feet and between two parallel rows of pews perpendicular to the image. Members of his hermandad will shortly settle in to pray rosaries and Stations of the Cross. At the back, four men were readying the deep purple curtain that will cover the decorated back wall of the church and the altar on Good Friday. As I left the church, I noticed the coffin that held and will again hold the Santo Entierro, sitting without candles or keepers in one of the side chapels. The four large candles that had marked its corners the day before were unceremoniously stacked inside.

The morning Mass, as on the preceding two days, is sponsored by the hermandad of Holy Wednesday, and the meal given by the mayordoma is the same as all those during the first part of Holy Week—breaded fish, beans, bread, and a sweet of fruit.

Holy Thursday

On Holy Thursday, after Wednesday's very busy day and evening, I was at San Vicente for what I thought was to be an 8:00 a.m. Mass.[8] The Mass began, in fact, at 9:00 a.m. What I did see at that earlier hour was the beginning of two and a half days of prayers by twelve men who take on the roles of the apostles. These two days—Holy Thursday and Good Friday—are also the core of Zapotec practice and belief during Holy Week; they are structured as a funeral and an acknowledgment of a revered relative and ancestor, Jesus Christ.

The twelve men, ranging in age from one in his twenties to the majority in their sixties and older, sat in two rows of folding chairs facing each other. Their helper, in his fifties, was seated behind them. The chairs were arranged perpendicular to the communion rail and in the space between it and where the pews began. Willow branches were lashed to the chair backs so that the appearance was of a forest or garden. A ba' yaa lay between the two rows of men. The foundation was a large woven mat, on top of which was laid a dark brown heavy cloth. The "body" consisted of guie' xhuuba' (jasmine of the Isthmus), which formed the shape of a body, head toward the altar.[9] As the day

---

8. Under the presidency of Ernesto Zedillo, Mexico adopted daylight savings time. While this was and is the official position, at least half the population pays no attention to it. Whenever a time is given for an event, it is usually modified by "*ora de Zedillo*," or "*ora de Dios*," (Zedillo's time or God's time) or in Juchitán, "*ora cubi*" or "*ora yooxho*" (new time or old time). If no modifier is given, people will usually ask but then will be unable to make the necessary transposition. I usually erred on the side of being too early, as in this case.

9. As I described in chapter 4, this position with the head toward the altar is the one used when the deceased was unmarried. It is fitting, then, that this ba' yaa for Christ should be oriented this way.

went on, other flowers would be added to the ba' yaa—frangipani, hibiscus, basil, cordoncillo, and petals of flor de china.

Father Pancho celebrated Mass, garlands of frangipani hung around his neck. When he finished, he left by the side door of the chancel. The twelve apostles began to pray—throughout the two and a half days, their prayers would sometimes be in Zapotec, sometimes in Spanish. (The only time there was a translation of Zapotec into Spanish was the Thursday liturgy of the seven words of Christ.) Each man recited the scripture first in Zapotec, then in Spanish. When they finished, they stood, and each was given a candle. The women of the hermandad were given vases of white gladiolas that had been next to the altar. The procession left the church—apostles, helper, prayer leader, the mayordomo, and the women with flowers. A band awaited them on the street outside the church and led them to the mayordomo's house, playing the kind of music associated with funerals. The mayordomo then gave them food and drink. The apostles made their way back to the church at noon, refreshed and ready to continue their cycle of prayers.

By 2:00 p.m., the women of the hermandad had set up tables in the court-yard of the church to sell ribbons and to receive contributions of money. The sound system played religious music with a tropical beat sung by a women's chorus. In the meanwhile, the apostles were in their seats in the church, alter-

Plate 34. Twelve men as the Apostles during the Holy Thursday liturgy. 2003. Photograph by Anya Peterson Royce.

Plate 35. Ba' yaa in front of the altar of San Vicente on Holy Thursday. 2003. Photograph by Anya Peterson Royce.

nately praying and resting. Delia and I returned at 5:40 p.m. for the 6:00 Mass only to discover that it was on the other time schedule that had preceded the new daylight savings time (an hour earlier), but we stayed through some of the apostles' prayers. When we returned at 7:00 p.m., the church was packed and waiting for the reenactment of the Last Supper.

A lone woman walked down the center aisle from the altar to the front door, scattering frangipani blossoms to make the way sweet. A young man carrying a cross faced the altar and walked slowly backward leading the procession—apostles, musicians, Father Pancho, and finally the congregation folding itself into the aisle. Once more, the notes of funereal music filled the church, followed the procession out into the courtyard, then to the table set under the arcades. Water and symbols of water were everywhere. The chairs sprouted willow branches; slices of watermelon and glasses filled with frangipani were at each place with the familiar Lenten fare of fish, bread, frijoles, and sweetened fruit in syrup. Small glasses of wine completed the meal. The apostles' helper poured cool water into each frangipani-filled glass, and other members of the hermandad passed shallow basins of watermelon through the crowd so we all could participate in this last supper. Father Pancho played the role of Christ, reading through the scripture of the first Eucharist. He and others followed with the commandment to love one another.

At the end of the meal, Father Pancho and the apostles stood and made their way slowly back into the church. We followed them back but found that many people had come into the church while we were outside so the pews were filled to capacity and beyond. After the Liturgy of the Word and a short homily, Father Pancho washed the feet of each apostle. Lay women distributed communion to the crowded church. At the end of the Mass, Father Pancho put the monstrance with the Blessed Sacrament on the altar, blessed some candles that people had brought, and left.

Christ of the Sacred Heart

It was past 8:00 p.m., but the observances continued. This time it was the turn of the hermandad de la Sagrado Corazón (the Society of the Sacred Heart). The image of Christ of the Sacred Heart had been displayed during the whole afternoon in front of the communion rail. Now the men who have vowed to care for him lifted the table on which he stood, carried it down the center aisle, and out the door. The congregation followed in silence. The men placed the image of Christ against the outside wall of the church to the right of the front door. He was dressed in a white satin robe with a red sash over his left shoulder and crossed at his right hip. One of the men bound his eyes with a black and grey neckerchief, while others brought willow branches that they leaned against the wall behind and on either side of him. Women of the Society of the Sacred Heart brought frangipani wreaths to hang around his neck. When they had finished, the men returned with two sections of barred fence and enclosed him in this prison. After the sections were lashed together, they wove more willows through the bars. During all of this, the congregation and the hermandad were singing "*El está con nosotros y no lo conocemos. Su nombre es el Señor*" ("He is among us and we do not know Him. His name is Lord"). It was a powerful moment, and tears flowed down many faces, young and old. Blind and bound, Christ drew a constant stream of people. They brought him candles and flowers; they stayed a moment, stretching their hands through the bars to touch his clothes and the frangipani wreaths. The Sacred Heart women settled in for the night in a wedged-shaped row of chairs facing the imprisoned Christ. They prayed, talked softly, straightened the candles, adding new ones when needed, and organizing the many flowers that people brought. Near them were tables set up with the various religious organizations selling ribbons and taking contributions. Inside the church, the members of those societies took turns keeping watch over the Blessed Sacrament. At the street entrance to the churchyard, women were doing their "work," selling garnachas, sweets, regañadas, curado (nanches or plums steeped in alcohol), cascarones, and candles. The street itself had become a huge fair, food sellers, beer vendors, bupu[10] vendors, and trampolines in wire cages and big plastic slides, which amused the children while their parents watched, stocked up on sweets, or visited Christ. From my second floor window, which faced onto the churchyard, I could hear the women's prayers floating on the night air, and when I looked out, I could see the blindfolded Christ lit by the flicker of dozens of candles.

Good Friday

Good Friday, 7:00 a.m.: Father Pancho is sitting with the women of the Sacred Heart who seem to be in no hurry to end their vigil. The apostles were already at their prayers, in Zapotec, inside the church. It will be another long day, filled with prayers, processions, the crucifixion, a final procession, and keeping vigil. The cast is large, beginning with the five saints who are the focal characters in this last day of Christ's Passion—La Virgen de Dolores, San Juan, La Virgen de la Soledad (representing Mary Magdalene), Nuestro Padre Jesucristo, and El Santo Entierro. The human cast includes the women and men of the hermandades, who care for the saints, pray to them, dress them, and ensure that they remain in people's hearts. This adds another 200 or so people. The clergy, of course, play a role, two attached to San Vicente, another four serving the city's remaining churches. Finally, the faithful, hundreds who move in and out of the various services, vigils, rituals, processions throughout the day, and for whom this is the most important observance of the religious calendar.

The early morning hours are spent dressing the saints and getting them into place on their *mesa del santo* or "saint's table" (a small table with poles for carrying). The two Virgins and San Juan are outside the communion rail—La Virgen de la Soledad and San Juan on the Epistle side and the Virgen de Dolores on the Gospel side. The two Virgins have white robes over their black gowns. The bloodied face of Christ is depicted on the front of each robe; La Soledad also has depictions of the crown of thorns and the nails with which Christ was crucified. The sides of her robe are stained with streaks of blood-red dye. San Juan is dressed in a white robe and has a gold stole. As they are being dressed and tied to the tables, they receive petitioners who leave flowers around their

---

10. *Bupu* is a festive drink available everywhere at this time of the year. It is a thin corn gruel (*atole*) with unsweetened chocolate and raw sugar. The *bupera* who makes the drink whips a froth of cacao, *panela* "unsweetened brown sugar," and frangipani blossoms, and serves it in a *xiga*, a *jícara*, or "hollow half gourd."

necks, at their feet, tucked into their hands, or in the folds of their robes. I watched as one woman emptied her bag of frangipani garlands, loose jasmine, and flor de china, then took out a branch of tuberose and tied it to the hand of San Juan, a fragrant sword for this beloved saint. In a short while, the images are so covered with flowers that you can no longer see the marks of the punishments or crucifixion.

Both the members of the hermandades and the petitioners are readying the saints for the first of the Good Friday processions; this one quite different in tone from the joyous entry of Christ into Jerusalem on Palm Sunday, less than a week ago. That one, from the church at the municipal cemetery to its final glorious arrival at the church of San Vicente, was filled with song, cries of "Long Live Christ the King," the waving of palms, and children and adults in festive clothes. This one represents the agonizing walk of Christ to his crucifixion, and it is accomplished in silence.

Plate 36. Image of La Dolorosa on Good Friday in San Vicente Ferrer. 2003. Photograph by Anya Peterson Royce.

Our Father Jesus Christ is alone at the end of the center aisle in the narthex. He is dressed in black, carrying the heavy black and silver cross on one shoulder. He faces the other images that surround the altar. The ba' yaa is gone now. Outside in the churchyard, the women still sit with the imprisoned Christ of the Sacred Heart, and the big wooden cross on which Christ will be crucified rests against the wall waiting to be brought into the church. The apostles are resting from their prayers, sitting in the shade of the arcades.

Procession of Christ, the Virgin, and Saint John

At 11:00 a.m. the apostles and members of several hermandades are assembled again in the church, and the prayers for Our Father Jesus Christ begin. At their close, four men lift him high on their shoulders, and preceded by the

Plate 37. Christ of the noon Good Friday procession. 2003. Photograph by Anya Peterson Royce.

apostles, leave the church. They walk on a thin carpet of flower petals, continually renewed by the petals thrown over the head of Christ. Women, dressed in *enagua de olán* (full, gathered skirt with a wide, white ruffle) follow the image. Men and women both join the procession just outside the churchyard and along the route. Umbrellas bob along high above the crowd offering some protection from the blaze of sun, if not from the heat.

As soon as the image of Christ leaves the church, the prayers begin for the Virgin of Sorrows (Virgen de Dolores). At their conclusion, she is lifted and carried by four women, all dressed in enagua de olán. Other women, walking behind, bathe the image with a soft rain of red flower petals. Women have a particular devotion to the Virgin of Sorrows. The colors today are colors of mourning—black, purple, dark blue, brown, or any of those combined with white. The men wear dark pants and white shirts and wear or carry their hats. The procession takes a different route from that followed by Christ.

Plate 38. La Dolorosa leaving San Vicente Ferrer for the noon Good Friday procession. 2003. Photograph by Anya Peterson Royce.

Finally, the image of San Juan exits the church, sent off by prayers and flower petals. He is carried by four men, and they and their followers take yet a third route through the streets. The interior of the church is quiet; the Virgen de la Soledad keeps watch as the men of the hermandad of the Santo Entierro begin discussing how to bring in the cross and raise it. The center aisle is all pink, red, and white from flor de china and guie' xhuuba' that were strewn before the saints.

People watch the processions from their doorways; some approach to scatter flowers in front of the image or leave them on the litter on which the image rests; others remain silent acknowledging their passage. More people join; more umbrellas punctuate the crowds. Each procession stops along its way for prayers at the places that were the Lenten Stations of the Cross. Everything moves slowly; the heat and dust are fierce; the images grow heavy; the crowds grow thicker. Silence reigns—dogs do not bark and children cease their play.

Plate 39. San Juan leaving San Vicente Ferrer for the noon Good Friday procession. 2003. Photograph by Anya Peterson Royce.

Perhaps two hours after leaving San Vicente, Christ, the Virgin, and John, the beloved disciple, come together (*el encuentro*) on the wide street in front of the Iglesia del Calvario. Christ and the Virgin approach each other; their bearers tip the images as if they are greeting each other: John approaches and looks on. Perhaps this is an enactment of Christ's speaking to Mary and John from the cross—he says to Mary, "Woman, here is your son," and to John, "Here is your mother" (John 19:27–28).

It is a deeply poignant moment; the crowd, in the hundreds even with the heat and the weariness of the processions, is utterly silent; tears make streaks through the dust that has settled on faces. It is the most human of moments—a mother encountering her son who is about to die in the most agonizing manner possible and a disciple who has given up everything to follow him. It is in moments such as these that we begin to glimpse what a theology of incarnation means. This is a story with which people are intimately familiar—it is no distant faith but one that is maintained through just such sacrifices and losses. It is a story so resonant in its fundamentals with the sacrifice, death, and rebirth of the Corn God so central to Mesoamerican cosmology that all the distance of centuries disappears.

The three processions become one, and it moves slowly back to San Vicente. The crowds are denser but just as silent. In San Vicente, the huge cross has been erected just to the Gospel side of the altar, and the Christ of the Santo Entierro has been hung on it. Four large mourning candles are stationed at the foot of the cross, and a purple curtain hides it all from view of the ever-growing congregation. The Virgen de la Soledad keeps her vigil in front of the communion rail. Identified by many as representing Mary Magdalene, her presence is supported by scripture, one of the women at the foot of the cross.

When the procession arrives a little after 2:00 p.m., the apostles lead it into the church. The Christ of Our Father stops at his accustomed place at the front of the sanctuary; the Virgin returns to her niche. Both images have been stripped of virtually all their flowers by people desiring their healing power. The image of John joins La Soledad in front of the communion rail. The apostles are back in their two lines of chairs in front of the altar. The women of the Sacred Heart occupy the front pews on the Gospel side.

Good Friday Vigil and Liturgy

We waited, in silence; only the whir of the fans disturbed the stillness. Shortly after 4:00 p.m., Father Pancho began the Good Friday liturgy by inviting the laity to pray the readings. He delivered a short homily, after which the women of the Sacred Heart hermandad read the Passion according to John, each woman taking turns at the lectern. They were followed by the apostles reciting the "seven last words of Christ," each one announcing his reading by saying, "*La* [*primera*] *palabra de Jesucristo*," doing the reading, and then repeating it in Zapotec.[11] Not all of the apostles were able to or wanted to do the readings in both languages, and so the readings fell to four rather than seven. After these readings, Father Pancho strode to the narthex where he picked up a large crucifix covered with a cloth. He raised it high in front of himself and brought it down the aisle, stopping twice to uncover more of the Christ and asking the congregation to look at it. He was met at the bottom of the chancel steps by a man who took the crucifix and held it in front of him, one end of the cross resting on the marble floor. Next to it was a chair with a woven basket on it meant to receive donations. Pancho invited the congregation to come up and adore the crucified Christ. People would approach, say a short prayer or not, leave a donation or not, but all would touch or kiss the cross or Christ. Returning to our seats, we found them filled by people who had come late, and had been standing at the back of the church. We sat through the remainder of the service seven or eight to pews that normally seat five.

Communion followed, rushed because Father Pancho had begun late, and, according to the liturgy, Christ had to be lowered from the cross by 6:00 p.m. Because of the large number of congregants, Communion was distributed by laywomen. After Communion, we moved into the last and in many ways the most moving part of the service. Four of the apostles donned white lace over-garments with black insets. These were the ones who would lower Christ from the cross. Others moved San Juan and the Virgen de la Soledad so that they faced each other, the Virgin the farthest on the Epistle side. The Centurion, made anonymous by his mask and leather dress, was led by two apostles over to the cross, and made his menacing approach, three long steps, each punctuated by the slash of his sword through the air. On the third and last step, he bent and kissed the base of the cross just as in the Stations of the Cross, he had kissed the frangipani hung around the cross. This reenactment of his threat to Christ that was part of the drama of the Stations of the Cross made a powerful impression on this most solemn of the church's observances.

Descent from the Cross

The descent from the cross was accomplished by four of the apostles working as a team. Two of the apostles dressed in the white and black garments climbed the ladders at the back of the cross, and untied the first set of white cloths that

---

11. Assigning origins to parts of ritual is always difficult, in this case, to what is on one level a Roman Catholic liturgy. It might be that what is here called the seven last words of Christ are part of the old Sarum rite in which Christ recounts what he has done for his people in bringing them out of Egypt and how he is repaid with crucifixion. Much of this is also incorporated in the liturgy of the Stations of the Cross.

held Christ to the cross. They handed these to the two other apostles waiting at the foot of the cross. These two then "presented" the cloths first to the Virgin of the Soledad, then to San Juan, before setting them aside to be packed away later. The presentation used the same three steps of the Centurion, and the tables on which the images stood were tilted as if acknowledging the presentation. The four working together repeated this a total of three times before all the bindings were loosed, presented, and put aside. The Centurion was then allowed to approach the two saints; on the third approach, he "kissed" them, the helpers holding the tables tipping them so that the Centurion could kiss the flowers around their necks, and by that gesture, earning their forgiveness.

Procession to the Chapel of the Misericordia

When Christ was finally unbound and lowered from the cross, the four apostles carried him to his coffin, placing him inside, wrapping him completely in the black and silver cloth. A band composed of five saxophones and one trumpet had entered the chancel from the side door, and now began to play a somber and sacred piece, the first time with a solo sax. Then they played as a group. When the last notes died out, a young man carrying a large sunburst cross began walking backward down the central aisle. The musicians followed first, then the apostles. Some carried the large glass-paned coffin; others carried the purple canopy on its four poles raising it over the coffin. The Centurion followed immediately behind the coffin. A mass of women dressed in mourning clothing brought up the rear. The procession stopped once inside the church, then once again outside in the churchyard. There, the two sets of mayordomos met the procession, kneeling on large woven mats with an incense burner in front of them. The women were in black with black lace head coverings; the men wore white guayaberas (a formal shirt worn outside the pants) with black armbands. One of the apostles censed the coffin while people heaped flowers— frangipani, jasmine, hibiscus—on top, hanging them especially around the cross that stands up at the one end but placing them wherever they could reach. More flowers were strewn on the ground in front of the coffin and showered over it. After this acknowledgment of Christ's passion by the mayordomos, the procession began again, stopping along the route to say rosaries, cense the coffin, and refresh the flowers. The streets were lined with men standing silently, hats and candles in hand.

As in the earlier procession, the Virgen de Dolores left the church next, carried by women. And finally, San Juan exited, attended by a small group of men and boys. The three images made their slow procession, silent except for the prayers, to the Chapel of the Misericordia. A stain of flowers and petals marked their passage.

Both change and continuity characterize this Good Friday procession. In 1972, it took place at dusk (Mexico was not then on daylight savings time)

Plate 40. Coffin with the crucified Christ in procession late on Good Friday from the parish church to the Chapel of La Misericordia. 2003. Photograph by Anya Peterson Royce.

and the impact of the lit candles was overwhelming. The crowds of followers were huge in comparison to this one in 2003, probably in the thousands rather than the hundreds, and double rows of men with hats lined the entire route. The reduced number does not mean that this commemoration has lost its significance, but rather has everything to do with the elevation of four chapels to the status of churches. As churches, they have their own images and may celebrate Masses as well as conduct the Holy Week liturgy. The Iglesia de Martes Santo (Holy Tuesday), the Iglesia de Angelica Pipi, the Iglesia de la Santísima Trinidad (Holy Trinity), and the Iglesia de Esquipulas (the Black Christ) all have images of the Virgin, St. John, and, most important, el Santo Entierro. In fact, there are now five Good Friday observances and processions. In 1972, there was only one.

On the other hand, the images housed in San Vicente have not changed, nor have notions about dress, order of procession including the Centurion who follows the coffin, and the use of specific flowers. Similarly unchanged is the return of the Virgin and St. John to San Vicente late on Good Friday while the Santo Entierro lies in state in the Chapel of the Misericordia. He is brought back late on Holy Saturday with no particular procession or ritual. Both Holy Thursday and Good Friday remain quintessentially Zapotec observances of death. Even the traditional Catholic blessing of water done on Good Friday by the priest has its Zapotec side. People bring their water in containers in which frangipani blossoms abound.[12]

The Great Vigil of Easter

The Great Vigil of Easter, which begins late on Saturday, the Paschal light leaving the Chapel of el Señor de la Piedad about 9:00 p.m., is now celebrated *con más pompa* (with more pomp) than before. In earlier times, it was simply the first Mass of Eastertide, often celebrated early on Sunday morning. Now, there is an hermandad for Jesús Resucitado (the Christ of the Resurrection) and its obligations are like any of the other hermandades—its members give Masses at specific times during the year; they are responsible for the care of the image; at Easter, they gather to light the Paschal candle, then bring it through the streets with music and fireworks to San Vicente; they sponsor the Mass that follows, and afterward hold a dance in the churchyard with music and food. In the morning, they are the principal participants in the 5:00 a.m. Mass of the Resurrection, and also in the 6:00 or 7:00 a.m. Mass of the mayordomía. The image of this Christ is the newest in the church and the hermandad also the newest. While the celebratory aspects of the observance of the Great Vigil are identical to any other Zapotec celebration, the liturgy is predominantly Roman Catholic. This stands in strong distinction to the liturgies of Holy Thursday and Good Friday.

At the heart of this distinction lies the fundamental Zapotec notion of death as a slow passage from one state to another—from wet to dry, from town to cemetery. Pre-Columbian Zapotec belief did not include an equivalent of heaven or hell, which makes sense only if one has some notion of sin. Christ is sacrificed for us, just as the Corn God was sacrificed for the continuity of a community dependent on corn for sustenance. The Corn God was months on his journey back to life. The Zapotec honor Christ's death and send him off as they would any beloved relative. They remember him as they do every ancestor, and they expect him to receive their petitions and prayers.

Were there any doubt, a visit to the Chapel of the Misericordia at the close of Good Friday or the morning of Holy Saturday would suffice to dispel it. After the crowds have left, one's eye is drawn immediately to Christ's cof-

---

12. Elsie Clews Parsons (1938), writing about the Mitla of the 1930s, describes a very similar custom. In this case, women bring vessels of water to the church to be blessed early in the morning of Holy Saturday. The water containers were pottery, glass, or tin and had flowers encircling them. She describes one green glazed pitcher that was wrapped with pink hollyhocks. Corn and flowers appear in abundance. Bowls of sprouted corn planted a month before Holy Week are placed on the altar together with ears of corn. Corn and beans in baskets wait to be asperged with holy water. Corn stalks and banana stalks decorate the back walls and corners, and flowers are heaped at the feet of the Virgen de Dolores (pp. 275–76).

fin resting on a long table in front of the back wall. The table beneath the coffin is brimming with flowers—mostly white and fragrant, punctuated here and there by the red of hibiscus. The coffin itself is nearly invisible beneath its burden of flowers. Four large funeral candles mark the corners of the table and its coffin. Behind, in the elaborately decorated wall is the image of the crucified Christ after which the chapel is named; other saints' images flank him. On the shelf in front of the images, dozens of candles burn. The altar in front of the coffin holds masses of veladoras that, like the other candles, are constantly replenished by people sharing the funeral vigil. Just in front of the altar stands another tall candle. Yet another table stands in front of the candle—a table with sharp pegs on which to stake tapers. Beneath the table and all around it are heaped the tapers brought by the earlier visitors, many of whom came with the procession.

Delia and I stepped into the chapel from the blinding sun of the street. The inside was dim and cool and so very fragrant. We both stood silently, overwhelmed by the presence of Christ at his most powerful healing moment, the sort of healing so thoroughly embedded in Zapotec belief. The flowers that covered him in his coffin healed the bodies and spirits of those who came and touched them. Their coolness soothed the heat of illness and despair. We sat on one of the benches that lined the side of the chapel, feeling the brush of the willow branches, feeling surrounded by green freshness (nayaa). A steady flow of women came, prayed, rested, and left. Into the quiet of whispered prayers came the song of a bere lele—a mourning song whose notes seemed to cascade over the coffin. The bird's song reminded me of another funeral long ago.

Saturday in San Vicente was a time for cleaning up. Na Nati was wiping down the pews while she waited for her companions of the hermandad to arrive. They were going to arrange the flowers that would go into the large vases on either side of Jesús Resucitado—white and yellow, she said, because Christ was Light. Guillermina, one of the sextons, scraped the wax from around all the images of the saints where candles had stood puddled in their own wax. Antonio, the sacristan, swept and bustled. I noticed that the Christ of the Sacred Heart was back in his niche but was still blindfolded. When I mentioned this, Antonio and Guillermina both rushed to remove the blindfold and the frangipani wreaths. When they handed the wreaths to me, I was struck by their freshness, even after they had hung there all night and part of the morning. When I took them home, we put them in a basin of water. Revived and still powerful from their contact with Christ, the family hung them about their necks to refresh themselves, and to draw healing from them. It was easy to understand why the power to heal is so consistently attributed to them.

By the time the Paschal candle leaves the Capilla del Señor de la Piedad with the mayordomos, San Vicente is ready for the Great Vigil. Jesús Resucitado stands on the Gospel side of the altar surrounded by jars of yellow and white lilies and gladiolas, frangipani hanging from his upheld arm; chairs are set up in the churchyard for the arrival and for the overflow; the loudspeakers have been tested; tables for the food are set out.

We can hear the procession as it winds through the streets, alternating between music, fireworks, prayers, and the reading of the designated Easter lessons. It arrives at 11:00 p.m., preceded by the augmented band of Carlos Robles playing a paso doble and by a *cohetero* (a person who sets off fireworks) blasting off the loud double rockets. The lighted Paschal candle is somewhere in the midst of the crowds. Carlos Robles and his musicians segue into "Dios nunca muere" ("God Never Dies"), always played at funerals, and people began lighting their candles from the Paschal candle. It looked as though a swarm of fireflies had descended on the darkened churchyard. When most of the candles have been lit, Father Pancho leads the congregation into the church with a shout of, "*Luz de Cristo*" (Light of Christ). The bells begin ringing for the first time in forty days, and the band, which has also entered the church, plays a "Diana," a son always played on the arrival of mayordomos. The women and men have shed their mourning clothes, the women now wearing brightly colored enagua de olán, with flowers and paper flags in their braided hair, and the men in festive dress of dark pants and white guayaberas.

The Mass is not long because the lessons had already been read at the mayordomo's house and in the procession, and because there are no baptisms. By 12:30 a.m., the congregation has left the church and the party begins. The band launches into sones, and the women of the hermandad appropriate the dance space. Other women pass out the plates of food and hand around drinks, including horchata especially for this occasion. The men stand in the back, eating and drinking. The band alternates between sones and piezas (contemporary Latin dance music), taking breaks to eat and drink. At 1:45 a.m. or 2:45 a.m., depending on which time you reckon, the party comes to a close. I watched the musicians packing up their instruments out by the basketball court in front of the churchyard. Some walked off into the night; some had cars or found taxis; one got onto his bicycle after a few tries, and wobbled off, his saxophone in its case over the back.

Everything was blessedly still—except for the night janitor who was sweeping up the debris from the party, plastic soft drink bottles and beer cans. The janitor let loose the big, mean dog and, enjoying its hours of freedom, it raced around the churchyard, sniffing at all the human signs left behind. Finally, not even the rattle of the plastic bottles could keep me awake.

Easter Sunday

I was awakened after a few short hours by "Las mañanitas," played by the double band of Carlos Robles, and blaring through the early dawn—it was 4:45 a.m.

and still dark, but all the members of the hermandad were assembled, acknowledging the resurrection of Christ. "Las mañanitas" is the song traditionally sung at the earliest possible hour of the day for those celebrating birthdays. Typically, a band will play it in the churchyard at dawn on the major saints' days. On this day, the band continued its serenade of the risen Christ until 6:00 a.m. The first Mass of Easter Sunday began at its usual time of 7:00 a.m. Much of it was a standard Roman Catholic Mass but it ended with the band, inside the church, playing "La Sandunga" (one of the most famous sones of the Isthmus). Afterward, the women of the hermandad gave out plates of food—tamales and bread, with a half-gourd of bupu. Fireworks, including a *castillo* (palm frame loaded with rockets and other fireworks), blasted off, bringing the festivities to a fitting, noisy, ear-splitting end.

After a relatively lazy day—everyone in the family had either participated in many of yesterday's events or had been kept awake by them, Delia and I went to the 6:00 p.m. Mass at San Vicente. Father Esau kept it short—he was suffering from a bad cold. The Santo Entierro was back in his usual place, in the glass coffin underneath the image of the Virgin of Sorrows. San Sebastian, who had the misfortune of having his name day fall on Easter so missing his normal celebration, was behind the communion rail on the Epistle side of the altar. In front of the rail on that side was San Juan. The focus of attention was Jesús Resucitado, behind the rail on the Gospel side, surrounded by white and yellow lilies, and adorned with yellow frangipani. The Paschal candle, still on the table on which it is carried through the streets, stood in front of the rail on that same side.

Juchitecos are exhausted after the nine days of observance both of the Easter Passion and of their own departed relatives. What they say, in describing this time, is that they have done their work, their dxiiña'. As described in chapter 9, the visits to the cemeteries are obligations of reciprocity and community. The dead remain part of the community, becoming ancestors who have some power to fulfill hopes and desires of their living relatives. It is a continuation from its original state in which the ancestors were mediators between the living and the gods and were objects of worship.[13] Today, Juchitecos honor their dead, and ask for their advice and intercession.

---

13. Both Ronald Spores (1965) and Joyce Marcus (1978) include ancestor worship and an ancestor cult as characteristic of pre-Columbian Zapotec religious belief. Marcus is especially clear: "the Zapotec had great reverence for their ancestors, who were thought to take part in community affairs even after death. If well treated, one's ancestors could intercede on one's behalf with lightning or the other supernaturals with whom they now resided. The ancestors of royalty were . . . often commemorated and sacrificed to as divine beings" (p. 175).

The Mesoamerican Corn God

Holy Week, as a Roman Catholic institution, has been overlain on spring rites that guaranteed the continuity of life through propitiation of particular deities, the Corn God above all. His was a ritual sacrifice, enacted each year, to make the crops grow. Alcina Franch (1993) grants him the same status as Cocijo, the God of Rain. In old codices, he is depicted as a corn plant with the face of a man. He appears in tomb 104 of Monte Albán, an example of the Classic Period in Zapotec civilization, as Pitao Cozobi, the God of Maize. In front of the niche in that tomb is a parrot with a kernel of maize in its beak (Caso 1965:866–87). In contemporary communities scattered throughout Oaxaca, seed corn is planted in pottery or glass containers in the month preceding Holy Week so that it is sprouted by Easter Sunday; similarly, in some Oaxacan towns corn is sown in the ba' yaa so that it will sprout at the end of the nine days of prayers. In Juchitán, it is clear from following the days of Nabaana Ró that very old beliefs about life and death shape practice. The explicit use of flowers of the wild for their moistness and their healing properties; their use in contexts where the dead especially are in need of moistness, that is, their appropriateness in the context of death, burial, and novenas—all of these speak to the interpretation of Holy Thursday and Good Friday as the death, funeral, and burial of a beloved ancestor. Christ has sacrificed himself for them, and he is in a position to intercede for them. The laying out of the ba' yaa on Holy Thursday, head toward the altar, and the willow branches decorating the chairs of the apostles both in the church and at the enactment of the Last Supper speak clearly to the paramount observance here—death and the correct way in which to acknowledge and honor it. The contrast with this and the events of Holy Saturday and the Great Vigil is the contrast between Zapotec belief and Roman Catholic belief. First of all, the Vigil was not until recently an event of great significance. Even now, many do not participate whereas most either participate in or acknowledge the importance of the events of Thursday and Friday. The Vigil makes sense as another opportunity for people to participate in a hermandad, to do their work of feasting other community members, and to satisfy their spiritual yearnings. Of all the Holy Week liturgically-based observances, this is the one with the most aspects of Zapotec festive as opposed to mourning culture. Some specific examples would include the playing of "Diana"s to acknowledge the arrival of the mayordomos and the use of flowers of the town—cultivated lilies—for the image of the Risen Christ.

Conclusions

The Zapotec have made choices about what Holy Week means, which dictate how they will observe it. In those areas where Roman Catholic practice is consonant with or at least does not conflict with Zapotec belief, it is incorporated. This is the same strategy of flexibility in accommodation that Zapotec have practiced throughout all domains of life. Someone once described the Zapotec as being very good at carrying water on both shoulders; that is certainly supported by my observations of Holy Week as well as by the choices people make about illness, healing, and where to go for medical assistance. The fiesta cycle, more elaborate than that of any surrounding communities and perhaps than anywhere else in Mexico, shows similar choices about incorporation and exclusion. The examination of this particular instance of religious observance is important precisely because it provides another model for understanding change and accommodation, one more complicated than older models that have described either-or choices or syncretism as the only two possibilities when two or more peoples encounter each other. What the Zapotec have achieved is a way of listening to the ancestors and seeing the merit of other practices, of maintaining practices that have guided them over centuries while adding new ones that enhance their self-presentation. In the case of Nabaana Ro, Zapotec belief determines the manner of celebration and the meanings one takes from it. And Zapotec belief rests on the fundamental transformation brought about by prayer and flowers mediated through public ritual that sustains the communities of the living and of the ancestors.

9

Nabaana Ro

Invitations from the Departed

Ne xinaxhi riale lu guie', ca rigola que,
Saa dunabé sicarú gulá'quica', biindaca' ne biyaaca'
Lu bi, lu za, lu bacaanda' ya'ni' xtica.

—From "Ca binnizá" by Maestro Enedino Jiménez

With the light breeze of flowers, the old ones
arranged symphonies; they lifted their song and dance
on the wind, the clouds, and the splendor of dreams.

—From "The Zapotecs," translated by Anya Peterson Royce

Palm Sunday

Even before the predawn procession of San Salvador del Mundo (Savior of the World image of Christ) left the chapel of the Panteón Cubi, the municipal cemetery hummed with activity. It was Domingo de Ramos, Palm Sunday, the day all the departed whose homes lie in that cemetery expect their friends and relatives to visit and stay for the fiesta of the souls.

When we arrived at 6:00 a.m. burdened with armfuls of flowers on our first of three trips, the sun was not yet up but oxcarts filled with palms, trucks overflowing with palms and willows, women already settling in for a day of business selling regañadas, others selling soft drinks and the syrupy raspados, still others with huge basins of glistening dxiña'—mango, papaya, sweet potato, lemon, plum, cherry, nanche, almond, all boiled in pounds of sugar until they are a heavy, sweet mass—all these jostle each other as they unload wares and find the best location. Men and women have little pushcarts offering hamburgers and hot dogs, competing with the vendors of tacos and garnachas. The beer sellers will arrive later although some have sent children or helpers to stake out a good place.

We were not the first arrivals among those coming to clean and decorate family tombs. The large water tank closest to Na Berta's tomb was already drained of half its water. Vicente filled the buckets quickly before the water level dropped even lower. The rest of us—all the still living children of Berta (Mavis and Berta from Mexico City, Irma, and Rosinda, the oldest) and I—fell into our accustomed roles, Irma passing the wilted flowers from the tomb to Vicente and Rosinda who sorted them into those to be discarded and those to be kept for other tombs we had to visit. Vicente cut the long stems to fit the vases, and stripped the lower leaves. I sorted the bundles of new flowers into piles based on color and size. Berta and Mavis swept and mopped the floor of the tomb. Irma stood inside the tomb and arranged the flowers passed to her by me and Vicente. Rosinda and I had bought arrangements in the flower market. This is a new service, and Rosinda's use of it has much to do with her increasing lack of mobility. The purchased arrangements fit nicely in the space between the large vases on the floor and on the upper shelf. For a newly departed soul, that space would be filled with a ba' yaa or a circlet of fresh flowers of the wild.

Plate 41. Panteón Domingo de Ramos, also called Panteón Cubi. 2001. Photograph by Anya Peterson Royce.

Plate 42. Repairing tombs for Palm Sunday at the Panteón Domingo de Ramos. 2003.
Photograph by Anya Peterson Royce.

When we had finished, Berta's tomb was filled from top to bottom with
white Easter lilies (*lilias de San José*), baby's breath, and daisy mums in shades
of lavender, rose, and light rust. The arrangements Rosinda and I contributed
were of pink carnations and white mums in the one, and red, yellow, purple,
pink, and white mums in the other.

Following our custom, we moved on to the tomb of Leonarda, one of
Berta's sisters who had died in her late twenties. We swept and mopped the
tomb, replaced the faded flowers with new ones—mums and baby's breath,
using some of the flowers from the last visit. Rosinda had ordered an arrangement for Leonarda too. Then, still following the familiar route, we went to
Tío Chito's tomb. He was Rosinda's youngest brother, dying quite suddenly of
a heart attack several years ago. His widow and daughter had come the day
before with flowers, filling the space with huge arrangements of yellow Asiatic
lilies. Irma and Berta put Easter lilies in the small vases on the shelf, and we
placed Rosinda's last arrangement on the floor in the center. Irma and I took
a brief rest to drink some refreshing bupu.

Plate 43. Tomb of José Fuentes Pineda "Tío Chito," Palm Sunday at the Panteón Domingo de Ramos. 2003. Photograph by Anya Peterson Royce.

Plate 44. Drinking *bupu* at the Panteón Domingo de Ramos on Palm Sunday. 2003. Photograph by Enrique Lemus.

I passed two tombs that represented the two ends of the continuum along which these Palm Sunday offerings lie. One, just down the path from Chito, had a screen of growing plants just inside the wrought iron and glass front. On the floor, someone had carefully placed eight large vases filled with red roses, baby's breath, and white lilies. In the process of construction were two ba' yaa of pine boughs, broken into fine pieces. Family members had spent a lot of time and care making the tomb fresh, fragrant, and beautiful. In the other direction, lay the tombs of some of the Musalem family—Sofia, Cecilia, Salvador, and Miguel, the eldest who had brought them all to Juchitán. Unlike most older tombs, and newer ones as well, these were side by side and open—no structure around them. Dead flowers lay scattered across the tops and debris had blown in between them. In March 2006, I went to the cemetery with Irma and Vicente, and Vicente took me to where his friend Julio "Chiquis" Musalem was buried. As is the case for many recent deaths, his tomb was a thatched palm structure, open at one end. Unlike most recent deaths, however, there were no flowers or candles or glasses of water. That someone recently dead has no flowers or candles is sad.[1] The Musalem family has been a powerful force in the city, but now all but Emma and a sister have died or left the city. Emma's mother is buried in the Panteón Miércoles Santo, and Emma visits her tomb weekly. After visiting the tomb of my friend Gudelia Pineda Luna, I left with the family, making a note to bring basil and frangipani for Gude on our return.

We had a constant stream of visitors at the house, family who had come to visit their dead. The Manuel part of the family on Na Berta's side came from Arriaga, a four-hour bus ride away, and most return each year for the Palm Sunday cemetery visits.

At 6:00 p.m., Mavis, Irma, Berta and I took a taxi back to the panteón for the real cycle of visiting with the living and the dead. Crowded already in the morning, now the cemetery was overflowing with humanity of all shapes, sizes, ages, and genders. Vendors were busily selling everything from iguana puppets and hats and glow-in-the-dark images of Christ and the Virgin to all manner of food and drink. Musicians, bands, trios of guitars, even a mariachi ensemble, strolled purposefully around, waiting to be hired. A band was play-

---

1. The expectation is that the dead, especially the recently dead, will be visited in their cemetery homes, not only during Holy Week but also on Sundays throughout the year. Surviving spouses and children, regardless of gender, are the usual caretakers. In reality, not everyone complies with the expectation. In the case of Gudelia Pineda, her sisters live outside Juchitán and her mother spends most of her time visiting them so flower offerings are irregular, although they always appear on Palm Sunday. Because Gude was my friend, I take her flowers when I am in Juchitán. The painter Jesús Urbieta has a huge monument from the city but not a single flower. His widow is remarried and does not visit. Vicente's response, "It is sad," is a good description of how people feel when someone is no longer cared for, sad that the person is alone, sad that he or she is no longer connected to the community of the living.

Plate 45. Afternoon of Palm Sunday at the Panteón Domingo de Ramos. 2003. Photograph by Anya Peterson Royce.

ing sones and piezas in front of the chapel, and members of the hermandad of San Salvador, after a long day of processions and Masses, were seated as if at a fiesta, consuming beer and snacks. People would enter the chapel, light votive candles, and touch the three crosses. One woman picked a red gladiola blossom from the base of one of the crosses, and rubbed it over her son's arms and head.

Preteens of both sexes scampered across the tops of the tombs, ignoring the half-hearted chiding of parents. Their younger counterparts chased each other with cascarones, some filled with flour, some with confetti. People came dressed as for a lesser fiesta—*rabonas*[2]—for both women and little girls, and

2. Traditional dress for Zapotec women varies according to the occasion. A *rabona* is a long, full, gathered skirt with a ruffle of the same material at the bottom. It is more formal than an *enagua*, the same form without the ruffle, but less formal than the *enagua olán* (long, gathered skirt with a starched white lace ruffle) or the *traje* (matching skirt and blouse with the starched white ruffle). The *rabona* is the appropriate dress for these annual visits to the cemeteries to visit the departed.

men in white shirts. The tombs were open so that people could sit inside the larger ones, or in front of or across the way in the case of smaller ones. We scattered, each going to visit some relative or friend, always making sure that someone was there with Na Berta or Chito, those two being the most recent family deaths in this cemetery. When we visited Leonarda's tomb, the relatives of the deceased in the adjacent tomb invited us to share in their array of food and drink—barbacoa, salsa, tortillas, potato puree, and soft drinks and beer from a picnic cooler. Other food items likely to be offered include iguana tamales and tamales del horno. In the case of recent deaths, the family is expected to provide either or both of those kinds of tamales. Anyone who comes to visit a tomb has to be given food and invited to sit, just as visitors to one's house are treated. In a sense, the living are acting on behalf of their dead relatives in providing the kind of hospitality that Juchitecos expect to give and receive. One can also buy all types of food and drink from the vendors stationed along the main streets of the cemetery, spilling onto the space in front of the big entrance. All the photographs of the departed are in the tombs, like the hosts of a fiesta. In an election year, all the local candidates appear at these cemetery visits campaigning because they know they will see and be seen by everyone. When it begins to get dark, the lights come on, and the parties continue around each tomb and at the chapel. Approaching midnight, the vendors begin to pack up, musicians put away their instruments, children fall asleep in their parents' arms, and the living bid goodbye to the dead.

Holy Monday

This is the day traditionally set aside for the dead of the Panteón Saltillo to feast their living relatives. This was the place where the Gómez families buried their dead and the followers of Che Gómez as well.[3] It has fallen out of use in

---

3. José F. Gómez was a popular, elected municipal president at the time of the Mexican Revolution. In 1911, when the governor of the state of Oaxaca sent yet another political boss to control what they perceived to be the always troublesome Juchitecos, the latter, rallying behind Gómez, resisted the imposition of this outsider. They succeeded in keeping the state's agent away, defeated the troops that were sent to quell the rebellion, and maintained their independence. Gómez had begun talks with Francisco Madero, the new leader of Mexico, and was on his way to met with Madero when he was ambushed and killed by the governor's troops. Che Gómez's remains were laid to rest on the family land, which later was ceded to the parish of San Vicente. One of the conditions was that his tomb, a rather imposing structure, would remain intact. It did, until 2003, when the parish priest built a long arcade and tore down the tomb, which lay in the middle of it. There is a bust of Gómez against the far wall of the arcade and his name in letters on the opposite wall. This was very distressing for many in the community for whom the physical presence of the departed is necessary for commemorations.

recent years, sometimes acting as a stopgap measure when someone dies, and for whatever reason, cannot be buried in the Panteón Domingo de Ramos. When we went in the evening, however, the party was every bit as loud, packed, and boisterous as it had been the day before in the Panteón Domingo de Ramos. Even the bridge across the river leading to Saltillo was filled with people coming and going. Once on the Saltillo side, we found ourselves in a dense, packed mass of young, old, babies, drunks, teenage boys showing off for teenage girls, women selling cascarones, regañadas, garnachas, dxiña', and soft drinks. There were dozens of strolling vendors of candles. Three trampolines inside cylindrical wire cages were filled with children jumping wildly while others lined up impatiently waiting their turn. Games of chance lined the streets; air rifles to shoot at targets for prizes; beer sellers—it was a gigantic fair.

Chiñas (my longtime field assistant, Roberto Guerra Chiñas), Delia, Karime (Delia's niece), and I pushed our way through the crowds to reach the old cemetery. Three families were sitting outside tombs; one, a child's tomb from 1988; another the tomb of an uncle of Chiñas buried there because he died during a period of heavy rains and could not be buried in the flooded Panteón Cubi; the third, a tomb near the street, closest to the old chapel and in disrepair. All three had flowers of the gui'xhi' and votive candles casting a flickering light across the faces of family sitting in front. Chiñas said that while his mother was alive they used to come to visit the uncle but now he does not have time for both the uncle in the Panteón Saltillo and his mother in the Panteón Domingo de Ramos. This is probably the case for many people who have to make choices when relatives occupy different cemeteries. Some attempt had been made to clean the weeds from around the tombs, and four other tombs had votive candles but no flowers or visitors.

The new chapel (La Capilla de Lunes Santo) attracted people who went to leave votive candles and flowers, and to pray. People were packed so tightly inside, and there were so many candles, that the heat was suffocating. People filled the pews, crammed the center aisle, and milled around the images, lighting their candles and leaving them as petitions. We quickly escaped to the front where a band was playing sones and piezas. It was a lively celebration with neighbors greeting one another, enjoying the music, and eating sweets.

Holy Tuesday

This used to be a busy day for the living and the dead in the neighborhood of Calvario. The chapel is still one of the most active in the city, and the neighborhood has its own vela, the Vela Calvario. The cemetery that once was there, however, is buried under a plaza of cement. No one could tell me where the graves and their occupants had gone. There is one remaining small, houselike tomb with a cross on top. On my last visit, it was being used to store bowls. On our way to Salina Cruz about 4:00 p.m., we made a detour to the chapel to see if anything was happening—nothing and no one except for a municipal worker who was sweeping the front and sides of the chapel. Gloria and I returned at 8:45 p.m. to find a lively crowd, smaller than that at Saltillo on the preceding day, but just as interested in visiting, listening to the music, and treating themselves to dxiña' and regañadas. The same women were there selling sweets, the same trampolines. On the side of the street opposite the chapel, there was a very large plastic slide, children shrieking their way down and racing back to go again. Members of the hermandad of the chapel were sitting behind tables at the entrance selling ribbons with the name of the chapel on them. Buy one, place it around someone's neck, and you are godparent to that person. This is the kind of godparenthood that lies between a baptismal or marriage relationship and the sort referred to as *sumpirinisa*, the Zapotec term for "dragonfly." It does not carry all the obligations of the former but is ongoing, unlike the latter. It requires one to greet the godparent respectfully with the term for godparent and to stand when the godparent enters the home and again when he or she leaves.

After a brief visit inside the chapel, we escaped to where it was not quite so stifling as the chapel in Saltillo, sitting on the stone benches along the two sides of the patio and listening to the flute and drum musicians playing sones. They had not been in evidence at either of the other two celebrations. The lovely harmonies of this old-style music were cut off by the arrival of the mayordoma of the hermandad, preceded by a band playing a diana. They marched up the steps, and took over the front benches and chairs, setting up food stands and coolers.

This is one alternative to the style of fiesta when there are actually tombs and dead to visit. Each of the four chapels has an hermandad devoted to the saints of their chapel and each sells sweets and ribbons, sometimes votive candles, as a way of earning cash for the upkeep of the saints and their home. Calvario has always been a vital neighborhood with a sense of its special identity—it has its own vela, so it is not surprising that the Holy Week visit has taken on this form rather than dying out altogether.

Holy Wednesday

Because Ta Chu and Rosinda's mother-in-law and father-in-law are buried in Cheguigo, she and her family are obligated to visit them on Holy Wednesday. This means Tomasa and Antonia as well because they are Chu's sisters. We had bought the flowers the day before and set out early in the morning to clean the tomb and arrange the flowers. Gloria drove Rosinda, Karime, Delia, and me. The streets were crowded even at that hour with people walking to the cemetery, loaded down with flowers and candles. When we got closer, we could see that the usual access points had been blocked off. We drove all around the cemetery to enter from the back but that was closed too. The municipal police said that it was to keep vendors from setting up their stalls in the cemetery. This was puzzling because selling food and drink is quite customary in the Panteón Domingo de Ramos. What it did mean, however, was that Rosinda could not participate in decorating her husband's tomb because she cannot walk long distances, and we could not park close to the tomb. After futile pleading conversations with several police who said the orders came from the municipal president, we gave up and drove Rosinda back home. She said that Chu would understand that she had done her best to comply with her obligations and that it was not her fault. She thus put a brave face on what was a very painful event for her.

When we returned and walked all the way to the tomb carrying flowers, buckets, scissors, and small chairs, it was more crowded than ever. The tank of water nearest to Chu's tomb was practically empty, and there were long lines waiting for what little there was. We swept and cleaned the tomb, saved what good flowers remained from the previous visit, and began filling the vases. Every so often, a friend or a family member would stop by and exchange greetings. Because the tomb faces to the west, we rigged a shade of palm so that the flowers would not wilt in the sun. When we finished, we had four large vases of flowers and two smaller ones. We lit a new votive candle in the center, swung the heavy door closed and locked it. We trudged back to the car in the already oppressive heat.

When we got back to the house, we described the flower arrangements for Rosinda who was still feeling upset at not being able to participate. She would also be unable to host the visitors who would come to Chu's tomb later in the day.

Although her absence was keenly felt and much commented on, the family sent as many representatives as we could gather: Delia and I as the daughters; Antonia and Tomasa as Chu's sisters; Ton (Vicente's son but, more important, someone beloved by Chu), his wife Gloria who goes every Sunday and most Thursdays to help with the flowers, and their children—Karime, home from medical school, Gibran, home from college in Mexico City, and Rosindita, the youngest. We carried dozens of tamales with us to give out to visitors, and took turns sitting in or just outside the tomb. I spent some time with the daughter of a woman whose tomb is diagonally across the way from Chu. We talked a lot about her mother, about her funeral, nine days, and forty-day Masses. The flowers in the tomb included many of the wild made into coronas on the floor of the tomb. "My mother always loved these simple flowers," the daughter said. Several vendors passed by, somehow having escaped the vigilant eye of the municipal police, and we bought string cheese in a chile salsa from one of them.

Many vendors had set up their stands just outside the walls of the cemetery so one had only to step outside to buy almost anything one might want.

The main street that makes the eastern boundary of the cemetery and on which is located the Capilla de Miércoles Santo had the by now familiar atmosphere of carnival. Women selling dxiña and regañadas, younger women with raspado stands, sellers of soft drinks, sellers of beer, smoking braziers producing dozens of garnachas, tacos, and clayudas, peanuts with chile and limón, cotton candy, ice cream; men strolling up and down hawking balloons; more games of chance; the ubiquitous trampolines. Families sat around the stands eating a meal; children raced back and forth across the basketball court opposite the chapel; a few women visited the chapel with candles; musicians downed cold beers. As I walked back through the cemetery, I saw tombs filling up with family, people visiting the tombs of their friends, musicians serenading the dead with sad songs for the very recent departed, livelier ones for the longer dead, and songs that the departed particularly liked. A group of mariachis was resplendent in the regulation black and silver costumes, silver buttons gleaming. It looked and sounded like a very large and lively block party.

We stayed until after it got dark and most of the visitors we could expect had come and gone, staying a bit to talk, then moving on the next relative. When we returned to the house, we sat down for a late supper with Rosinda and told her who had come to visit Chu and as much of the conversations as we remembered.

Plate 46. Panteón Miércoles Santo carnival during Holy Week. 2003. Photograph by Anya Peterson Royce.

Comparisons

Clearly, the two most fully elaborated commemorations of the dead are those in the Panteón Domingo de Ramos and the Panteón Miercoles Santo. These are the two newest cemeteries and the largest. Indeed, both are gobbling up adjacent parcels of land at an alarming rate. In both these cemeteries, there is a large community of the dead whom the living visit regularly but especially on Palm Sunday and Holy Wednesday. With its small number of dead, the Panteón Saltillo (or Panteón Lunes Santo) has begun to shift from a commemoration of the dead who have invited the living to a time for the living of the neighborhood to come together and eat and drink. Not insignificantly, they also visit the chapel to make supplications to its saints and intercessions for their departed friends and family. There are still graves here and they are visited; even the ones who had no family visible had votive candles. Calvario has changed the most because it no longer is a cemetery at all. Like good Zapotec, however, the people who live in that neighborhood see no reason to lose an opportunity to gather the community together. The hermandad of the chapel is the official sponsor of the festivities, and everyone who lives nearby comes and stays into the evening. It may well be that the Saltillo celebration will gradually become like that of Calvario because there are few graves now with living relatives, and the cemetery is not really an active one. The two large, active cemeteries are quite unlikely to fall into disuse anytime soon; rather, they are expanding. Given the number of children one sees during these observances, there will be many family members to remember the dead well into the future.

Competing Claims

Many families are like mine with close relatives in more than one cemetery. Sometimes this breaks down into blood kin in one and affines in another as is the case for Rosinda. Her parents and siblings, aunts and uncles are in the Panteón Domingo de Ramos; her spouse and his kin are in the Panteón Miercoles Santo. She and Delia and I, when I am there, visit both sets of kin, although Rosinda's siblings Vicente and Irma have undertaken most of the responsibility for the family buried in the Panteón Domingo de Ramos. Rosinda's primary obligation is to her spouse. When I raised the question of where Rosinda would be buried, she said that her place is with her husband. Delia said that she, of course, would be with her parents, but she has no competing allegiance, being unmarried. It seems that my place would also be with Chu, Rosinda, and Delia. Delia confirms this, and it is taken for granted by other family members.

Family but No Body

Having no physical body at the center of the rituals for the dead is a much rarer occurrence, and one that causes great distress. The one instance I know well is that of a young woman who died of kidney failure while undergoing treatment in Mexico City. She left a twelve-year-old daughter and a husband. Thinking of them, she had left instructions that she was to be cremated. She could not imagine her young daughter and a husband unfamiliar with Zapotec customs being able to meet all of the complicated rituals involved in burying a body. Her ashes eventually came back to Juchitán where they sat in a cardboard box on a shelf in the family living room. Her other relatives and friends were quite disturbed. First, her cremation had brought to an abrupt end the whole slow transition from living to dead. Second, there was no body from which to take one's leave. How important this leave-taking is can be demonstrated by the case of Gudelia, a young Juchiteca who was killed in an automobile accident in Mexico City. Her body was badly broken but they brought her back to Juchitán, and family and friends gathered around the open casket to see her one last time and to say goodbye. The well-intentioned decision of the young mother left people unable to say goodbye or see her off with the comforting rituals—no viewing, no funeral, no nine days of prayers or forty-day Mass for the dead. It did not seem right. Finally, a relative gave a portion of her family's tomb so that the ashes could be laid to rest. At last there was a location to commemorate even though there was no body. In the case of Humberto López Lena, the family did bring the ashes back to Juchitán and held the full nine days of prayers at the home altar with a ba' yaa laid out in front. While not quite orthodox in terms of grieving with a body, this did seem to satisfy the community's need for a proper observance. Manuel Pineda's death was yet another variation. He died in Huatulco where he had lived for many years; his cremated remains came to Juchitán for the nine days of prayers; he eventually returned to Huatulco to be with his son.

Significance

These visits to the dead in their cemetery homes during Holy Week are the second of the two large communal observances of death. To my knowledge, no other community or group in Mexico has anything comparable. As I mentioned earlier, it may be connected to the pre-Columbian practice of transporting the dead of high rank and certain social roles to Mitla, Stibaa, or Liobá, places that were essentially cemetery-pantheons. Commemorations of those persons would have happened in the place of their burial. We do know that the staircases and openings in the tombs were there so that people could come and leave offerings. That they were powerful ancestors meant that people would come regularly to petition them with prayers of intercession.

Many communities throughout Mexico celebrate the Day of the Dead with visits to the cemeteries, the most famous of these being in Janitzio, Michoacan. The timing of the Juchitán visits then becomes an issue. Why Holy Week? Why a separate occasion? What Elsie Clews Parsons (1936) tells us about the sowing of corn kernels in offerings to the dead just before Holy Week so that they have sprouted by Easter is most likely part of old rites for the Corn God, sacrificed and brought back to life every year. The rainy season—gusiguié ("season of flowers")—heralded by Holy Week, is always the time of renewal, when plants begin to flower and the world turns green (nayaa) once again. In Juchitán, this is also the time of weddings, baptisms, and the great cycle of velas. Fall and winter—gusibá ("season of the tomb")—after the big velas of August and the beginning of September and the third harvest of crops, settles into being a "dead" time. There may be weddings, baptisms, birthday parties, but there are no communitywide observances until the Day of the Dead. This is followed, still in the dry season, by Christmas, celebrated but purely as a Western holiday. The forty days of Lent, a time when no healing services are offered and no weddings are celebrated, marks the end of the dry season.

The Holy Week visits are also fundamentally a matter of reciprocity. The dead, who are still part of the community, are meeting their obligations to feast the living to whose homes they went during the Day of the Dead. That the living acknowledge the new homes of the dead in this way is part of their concern that the dead be content where they are. Troubled, unhappy spirits can bring illness and bad fortune. The numbers of people who visit the espiritistas (spiritualist healers) on November 1 for the passing of the souls attest to this concern. There are healers or mediums who can contact the spirits at other times if so asked. People will consult them for advice or if someone in the family has an illness that seems unusual.

Those who died within forty days of the Day of the Dead would have to wait more than a year for any sort of communitywide commemoration were it not for the Holy Week visits. The regular timing of individual observances for the dead suggests that such recognition is important for the spirit to make its transition smoothly. It may be that this springtime observance functions in this way most particularly for those who have not yet been honored at Day of the Dead.

Annual Cycle

When one looks at the annual cycle of major rituals and observances, it is striking that the half of the year that begins at the end of March and ends

Plate 47. Flowers of the wild and town flowers in a tomb in the Panteón Miércoles Santo. 2007. Photograph by Anya Peterson Royce.

at the beginning of October contains all the major communal celebrations with the exception of Day of the Dead and Christmas. Holy Week—Nabaana ro—which is the most important religious observance of the year, several velas in April, the great velas of May, each of which has religious significance, the four velas of August and September, again with religious connections, are the communitywide celebrations for which those living outside Juchitán return. The other half of the year is meager indeed, with only the Day of the Dead and Christmas. The local population of muxe' have claimed December as the time for the two new velas that they sponsor. That choice may have much to do with the fact that there is hardly any other time of the year not already crowded with velas or other celebrations. Superimposed on the agricultural or seasonal cycles, the pattern of communal activity takes on additional meaning. While this region of Mexico does not have a winter and a summer in terms of temperature, periods are marked by the dry, cool winds called *nortes* and the hot, wet winds off the Pacific. It is a year divided into a dry, cooler season of little activity or growth, and a wet, hot season packed with both communal and family activities, the season of bountiful crops and flowers. In the dry season, when the nortes scour the streets, people venture out only for necessities. As a friend remarked, "I dislike this time of the nortes because there is no one on the streets; there is no *alegría* (good times, joy)." As much as I suffer from the heat, I find it preferable to those times when the winds blow without ceasing for weeks at a time and the air is dark and thick with dust.[4]

Given all the associations of wet and dry with the process of dying and becoming a member of the community of the dead, eventually becoming an ancestor, an observance in the spring at the very time when the earth is the most fertile, the wettest, would benefit the dead who are being transformed. It may be that then, they, like the corn, are being revived by the very moistness and fecundity of the earth itself. The other communal recognition, Day of the Dead, while it occurs during the "dead" time of year, counteracts that by the abundant use of plants and flowers of the wild, providing the spirits of the dead with the moistness they crave.

Dxiña

One of the most striking characteristics of Holy Week celebrations is the abundance of sweets—dxiña or nanaxhi or cuananaxhi. These are fruits that have been boiled down with sugar until they are soft and syrupy and very sweet. Every kermess (fund-raising fiestas for churches and chapels) of every religious society with a celebration at the end of Lent or during Holy Week attracts the makers of these sweets. They are sold outside every cemetery including Calvario, which is no longer a cemetery, during Holy Week. Women bring them to the homes as well. Juchitecos consume great quantities of them during this concentrated period of time because they are not so commonly had during the rest of the year. Coming right after Lent, a period of self-deprivation, these sweets would be especially attractive. The craving for this treat is irresistible, yet people do without it for most of the year. It makes sense that sweets would be the food craving

---

4. The Yaqui or Yoeme, an indigenous people of the Uto-Aztecan language family who live primarily in the state of Sonora, divide their annual cycle into dry and wet. The dry season is presided over by Christ who appears as an old Yaqui man. The wet season belongs to the Virgin Mary or Our Mother in the pre-Christian belief system.

of the Isthmus Zapotec. It would have been the thing in shortest supply. The pre-Columbian diet, especially in the Isthmus, had a lot of high-quality protein in both freshwater and ocean fish, game animals, and birds. Some of those would have provided a reasonable amount of fat. Starches would have come in corn, beans, and squash. Natural sweets would have been found in fruit, especially of the tropical variety of the Isthmus, and honey, when available. We know that the early Zapotec made little cakes of honey and amaranth as offerings for the dead. But compared to the other tastes, sweet foods would have been the most scarce.

Most of the fruits that are made into dxiña are available all year so the seasonality of the treat cannot be explained on the basis of availability. Dxiña most likely falls into that category of "special" foods consumed only at particular times. On Christmas and after the New Year's Day main meal, people eat *estorrejas*, a kind of French toast served in heavy sugar syrup. The Christmas posadas feature horchata, a drink made of ground rice sweetened with sugar and cinnamon. This drink is available at other times of the year, but it becomes a special feature of the posadas. Sweetened chocolate is given to the women who attend the prayers for the dead, and the bread is slightly sweetened, too. There is nothing, however, to compare to the orgy of sweet, cooked fruits, which is one of the eagerly awaited highlights of Holy Week.

Balance

All things in good time and measure is a constant theme for the Zapotec. This does not mean that they maintain a steady hum of moderation. At the level of the annual cycle, the crush of activities in the wet season is balanced by the quiet of the dry season. The two communitywide commemorations of the dead balance each other, one in the fall or dry season, the other in the spring or wet season. Those achieve a kind of symmetry, with the Day of the Dead at the homes of the living and Holy Week visits at the homes of the dead. The extraordinary consumption of a particular kind of sweet during Holy Week is balanced by relative abstinence the rest of the year. One exception would be the high consumption of the very sweet regañadas (thin flour tortillas toasted and sprinkled with colored sugar) during Lent.

Community

The obligations of community are many and varied during Holy Week. First, the observances by their public nature remind everyone that death does not sever the ties of community. One of the saddest figures in Juchitán is the person who outlives all his family. Don Silain was one of these—he had only a daughter-in-law remaining when he died and she lived six hours across the Isthmus in Coatzacoalcos. Had he not maintained his commitment to community even though he had virtually no means with which to do so, he would have had no one to grieve for him, and he would have no one to do all those things that are essential to a proper death and journey. As it was, people who were part of his community "family" honored him with all the proper rituals. The obligations of care and remembrance bind the living and the dead just as the living are bound. The occasions and the rituals are different but the purpose is the same. Physical distance does not obviate the obligation. Buses to and from the Isthmus during Day of the Dead and Holy Week are packed, and, as sometimes happens, if illness or other family obligations prevent coming in person, individuals will send flowers, candles, fruit, bread, or other tokens in their place. People passing those uncared for tombs shake their heads sadly, often crossing themselves as if to prevent the same happening to them or their loved ones. Abandoned dead are truly dead.

These commemorations also bind the living to each other. Much of the time at the cemeteries is spent in visiting relatives and friends who are remembering their dead. This is especially important the first or second year after a death. People remember who came just as they do at fiestas. The public nature reminds people who those are who understand what it means to belong to the community. It is used as a way to teach children about obligation, and, indirectly, to scold those who have been negligent. These reciprocal expectations are not one for one, each one a completed transaction. It is vital to keep relationships always a bit uneven so that continuity is ensured. People are tolerant of demands on others that might prevent them from fulfilling an obligation at the proper time. But once a persistent pattern appears of not meeting one's obligations, then that person can expect to be dropped from the web of relationships and support.

Transformation

One of the most important functions of these Holy Week celebrations is to sustain the progress of the spirit in its transformation. By acknowledging relationship, providing flowers that help the spirit make an orderly shift from living to dead, supporting the endpoint of the process by this spring celebration of life, and by coming to the homes of the dead, the living are saying that there is and should be a gradual transformation, and that they are obligated to ensure it for their loved ones. Cemeteries are communities of the transformed and so not to be feared. It is the restless spirits, those who have not been able to accept their state, who met a violent death, or for whom the proper rituals have not been done, who pose problems for the living. When they do, it is because they are "out of their place"; they are wandering in the space of the living. Espiritistas are called on to calm these restless spirits and to try to get them on the path of transformation.

One incident that illustrates the power and potential for harm of such spirits was the subject of a conversation while several of us were changing the flowers in Ta Chu's tomb one Sunday morning. "This is something hard to believe, and it happened just last week," Paco began.

> A young girl, in her teens, fell into a faint at her school, fainted in front of everyone. People ran to get alcohol to revive her but before they could use it, a voice came from her—a deep, hoarse male voice, "Stand back; she belongs to me," the voice said. Everyone was startled and afraid. The voice continued, "Put away all your crucifixes and crosses. I don't like them." He told them then that he was the student who had been killed at that school. "What do you want?" people asked him. "I want you to light candles for me. If you do this just as I say, I will leave this girl alone."

Paco continued:

> They took the young girl to her house where her mother was crying. A neighbor brought an egg and two bunches of basil—they just had them there; they had not done any healing with them yet. "Get them away," the deep voice said, "they are hurting me. Do as I said and get the candles." As soon as he said that, the girl fell limp and another voice came out of her. This time it was the voice of a young woman—"Don't worry. I will be with your daughter and no harm will come to her." The mother was afraid to do what the spirit wanted but the young woman said it would be alright, she would be with them. Then the young girl woke up—"Where am I? What happened?" She didn't remember anything.

The family lit the candles at the time and place that the spirit had indicated, and he did not return.[5]

---

5. This is but the most extreme instance of what can happen when the spirit of a dead person is restless and unhappy. For the most part, Juchitecos think of the departed as benevolent and in a position to intercede for them. But there can be a sense of anxiety, especially around the Day of the Dead when souls will sometimes return and speak through the adepts at various temples. Will they be content with how we have honored them? Will they have made good progress on their journey? There is also a certain fearfulness surrounding those occasions when someone will ask a healer to contact the spirit of a deceased relative, especially because these "raisings" usually happen at midnight. Illness is sometimes caused by restless spirits who want something from the living. This is most often diagnosed by a healer who will also tell the suffering person what they must do to make this right.

Conclusion

The Holy Week commemorations of the dead are vital to the health of the living and the dead. Through them, one sees fundamental values and oppositions at work. Honoring the ancestors, seeing them as intercessors and advisors, wanting the dead to be content so that they will not wander and cause grief to the living, keeping them involved in the reciprocal relationships that underlie community—these are all important motivations for the Holy Week celebrations. One can also see parallels in other domains, especially in that of illness and healing. The celebrations and their dry season counterpart, the Day of the Dead, are integrated into the life and breath of the community. They occur, as we saw chapter 8, at the same time as the liturgies of Holy Week, both lay and clerical. The commemoration of Christ's dying is just one commemoration of the many that are recognized during this hallowed time. Through the medium of the dead, the living are bound together and community is honored.

10

Becoming an Ancestor

Yacati' cueelú gubidxa.
Guza' bi'lunu guibá'
Guzé' ruaanu xtiidxa' ca rigola za.
Gurúbanu guendanayeche' ndaani' yoo.
Guiba' zuunda' nezalunu
Guirá' ni guizaaca lu dxi cayalegasi xtinu.
Xtiidxa' ca rigola za
zutale xquite ladxido' no,
zandisa' ne zucuaani'
guendabiaani' xtinu'.

—From *"Siadó guié,"*
by Maestro Enedino Jiménez

With the opening of each dawn-flower,
we raise our gaze to the heavens
we hear the voice of the ancestors
reborn on our lips
and tenderness rains in our homes.
Our eyes will see heaven announcing
the meaning of the days in which we flower.
The voice of the ancestors
will nourish our souls with joy
and will awaken our understanding.[1]

—From *The Flower of Dawn*,
translated by Anya Peterson Royce

---

1. This is a stanza of a poem by Enedino Jiménez. The poem appears in both Zapotec and Spanish in *Ti guchachi' cuxooñe' guidxilayú: Una iguana recorre el mundo* (Oaxaca, Oax.: Instituto Estatal de Educación Pública de Oaxaca, 2004), p. 72.

Maestro Jiménez speaks for all the Juchitecos when he describes the voice of the ancestors. They instruct; they are the memory of the past and the portent of the future; they fill our souls with joy. They continue to be deeply part of the community of the living.

On August 27, 2005, one year after his death, we celebrated the life of poet, teacher, and revolutionary Enedino Jiménez Jiménez with a Mass in the parish church of San Vicente Ferrer. At 9:00 A.M., it was already brilliantly hot and clear as family, friends, students, and colleagues gathered to remember this remarkable man. When the liturgy was concluded, the prayer leader came forward, and kneeling in front of the large photo of Enedino, he led us in the prayers for the repose of the souls in purgatory. At the conclusion of the prayers, four men lifted the large candles, the lacquered wooden holders were portioned out to the women, and Enedino's photograph went to a young girl. The procession got itself in order, everyone knowing the practice of the familiar—prayer leader, young girl, men with candles, women with candleholders and flowers that had been at the foot of the altar, and guests. Just outside the church men were carrying huge coronas of white flowers that had been sent by the communities in which Enedino had been a prominent figure—his political party, the union, teachers, and students. The band members had also gathered and the band and the prayer leader took turns playing and praying as they led the procession to Enedino's home. I remembered my last visit to this house with its cool patio shaded by flowering trees and graced by bougainvillea, jasmine, and hibiscus in massive clay pots. It was to talk with Enedino about his poetry and to listen to him read. Now the patio was filled to overflowing with people who came to help the family remember this man. When we entered the house, the *rezador* was leading a small group of women in prayers in front of the altar. Na Enilda Vasquez, Enedino's widow, was receiving the greetings of visitors; a strong, gracious woman, with a few words or a touch she made everyone feel cared for and honored their memories of her husband. "Your husband's poetry gladdened my heart," I told her. "Thank you," she replied, "He would like that."

Relationship and Community

One important lesson to be learned from this exploration of death is the centrality of relationship that is displayed, reinforced, and honored in every remembrance of a death, whether familial or communal. The death of a loved one creates an empty space where once was a web of human connections— kin, spouse, parent, child, friend. From burial to Masses for the dead, all the observances serve to transform original relationships into new ones for family and friends. And as we see in Na Enilda's behavior toward those who came to mourn and remember, each person belongs to the community of friends and family in death just as in life.

The individual's relationship to community is acknowledged publically most clearly and consistently in death. The fundamental elements of all the communal activities are bread, flowers, and prayer. Bread and flowers are exchanged in recognition of relationship and obligation. Bread is given to those who help mourn; flowers are given by the mourners to the departed through her family. Prayer is offered in intercession for the soul of the departed by both family and mourning friends. The community beyond the family and mourners is made witness to the loss of one of its members through public rituals and processions. Mourners and community both give the weight of their attention and presence to all the sustaining and transforming rituals of death.

Community of the Dead

All the beliefs surrounding death revolve around transformation; the rituals, and their constitutive elements, are the mechanism of transformation. Grieving, both public and private, lends its emotional content to transformation. Transformation is necessary to mend the community of the living at the same time that it allows the departed to become part of the community of the dead. The elements essential to the transformation and translocation of the departed include water, flowers, and earth. Water and flowers of the wild, those that are the "wettest," give the departed the sustenance necessary to make her journey a gradual one—to give her time to leave the living and join the dead. Earth, in a very real sense, "grounds" the spirit by connecting it immediately to the earth that was its origin. The floor directly in front of the home altar is the preferred place for the newly departed to be laid. When the body itself is taken to be buried, the symbolic "body" of healing herbs, flowers, and sand takes its place on that spot, rooting the spirit which has not yet left the house. At the same time, the place of transformation is prepared in the tomb—a corona of the same elements as the ba' yaa occupies the floor directly over the body.

All the rituals of death bind the living around their common loss—prayer, grieving, visiting, bringing flowers, and giving bread and chocolate.[2] The Day of the Dead celebration brings together the small community of those closest to the dead and their living family around nine days of prayers at the home altar. More distant friends and relatives come together during the two days of visits to the altar when they bring flowers, candles, and a monetary offering.

---

2. Chocolate has been used in rituals that bind individuals together to remember and to celebrate since early Classic Mesoamerican times. There are women who dedicate themselves to making the chocolate tablets that are exchanged on these occasions. Na Victoria is regarded as one of the very best.

In return, they are given bread and tamales. They are bound by these gifts, by the common ritual, and by their shared remembrance of the departed.

COMMUNITY WORK

The community beyond family and friends is essential to give dying and death its proper recognition. The goods and services provided by bread makers, cooks, flower sellers, prayer leaders, and musicians bind the living to each other at the same time that they are the transformative forces that help the newly departed find their way to the community of the dead. The beauty with which these forces of transformation are created is an obligation felt by all who hold membership in the community. The family still carries the majority responsibility for particular observances, certainly in decision-making, and often in the work itself. Typically, hiring a cook or several cooks means that they will supervise the women of the family in the basic preparation of ingredients—chopping and peeling, stirring, mixing, assembling, and packaging, while they do the work

Plate 48. Na Victoria de la Cruz Martínez, chocolate maker. 2006. Photograph by Anya Peterson Royce.

that requires their particular skill. Bread makers nowadays do all the work of making the bread because very few households still have the large ovens necessary for baking enough bread for even a modest funeral or nine days celebration. Tía Nufa, Na Arnulfa Pineda vda de Pascal, the matriarch of the Pineda family when I first visited Juchitán, had just such an oven in her compound, and I remember Na Berta, Rosinda's mother, baking bread in it. But even if the family does not bake the bread, they are involved in all the decisions about what it takes to make the finest bread.

Prayer leaders are essential if the departed is to be effectively soothed, transformed, and given over to the care of a benevolent God and the company of the ancestors—binni gula'sa'. The combined voices of the family and friends,

Plate 49. Na Berta Pineda de Fuentes baking bread at Na Nufa Pineda's house. 1971. Photograph by Ronald R. Royce.

however, give the prayers power, and they, like the prayer leader, commit themselves to follow all the stages of commemoration of a particular death, giving the full force of their presence.

Like the prayer leaders, musicians are the public voice of acknowledgment. While the body lies in front of the altar as people say their good-byes, musician friends often come to sing familiar and beloved songs. They lead the many processions, and when those processions end at the home of the deceased, they sit outside, in public view, to play the songs of death. Their music goes out to the hearts of the mourners just as the smoke and fragrance of the incense rise to heaven.

The women who sell flowers, whether wild or cultivated, are utterly indispensable because death cannot be accomplished without the mediation of flowers. Their knowledge of custom means that they take care to have all the appropriate flowers available, both year-round for funerals and Masses, and at those two points in the year that call for the big communal celebrations. The women of the family, however, select the flowers and arrange them; for the first forty days, this is a daily obligation. For the later Masses, their obligation extends beyond the home altar to the floral arrangements in the church. And around the Day of the Dead and during the Holy Week visits, they spend long hours arranging flowers and healing herbs so that they honor and receive the dead.

Plate 50. Flowers for the tomb—bougainvilla, gardenia, jasmine, and hibiscus. 2007. Photograph by Anya Peterson Royce.

PUBLIC ASPECT OF DEATH

Death is never solitary.[3] In dying, a person is surrounded by family and friends. Those intimates become multiplied at death, concentric circles of intimacy that expand beyond family, friends, and relatives of the departed to include those who are related to anyone close to the person who has died to people living outside the city to the professionals who practice the crafts necessary to make the rituals surrounding death effective and pleasing.

The marks of mourning worn by women and men—black clothes or black armbands, announce the death to the community at large. Their more cloistered presence in the home and altar room and their absence from happier celebrations are a sign that death has touched them.

The processions, of course, are a public statement of relationship and obligation—burial processions from the house to the cemetery, forty-day, one-year and seven-year Masses for the dead processions from church to home, the pilgrimages involved in Stations of the Cross, and all the processions of Holy Week. The Day of the Dead, one of the largest, predictable commemorations of death, involves only the processions of the spirits of the dead to their former homes. The public nature, however, is clear in the symbols of death that mark the entryway to every house with an altar for its recently dead. Huge arches of banana stalks frame the doorways, and they are hung with green cocos, marigolds, and the bread of the dead. No one can miss these green invitations to the returning spirits. In a similar way, the reciprocal visits of the living to the tombs of their relatives during Holy Week are a public statement. The cleaning, repainting, and plastering of the tombs or the newly woven palm walls that replace the dried ones, the filling of the tombs with flowers, and fresh glasses of water announce that here are people honoring their relationship to the dead and the living. The cemeteries become hugely communal sites of visiting, remembering, exchanging food and drink, and listening to music with people settling in for the afternoon and evening. Those who do not remember their dead in this way face the opprobrium of the community. No one wants to think that they will not be remembered, that they will cease to be part of the memory of family and friends.

EQUALITY IN DEATH

No matter what one's standing is in Juchitán society, one's treatment in death will follow the same progress and rituals of commemoration. The first death I experienced was Don Silain's, an old man who had been Ta Chu's apprentice

---

3. The social nature of death may well be why suicide is so horrifying for Zapotec. It is the ultimate act of exclusion, a selfish drawing away from those closest to you. The Roman Catholic church defines it as a sin but that is not the source of the distaste most Juchitecos feel about it. Suicide denies relationship and one's obligation to community. It is not common in Juchitán.

and who had no living relatives. The whole structure of required observances was followed, and people pointed out that the community needed to see that Silain had friends who cared about him. He had tried, even with very reduced economic means, to maintain his social obligations and relationships, and that meant that people were bound to honor him in death. After the first rituals of burial, nine days, and forty days, however, the fact that he had no family meant that the other observances that fall to family were attenuated. The burial and subsequent observances for Na Berta followed exactly the same form only with vastly greater numbers of mourners and participants, flowers, and bread. Her family still remember her each week with fresh flowers. In the case of individuals who are disadvantaged economically or in terms of family, all those who were maintained by them in the rounds of reciprocal giving, remember their obligations when it comes to acknowledging the death.

The obligations to community are perhaps most clearly enunciated in the domain of death. Why this should be so is important to consider. First, unlike every other change in status except birth, death comes to everyone. In birth, the newly born member of the community has no history of relationship other than that to the parents. Even as recently as twenty years ago, the infant mortality rate in the first year was high enough so that one was unsure whether the baby was going to become a member of the community. Rituals for the newborn involve those that protect the infant from illnesses caused by *aire* (air or wind), envy, or other nonbiomedical causes of illness. Those are practiced within the confines of family or between family and a healer who specializes in infants. Baptism is the only public rite, and that happens usually after it is clear that the child will survive its first vulnerable months. The death of an infant is treated differently than that of an adult. Infants are regarded as pure souls, *angelitos*; the litany of the prayers acknowledges that. The coffin and the adornments are white, blue, or pink. Fireworks are set off at the beginning of the funeral procession to stand for the fireworks that are burned at weddings. The music is happy rather than somber. Subsequent rituals are more intimate. While the observances appear to be more celebratory, the grieving is every bit as wrenching as that for an adult.

Death usually takes those who have had time to become members of the community, those who have demonstrated their loyalty and ties to Juchitán. They have had time to establish relationships and those imply reciprocity. They have invested more in the community and the community in them. Regardless of their social station in life, if they have honored relationships, they will be treated as full members of the community in death.

Why Death?

The domain of death is for the Zapotec of Juchitán the encapsulation of all the values that have sustained them throughout generations of interaction with other cultural systems bent on eliminating, incorporating, assimilating, and otherwise changing who they are. In the first chapter, I offered the analogy of a great river as a way of understanding the genius of Zapotec persistence. The banks, where the river encounters obstacles, require nerve and the ability to transform oneself to take advantage of new opportunities or to avoid unexpected dangers. The banks are the site of innovation and transformation both for individuals and for the community. The current at the center of the river runs smooth and deep, unaffected by the swirls and eddies at the banks. This is where one finds community and relationship, the second fundamental Zapotec value. It offers the safety net of the known and the reliable so that people are willing to risk change. Balance between extremes of transformation or change and the conservative force of community is what allows the Zapotec to live lives of integrity, accommodating and initiating change that benefits them while resting assured in the continuity of community. Individual deaths are unanticipated—they are the river encountering the unexpected. Yes, we know that death comes to everyone but the manner and the time always catch us by surprise. The rituals of death envelop the departed and all the mourners in the comfort of community and relationship. The beauty of those rituals gives them power to transform and to bind. We can give ourselves into the keeping of that calm, deep current, trusting in the wisdom of the ancestors whose voices are reborn on our lips with the flowering of each dawn.

Epilogue

Many family, friends, and acquaintances have made the journey from the community of the living to the community of the dead since I first visited Juchitán in 1968. Some are still very present when I visit them in their cemetery homes or when I attend one of the Masses honoring them. They remain present because their lives touched mine just as my life touched theirs.

Like stones tossed into a pond, the ripples of our encounters have spread across the many years of my work here: Na Berta Pineda de Fuentes, Na Rosa Pineda de Ruiz, Ta Rufino Pineda, Na Bernarda Gurrión de Pineda, Na Paula Villalobos de Pineda, Na Arnulfa Pineda vda de Pascal, Na Orfia Carrasco Pineda, Na Corina Carrasco de Blas, Na Berta Pineda de Orozco, Na Rita Paz de Pineda, Ta Luis Pineda Cruz, Na Margarita Carrasco, Ta Conrado DeGyves Pineda, Na Ofelia Pineda, Pilarica Orozco Pineda, Ta Jesús Ramírez Escudero, Na Elodia Escudero de Ramírez, Salma Davar Gonzalez "Na Chema," Doctora Velma Pickett, Ta Silain Azcona, Na Eutiquia Castillejos de Deheza, Ta Victor Ramírez Escudero, Na Paula Hernandez, Doña Joaquina Peral, Ta Felix López Jiménez, Na María Cruz López, Na Adolfina Manuel Santiago, Ta Saureano López, Na Alicia DeGyves, José Fuentes Pineda, Gudelia Pineda, Tomasa Ramírez Escudero, Na Urania Dordelly de Nolasco, Julio Bustillo, Ta Manuel Pineda, Na Consuelo Valdivieso, Na Cirila Guerra Chiñas, Na Amparo Sol, Isabel Meneses, Ta Cecilio Z. Jiménez, Ta Enedino Jiménez Jiménez, Maestro Hebert Rasgado, Ta Macario Matus, Ta Adelfo Valdivieso, Na Soledad Santiago, Rogelio Santiago Cruz, Taurino López Cruz, Dr. Amador Zarate, Na Amelia González de Zarate, Teodoro Altamirano Robles, Ta Manuel Ferra, Na Juanita Ruiz de Ferra, José González Nazarala, Na Esperanza López Lena, Don Oscar Shibayama, Doña Matilde M. Hernandez, Paricutín Oshino, Doña María Luisa Musalem, Don Salvador Musalem, Julio César Musalem, and Gutu Wada.

When I speak their names, I remember stories told by them and about them. On the framework of the stories, I can layer the virtues of relationship, of community, of individual daring and confrontation. I see people who graced my life with remarkable gifts—some were poets, some healers, some musicians, many who were referred to collectively simply as "*las tías*," others were teachers, scholars, craftsmen, market women, entrepreneurs. Through the daily work of maintaining family and the work of celebration and commemoration, they crafted lives of grace and bountiful offering. They were my teachers, my friends, and my family, and they opened my eyes to a way of living based on community and transformation, on the fundamental importance of relationships, and of being present for one another. They have become those ancestors whose voices nourish our souls.

Diuxquixe pe' laatu

—Anya Peterson Royce
December 2010

Glossary of Isthmus Zapotec
and Spanish Terms

ba'. The body prepared for burial; the body in its coffin; the body, its coffin, and its immediate surroundings in the tomb; a tomb (*yoo ba'*), including its contents.

bandaga. A large leaf.

ba' yaa. lit. "moist, green, fresh *ba'*." A carpet of flowers laid out in the shape of a cross or body in front of the home altar for the nine days following burial.

bere lele. Bittern (Sp. *alcaraván*).

bidó'. The saint (Sp. *el santo*). Colloquially this refers to the home altar.

biduaa. Banana.

bidxi'. Toad.

bidxi ñee gaa. Frog.

biguié'. Altar, lit. "flower air or spirit."

bi nisa. The south wind, lit. "water wind."

binni guenda biaani'. Wise people, lit. "people of enlightenment."

binni gulasa'. Ancestors, old ones.

biruba gui'ña'. Hibiscus.

bi yooxho. The north wind, lit. "old wind."

botana. Appetizers.

bupu. A festive drink made from a thin corn gruel (*atole*) with froth on top made by whipping some of the atole with unsweetened chocolate, brown sugar (*panela*), and frangipani blossoms. It is served in hollowed half gourds, called *xiga* in Zapotec (Sp. *jícaras*).

211

castillo. A palm frame loaded with fireworks, carried in processions, and set off on commemorative occasions.

cheguiiña'. Venison stew.

cocotero. The coconut palm.

cohetero. A man who sets off fireworks; also refers to those who make fireworks.

cordoncillo. Any of several herbs from the genus that includes *Piper sanctum*. Multiple uses are based on their cleansing qualities.

cuananaxhi. The fruits that can be boiled in dark brown sugar to make a very sweet treat. This category also includes sweet potatoes.

curado. Plums (Sp. *nanches*) steeped in alcohol.

daa. A mat woven of palm fiber (Sp. *petate*).

diidxa' guie'. Poetry, lit. "flowery words."

doo yoo. Umbilical cord; placenta.

dxiibi. Fright.

dxiña. A sweet; sugar.

dxiña ridaa' bladu. Sweets served on a plate.

dxita. Bone; egg.

enagua. Long, full, gathered skirt without a ruffle.

enagua olán. Long, full, gathered skirt with a starched white lace pleated (or gathered) ruffle at the bottom.

espiritista. One of several categories of healers. They work by being intermediaries between the patient and the spirit world. They also use other healing techniques, but this is what distinguishes them from others.

garnachas. Small *tortas* topped with chopped meat or chicken, onions, and chiles cooked in lard on a griddle, and served with a spicy mixture of shredded cabbage, jalapeño peppers, and carrots.

guendahuara' bidxi. Dry sickness.

guendalisaa. Kinship relations; the duties and responsibilities engendered by kinship relations, either real or fictive.

gueta bicuuni bola. Small, thick, hard tortillas used for dipping in broth or coffee.

gueta biguii. Large tortillas baked in an earthen oven (Sp. *totopos*).

gueta guu beela za. Beef tamales made with lard.

guidxi. The town.

Guidxiguie'. Juchitán, lit. "town of flowers."

guie'. Flower.

guie' bi'chi'. Dragon's blood, *Croton draco.*

guie' bicohua. Rose of Castile (Sp. *Rosa de castilla*).

guie' bigaragu. Palm flower (Sp. *coyol,* lit. "flower of the palm.")

guie' biguá. Marigold, flower of the dead.

guie' biuxhe. Any of a category of wildflowers used for the ba' yaa (Sp. *flores sencillos*).

guie' chaachi. Frangipani, plumeria.

guie' chaachi doo. Frangipani blossoms strung on a cord for hanging.

guie' daana'. See *cordoncillo.*

guie' guidxi. Cultivated flowers, lit. "town flowers."

guie' gui'xhi'. Wildflowers; flowers that normally grow away from human habitation in wild, uninhabited places (Sp. *flores del monte*).

guie' ndase. Flowers suitable for scattering, as at the feet of images of saints or over their heads in processions; flowers set aside for this purpose.

guie' nisa. Mother of cacao (Sp. *madre de cacao*).

guie' stia. Basil.

guie' xhuuba'. Jasmine of the Isthmus.

gusibá. Dry season, lit. "time of the tomb."

gusiguié. Wet season; rainy season.

gui' xhi'. The wild, uninhabited places (Sp. *el monte*).

ique guidxi. Entry to the town, lit. "head of the town."

ladi. Outside of the body; can also refer to the body.

lad'xi'. All the organs inside the body, insides; pulp of a fruit.

ladxidó. Heart, stomach, the very center of the inside of the body.

liston, listones. Ribbon, ribbons.

lu bidó'. Lit. "Face of the altar"; a photograph or painting of the deceased that is placed on the altar.

marquesote. Rectangular loaf of sweet bread decorated with egg white in which is written the name of the deceased. It is placed on altars for the dead.

mudubina. A kind of water lily.

muxe'. A person belonging to the third Isthmus Zapotec social gender, neither male nor female.

Nabaana Ro. Holy Week; lit. "great anguish or grief."

nabidxi. Dry; also "frail," "thin," or "sickly."

nagá'. Lush; leafy (Sp. *frondoso*).

naguundu'. Dried up; wilted.

nananda. Cold.

nanche. Small, wild fruit usually steeped in alcohol (*Byrsonima crassifolia*).

nanaxhi. Sweet-smelling; fragrant.

nandá. Hot.

nayaa. Moist, green, fresh.

nisa. Water.

nisadó'. The sea.

nisa guie. Rain.

nisiaaba'. Corn gruel (Sp. *atole*).

nisiaabala'dxi'. Warm, sweetened corn gruel presented in a container.

pan bollo. A square bread roll, given to guests, especially at prayers for the dead.

pan de muerto. A thick round or oval loaf of sweet bread, decorated with designs in dough depicting a cross, tear drops, or bones. It is used on altars for the dead.

pan dulce. Sweetened bread.

rabona. A long, full, gathered skirt with a ruffle of the same material at the bottom.

reunión de señoritas. Clusters of small, fragrant blooms, which can be red or white, taken from a large shrub.

rezadora. A prayer leader.

rubidxi. Dry cough.

rusiguunda gue'tu'. Helping the dying to die accompanied by prayer (Sp. *encaminarlos*).

ruxhirini. To eat *almuerzo*, the larger, second breakfast of the day.

son gue'tu'. A musical piece played for the dead.

stagabe'ñe'. A kind of water lily. This and the *mudubina* are closely related.

sumpirinisa. A dragonfly.

torta. A large, rectangular bread, sweet and rich, given at Masses for the dead.

traje bordado. Women's costume including an embroidered, full, gathered skirt and a matching embroidered blouse.

traje de cadenilla. Women's costume including a gathered skirt and blouse, both decorated with geometric patterns of chain-stitching made by sewing machine.

traje tejido. Women's costume including a gathered skirt and matching blouse, decorated with crocheted geometric and floral patterns.

veladora. A large votive candle.

via crucis. Way of the Cross; Calvary.

Xandu'. Day of the Dead.

xandu'. Altar.

xandu' guiropa. The altar made for the second Day of the Dead after a person dies.

xandu' yaa. The altar made for the first Day of the Dead after a person dies.

xiga gueta. A painted and lacquered half-gourd (Sp. *jicalpextle*).

yaga gueza. Willow.

yemita. A small round loaf of bread made with many egg yolks.

yoo ba'. A tomb, including the entire structure and its contents.

References

Alcina Franch, José. 1993. *Calendario y religion entre los zapotecos.* México, D.F.: Universidad Nacional Autónoma de México.

Ariès, Philippe. 1981. *The Hour of Our Death.* New York: Knopf.

Badone, Ellen. 1989. *The Appointed Hour: Death, Worldview, and Social Change in Brittany.* Berkeley: University of California Press.

Bayer, Gabriela Kraemer. 2008. *Autonomía de los zapotecos del istmo.* Michoacan, Mexico: Universidad de Chapingo.

Bennholdt-Thomsen, Veronika, ed. 1997. *Juchitán, la ciudad de las mujeres.* Oaxaca, Oax.: Instituto Oaxaqueño de las Culturas.

Bloch, Maurice, and J. Parry, eds. 1981. *Death and the Regeneration of Life.* New York: Cambridge University Press.

Brandes, Stanley. 1997. "Sugar, Colonialism, and Death: On the Origins of Mexico's Day of the Dead." *Comparative Studies in Society and History* 39(2):270–99.

———. 2003. "Is There a Mexican View of Death?" *Ethos* 31(1):127–44.

———. 2006. *Skulls to the Living, Bread to the Dead: The Day of the Dead in Mexico and Beyond.* Malden, Mass.: Blackwell Publishing.

Brueske, Judith M. 1976. *The Petapa Zapotecs of the Inland Isthmus of Tehuantepec: An Ethnographic Description and an Exploration into the Status of Women.* PhD diss., University of California, Riverside.

Burgoa, Francisco de. 1934. *Geográfica descripción.* 2 vols. Publicaciones del Archivo General de la Nación 25 and 26. México, D.F.: Talleres Gráficos de la Nación.

Campbell, Edward, Leigh Binford, Miguel Bartolomé, and Alicia Barabas, eds. 1993. *Zapotec Struggles: Histories, Politics, and Representations from Juchitán, Oaxaca.* Washington, D.C.: Smithsonian Institution Press.

Caso, Alfonso. 1928. *Las estelas zapotecas.* Monografías del Museo Nacional de Arqueología, Historia, y Etnografía. México, D.F.: Secretaría de Educación Pública, Talleres Gráficos de la Nación.

———. 1938. *Exploraciones en Oaxaca, quinta y sexta temporada, 1936–1937.* Instituto Panamericano de Geografía e Historia, Publicación 34. México, D.F.: Instituto Panamericano de Geografía e Historia.

———. 1965. "Sculpture and Mural Painting of Oaxaca." In *Handbook of Middle American Indians.* Vol. 3, *Archaeology of Southern Mesoamerica, Part 2.* Edited by Gordon R. Willey, 849–70. Austin: University of Texas Press.

Chiñas, Beverly. 1973. *The Isthmus Zapotecs: Women's Roles in Cultural Context.* New York: Holt, Rinehart and Winston.

Covarrubias, Miguel. 1946. *Mexico South: The Isthmus of Tehuantepec.* New York: Knopf.

Córdoba, Juan de. 1987. *Vocabulario en lengua zapoteca, hecho y recopilado por el muy reverendo padre fray Juan de Córdoba.* Facsimile edition. México, D.F.: Ediciones Toledo, INAH.

Danforth, Loring M. 1982. *The Death Rituals of Rural Greece.* Princeton, N.J.: Princeton University Press.

De la Cruz, Victor. 2002. "Las creencias y prácticas religiosas de los descendientes de los binnigula'sa'." In *La religion de los binnigula'sa'.* Edited by Victor de la Cruz and Marcus Winter, 275–341. Oaxaca, Oax.: Fondo Editorial, IEEPO.

De la Cruz, Victor, and Marcus Winter, eds. 2002. *La religion de los binnigula'sa'.* Oaxaca, Oax.: Fondo Editorial, IEEPO.

Durkheim, Emile. 1946. *The Division of Labor in Society.* Translated by George Simpson. Glencoe, Ill.: Free Press.

El Guindi, Fadwa. 1986. *The Myth of Ritual: A Native's Ethnography of Zapotec Life-Crisis Rituals.* With the collaboration of Abel Hernández Jiménez. Tucson: University of Arizona Press.

Everts, Dana. 1990. *Women Are Flowers: The Exploration of a Dominant Metaphor in Isthmus Zapotec Expressive Culture.* Ann Arbor, Mich.: University Microfilms.

Flannery, Kent V., and Joyce Marcus. 1976. "Formative Oaxaca and the Zapotec Cosmos." *American Scientist* 64(4):374–83.

Foster, George M. 1960. *Culture and Conquest: America's Spanish Heritage.* New York: Cooper Square.

Frake, Charles O. 1964. "A Structural Description of Subanun 'Religious Behavior.'" In *Explorations in Cultural Anthropology.* Edited by Ward H. Goodenough, 111–29. New York: McGraw-Hill.

Henestrosa, Andrés. 1997. *Los hombres que dispersó la danza.* México, D.F.: Miguel Ángel Porrúa.

Hertz, Robert. 1960. *Death and the Right Hand.* Translated by Rodney and Claudia Needham. Glencoe, Ill.: Free Press.

Humphreys, Sarah C. 1993. *The Family, Women, and Death: Comparative Studies.* 2nd ed. Ann Arbor: University of Michigan Press.

Humphreys, Sarah C., and Helen King, eds. 1981. *Mortality and Immortality: The Anthropology and Archaeology of Death.* London: Academic Press.

Huntington, Richard, and Peter Metcalf. 1979. *Celebrations of Death: The Anthropology of Mortuary Ritual.* Cambridge: Cambridge University Press.

Jiménez, Enedino. 2004. *Ti guchache' cuxooñé guidxilayú: Una iguana recorre el mundo.* Oaxaca, Oax.: Instituto Estatal de Educación Pública de Oaxaca.

Jiménez Girón, Eustaquio. 1979. *Guía gráfico-fonémica para la escritura y lectura del zapoteco.* Juchitán, Oax.: Editorial Victoria Yan.

Kamar Al-Shimas. 1922. *The Mexican Southland.* Fowler, Ind.: Benton Review Shop.

Leigh, Howard. 1974. "The Evolution of the Zapotec Glyph C." In *Ancient Oaxaca: Discoveries in Mexican Archeology and History.* Edited by John Paddock, 256–69. Stanford, Calif.: Stanford University Press.

Leslie, Charles M. 1960. *Now We Are Civilized: A Study of the World View of the Zapotec Indians of Mitla, Oaxaca.* Detroit, Mich.: Wayne State University Press.

Lomnitz, Claudio. 2005. *Death and the Idea of Mexico.* Boston: MIT Press.

López Chiñas, Gabriel. 1969. *El concepto de la muerte entre los zapotecas.* México, D.F.: Vinnigulasa.

———. 1975. *Guendaxheela: El casamiento.* México, D.F.: Talleres de Complejo Editorial Mexicano.

Marcus, Joyce. 1978. "Archaeology and Religion: A Comparison of the Zapotec and Maya." *World Archaeology* 10(2):172–91.

Marcus, Joyce, and Kent V. Flannery. 1977. "Ethnoscience of the Sixteenth Century Valley Zapotec." In *The Nature and Status of Ethnobotany.* Edited by Richard I. Ford, 51–79. Museum of Anthropology, University of Michigan, Anthropological Papers 67. Ann Arbor: University of Michigan.

———. 1996. *Zapotec Civilization: How Urban Society Evolved in Mexico's Oaxaca Valley.* London: Thames and Hudson.

Mendieta y Núñez, Lucio. 1949. *Los zapotecos: Monografía histórica, etnográfica y económica.* México: Imprenta Universitaria.

Meneses Velasquez, Marina. 1996. "El camino de ser mujer en Juchitán." In *Juchitán, la ciudad de las mujeres,* ed. Veronika Bennholdt-Thomsen, 99–125. Oaxaca, Oax.: Instituto Oaxaqueño de las Culturas.

Messer, Ellen. 1975. *Zapotec Plant Knowledge: Classification, Uses, and Communication about Plants in Mitla, Oaxaca, Mexico.* PhD diss., University of Michigan.

———. 1978. "Present and Future Prospects of Herbal Medicine in a Mexican Community." In *The Nature and Status of Ethnobotany.* Edited by Richard I. Ford, 137–61. Museum of Anthropology, University of Michigan, Anthropological Papers 67. Ann Arbor: University of Michigan.

Montemayor, Carlos, and Donald. Frischmann, eds. 2005. *Words of the True Peoples: Anthology of Contemporary Mexican Indigenous-Language Writers.* Vol. 2, Poetry. Austin: University of Texas Press.

Miyazaki, Hirokazu. 2004. *The Method of Hope: Anthropology, Philosophy, and Fijian Knowledge.* Stanford, Calif.: Stanford University Press.

Miano Borrusco, Marinella. 2002. *Hombre, mujer y muxé en el Istmo de Tehuantepec.* México, D.F.: Instituto Nacional de Antropología e Historia/Plaza y Valdés.

Nácar, Pancho. 1973. *Diidxá stí Pancho Nácar.* Juchitán, Oax.: Patronato Casa de la Cultura del Istmo.

Needham, Rodney, ed. 1973. *Right and Left: Essays on Dual Classification.* Chicago: University of Chicago Press.

Norget, Kristin. 2006. *Days of Death, Days of Life: Ritual in the Popular Culture of Oaxaca.* New York: Columbia University Press.

Orozco, Gilberto. 1946. *Tradiciones y leyendas del Istmo de Tehuantepec.* México, D.F.: Revista Musical Mexicana.

Parsons, Elsie Clews. 1936. *Mitla: Town of the Souls.* Chicago: University of Chicago Press.

Pickett, Velma. 1971. *Vocabulario zapoteco del Istmo.* 4th ed. Serie de Vocabularios Indígenas Mariano Silva y Aceves 3. México, D.F.: Instituto Lingüístico de Verano.

Pineda Santiago, Irma. 2005. *Ndaani gueela: En el vientre de la noche.* Mexico City: Fundación Cultural Trabajadores de Pascual y del Arte A.C.

———. 2007. *Ti gueela' nacahuido': Una noche oscura* [Translations of Poems of Pancho Nácar]. Juchitán, Mexico: Bacaanda', ediciones.

Reko, Blas Pablo. 1945. *Mitobotánica zapoteca.* Tacubaya, D.F.

Ricard, Robert. 1966. *The Spiritual Conquest of Mexico.* Translated by Lesley Byrd Simpson. Berkeley: University of California Press.

Rosaldo, Renato. 1984. "Grief and a Headhunter's Rage: On the Cultural Forces of Emotion." In *Text, Play, and Story: The Construction and Reconstruction of Self and Society.* Edited by S. Plattner and Edward Bruner, 178–95. Washington, D.C.: American Ethnological Society.

Royce, Anya Peterson. 1975. *Prestigio y afiliación en una comunidad urbana: Juchitán, Oaxaca.* Translated by Carlos Guerrero. Serie de Antropología Social 37. México, D.F.: Instituto Nacional Indigenista/Secretaría de Educación Pública.

———. 1981. "Isthmus Zapotec Households: Economic Responses to Scarcity and Abundance." *Urban Anthropology* 10(3):269–86.

———. 1982. *Ethnic Identity: Strategies of Diversity.* Bloomington: Indiana University Press.

———. 1991. "Music, Dance, and Fiesta: Definitions of Isthmus Zapotec Community." *Latin American Anthropology Review* 3:51–60.

———. 2002. "Learning to See, Learning to Listen: Thirty-Five Years of Fieldwork with the Isthmus Zapotec." In *Chronicling Cultures: Long-Term Field Research in Anthropology.* Edited by Robert V. Kemper and Anya Peterson Royce, 8–33. Walnut Creek, Calif.: AltaMira Press.

———. 2004. *Anthropology of the Performing Arts: Artistry, Virtuosity, and Interpretation in Cross-Cultural Perspective.* Walnut Creek, Calif.: AltaMira Press.

———. 2008. "An Aesthetic of the Ordinary: Embodying Zapotec Gesture, Movement, and Craft." Paper presented at the annual meetings of the American Anthropological Association, November 19–23, San Francisco, Calif.

Sayer, Chloë, ed. 1990. *The Mexican Day of the Dead: An Anthology.* Boston: Shambala Publications.

Seremetakis, C. Nadia. 1990. *The Last Word: Women, Death, and Divination in Inner Mani.* Chicago: University of Chicago Press.

Spores, Ronald. 1965. The Zapotec and Mixtec at Spanish Contact." In *Handbook of Middle American Indians,* vol. 3, *Archaeology of Southern Mesoamerica, Part 2.* Edited by Gordon R. Willey, 962–87. Austin: University of Texas Press.

Stephen, Lynn. 2005. *Zapotec Women: Gender, Class, and Ethnicity in Globalized Oaxaca.* 2nd ed. Durham, N.C.: Duke University Press.

Strathern, Marilyn. 2006. "A Community of Critics? Thoughts on New Knowledge." *Journal of the Royal Anthropological Institute* 12(1):191–209.

Toren, Christina. 1988. "Making the Present, Revealing the Past: The Mutability and Continuity of Tradition as Process." *Man* (n.s.) 23(4):696–717.

Weckmann, Luis. 1992. *The Medieval Heritage of Mexico.* Translated by Frances M. López-Morillas. New York: Fordham University Press.

Zeitlin, Judith Frances. 2005. *Cultural Politics in Colonial Tehuantepec: Community and State among the Isthmus Zapotec.* Stanford, Calif.: Stanford University Press.

Index